AF324070

Mormons in American Politics

Mormons in American Politics

From Persecution to Power

Luke Perry and Christopher Cronin

 PRAEGER

AN IMPRINT OF ABC-CLIO, LLC
Santa Barbara, California • Denver, Colorado • Oxford, England

Library of Congress Cataloging-in-Publication Data

Perry, Luke.
   Mormons in American politics : from persecution to power / Luke Perry and Christopher Cronin.
       p. cm.
   Includes bibliographical references (p.   ) and index.
   ISBN 978–1–4408–0408–3 (hard copy : alk. paper) — ISBN 978–1–4408–0409–0 (e–book) 1. Church of Jesus Christ of Latter-day Saints—Political activity. 2. Mormon Church—Political activity. 3. United States—Politics and government. I. Cronin, Christopher. II. Title.
   BX8643.P6P47   2012
   305.6′89373—dc23   2012027718

ISBN: 978–1–4408–0408–3
EISBN: 978–1–4408–0409–0

16 15 14 13 12   1 2 3 4 5

This book is also available on the World Wide Web as an eBook.
Visit www.abc-clio.com for details.

Praeger
An Imprint of ABC-CLIO, LLC

ABC-CLIO, LLC
130 Cremona Drive, P.O. Box 1911
Santa Barbara, California 93116-1911

This book is printed on acid-free paper (∞)

Manufactured in the United States of America

Contents

Acknowledgments

I would like to thank my parents, Chad and Diane; my wife, Janelle; and the faculty and staff in the Department of Political Science and Criminal Justice at Southern Utah University for their caring and thoughtful support.

— Luke Perry

I would like to thank: my parents, Brian and Kim, for their support; Dr. Andrew Ziegler and the faculty and staff of Methodist University; my good friends for their reminders; and Marshall.

—Christopher Cronin

1

Introduction

In the small city of Panajachel, Guatemala, sits a church that is at once removed and at the center of life. The Iglesia de Jesucristo de los Santos de los Ultimos Dias is the city's Mormon church and is nestled among the bustling shops on one of three main streets. The name is a Spanish translation of the Church of Jesus Christ of Latter-day Saints. Most of the surrounding buildings are made of reinforced concrete and are in some level of disrepair. The city is a bustling tourist town sitting on the shores of Lake Atitlán, but is still in various stages of modernization. Compared to the surrounding buildings, the Mormon church is a meticulously maintained structure. It is a modest, single-story brick building. A tall metal fence with a locked gate prevents casual access. The lawn is closely cropped grass amidst a city of cobblestones and concrete streets poured one wheelbarrow-full at a time. The church is remarkably crisp, distinct, and quiet in the center of a bustling city. Noisy tuk-tuks, motorcycles, donkeys, and bicycles all race past the opaque windows of the still church. The building is set back from the gates 50 feet while all other buildings crowd the edge of the sidewalk. It is near the geographic center of the city and yet it stands removed in almost every way. This small church represents a modern religion that is at once removed and central to millions of lives. The Mormon faith is the fastest-growing religion in the world and yet is still shrouded in mystery to vast swatches of society. This mystery in the face of global success leads to some fear and trepidation on the part of those unfamiliar with the history and tenets of the Mormon Church.

Fear has been a common reaction to the Church since its early days in the northeastern United States. This fear produced plenty of persecution and strife for the young religion. Nevertheless, the Church survived and is now thriving. With growing power, the Church is now poised to capture new prominence in American politics. The church in Panajachel represents a religion that is uniquely American in its origins. Compared to the Catholic church in the city square, the Mormon church is a tiny structure. But the modest building connects local members to the legacy of American culture and a vision of future heavenly significance. Its limited access also illustrates part of the mystery that surrounds the Mormon faith. The Catholic church is open to any who wish to view the withered wooden ceiling and stone walls. The Mormon church is tucked away safely behind metal fencing and green grass. The gate is locked and the windows impenetrable. The church is accessible only to members of the Mormon faith.

The church is also evidence of the vast global expansion of the faith. Almost every corner of the globe is home to Mormon missionaries spreading the word and converting thousands. The implications are many for the politics of the world, but nowhere more pertinent than in the nation of origin. Mormonism in the United States is growing while many more traditional religions struggle to maintain membership. For many years Mormons were persecuted and isolated. Now the faith rises with the strength of millions of American citizens and financial wealth that exceeds other religions' resources. Despite many years of steady growth, the Church has been hesitant to enter the realm of politics. A difficult history of interaction with the American state led to many years of isolation for the Church as an organization. In recent years, however, the Mormon faith has been more active in select policy battles, and the number of Mormon politicians in office or running for positions of political power is on the rise.

A study of the Mormon Church in American politics reveals more than the struggle of one religion. It reveals the struggle of any divergent minority population within a majority culture. The history of the Mormon Church is a case study in the competing tensions of individual rights and popular sovereignty. Much of the Church's early existence rests on a religious pluralism that thrives in the United States due to some secured rights for individuals to practice spiritual belief as they please. However, the Church has needed to adapt and change its theology merely to survive the pressure of a majority culture that pushed Mormonism to the edges of the frontier. For many years American culture and government marginalized the faith and treated it as a cult to be destroyed. From the brink of violent confrontation with its host nation, the Mormon Church has stormed back to represent a vibrant faith that is committed to the nation and to its core political values. Once under the heel of majority politics, the Church now finds itself with enough political power to work through the very processes of democracy that harness majority power. Once a fringe religion cast as moral deviancy, the Church is now firmly entrenched as a representative of traditional conservative American values. How the Church managed this turnaround is a remarkable story that illustrates the potential and danger involved in balancing majority power with the classic rights of liberalism.

The Mormon story is also one of transition from an obscure part of American culture to one now often in the spotlight. Aside from how the Church made this transition, it is important to consider how the spotlight may affect the religion and its place in American politics. Obscurity may not bring much in the way of political power, but it does assure some insulation from the pressures of modern social norms. Living at the margins allows a religion to purify its beliefs in the same way early American Puritans sought the wilderness to purify their Christianity. Moving into the spotlight of political and cultural power likely means a level of scrutiny greater than any other time in the Church's history. The relative youth of the faith leads many outsiders to dismiss the theology and organization altogether as a cult. The mystery that surrounds the more detailed spiritual beliefs of Mormons further exacerbates this dismissal. The Church is likely to face many years of scrutiny and public relations work. This is true, though, for any religion that is new to political power. The quirks of religious practice are easily fodder for persecution when first presented. As the religion becomes more successful and more integrated into the political process, these quirks become the detailed behaviors of a mainstream religious background that is no longer scrutinized beyond the implications for political decision making. Just as Catholicism burst onto the political scene with the candidacy of John F. Kennedy for president, so too has Mormonism with the candidacy of Mitt Romney. Kennedy faced the scrutiny of a Protestant majority culture that found parts of the organizational practice of Catholics to be potential threats. The role of the pope in the life of American Catholic politicians was examined thoroughly along with the doctrinal differences central to the persistent Protestant-Catholic divide. Nevertheless, in contemporary American politics a Catholic candidate no longer faces such scrutiny specific to his or her faith. If the Mormon Church's history of successful integration into American culture is any indication, the same fate likely awaits the Mormon candidates of the future.

The more distinct a religious tradition is, the more possibility for cultural disdain. The more accessible a religious tradition is, the less theological distinction likely exists. This tension has shaped much of the Mormon story. Fitting into the American cultural and political mold has required many central tenets to be altered or done away with entirely. The process has significantly changed the theology of the Church. Some of the aspects of Mormonism that made it such a distinct new movement are the very aspects that have disappeared to accommodate assimilation into the mainstream United States. This assimilation allows for greater political power, but at the expense of some detailed theological tenets. What a greater Mormon presence in American politics looks like depends somewhat on how the process of assimilation has affected the political beliefs of the Church. Mormon political actors, like those of any religious tradition, are free to believe whatever portion of religious principles suits them best. Individual actions cannot be predicted precisely by understanding the overall politics of a church, but the aggregate cultural and political leanings of a tradition can provide some indication of political preference. The Mormon Church is relatively successful at maintaining solidarity throughout its membership, and this means that understanding the politics of the Mormon Church allows for somewhat more reliable predictions for individual politicians and voters.

The tension between maintaining a distinct religious tradition and one that is accessible to new members is related to the tension between isolation and integration. The more isolated the Church was in its history, the more freedom it had from outside scrutiny and intervention. As it has integrated into the national political system, it has lost the freedom to believe in tenets that lie outside of traditional American values. For the most part, the Church has been happy to embrace the socially conservative values that come with mainstream American culture. There is a flip side to this equation, however, which is the socially questionable morals of modern society. While isolated, the Church was insulated from what the faith views as the moral degradation of modern society. Thus, as the Church has integrated, it has been exposed to more of the larger American culture, and some of that culture is an affront to Mormonism. The Mormon faith now finds itself in the middle of what it considers to be a war between traditional conservative values and the moral decline of modernism and postmodernism.

The culture war piece of the contemporary Mormon worldview has a great deal to do with the Church's political leanings. Like any religion, the Church has some tenets it holds to be sacred lasting truths. As these truths are challenged or endangered by the world, they must be protected and defended. This brings the Church in line with much of conservative American religion in terms of social issue politics. Though once persecuted by conservative Protestantism, the Mormon faith is now aligned with conservative Protestantism and Catholicism on issues like abortion and gay marriage. These political issues have become the focus of Mormon politics in terms of specific mobilization and expenditures. The Church maintains partisan neutrality, but is in clear support of Republican positions on these cultural issues. There are indeed Mormon Democrats, but these tend to be socially conservative Democrats. As with conservative Protestantism, culture war politics has little to do with economic issues beyond a general support for the dynamic productivity of American capitalism. This has not always been the case for the Mormon tradition. There are many examples of more communal understandings of economic activity in the Church's theology and history. These communal impulses, however, have given way to an embrace of American capitalism. Embrace here is meant to imply a full acceptance of and successful integration into market economics for Mormonism. On the whole, the Mormon religion is more financially successful than any other major religion. With social issues dominating the Mormon call to political action, the Church in contemporary politics supports conservative ideology.

Considering the size of the Mormon religion, the political activities and effects of mobilization have been minimal. The Church is trending more active, and the future likely holds more involvement for Church members at least in terms of social issue politics. For many years, the Church was content to remain neutral in partisan American politics. Even the early years of the Church saw the use of party politics in essentially instrumental ways with no real attachment to the ideology of either party. Contemporary Church politics remains nonpartisan, but the electoral reality is that Mormons are overwhelmingly Republican voters. The connection of the Church to American political power is partially related to the theological connection of the physical and spiritual worlds. For many other conservative religious traditions, the temporal world of politics is a sordid world that is doomed to fail. Upon this failure, many traditions hold, the end of the world will usher in a new heavenly dominion. The Mormon faith teaches of a new Zion to be located in the United States. Though the political system may still be doomed in some sense, the Church sees itself coming to the rescue of the Constitution. There is a more hopeful attitude toward the American political system, with some heavenly guidance believed to be the inspiration for the nation's founding documents. These considerations make it easier to see the connection between the spiritual world of eternal worth and the temporal world of corporeal values.

The role the family plays in the Mormon faith is a big factor in Mormon politics. The family is central and eternal. Bonds consecrated by the Church are secured not merely for life spent on earth, but for all eternal spiritual existence. The traditional model of the family may not have always been the model for Mormon marriage, but contemporary Mormonism is committed to a traditional understanding of the American family. The bonds between male and female companions are eternal as are their relationships with their children. The importance of bearing children exceeds the fulfillment of a set of traditional values and provides for the spiritual development of the individual. The value placed on childbirth and the spiritual benefits yielded from a large family lead Mormons to favor those political positions that secure the traditional model and to oppose deviations from the traditional mold.

The Church of Jesus Christ of Latter-day Saints teaches its members to be loyal citizens of their given nations. For the American context this means that Mormons are rather patriotic. Support for the nation is deeper than the patriotism expressed by many conservative religious traditions because it includes the constitutional structure of government. Most citizens who express patriotism generally mean it in relation to the underlying principles of the American regime. Those same citizens rarely connect feelings of patriotism to the actual government. Mormons believe in the founding documents as part of a larger plan for a future kingdom of heaven on earth. This kind of nationalism leads to nationalist politics and strong support for the U.S. armed forces. The place of the United States in the world is second only to the place of Mormon missionary work in the world. This sacred rite of passage takes young adult Mormons into two years of intense service. This service, whether conducted abroad or within the United States, tests individuals and signifies a transition into adult dedication and belief. In the meantime, the work done through missionary service spreads the Mormon faith around the globe. Mormon politics as it relates to foreign policy tends to favor actions that secure missionary work while maintaining the United States' position in the world.

The Church favors domestic politics that support its commitment to the family. Mormonism requires much discipline and time from its members. The cultural aptitude for entrepreneurial activity and market economics is shown in the Church's members' high per capita incomes. Furthermore, the strict tithing of members has secured the Church organization's financial prosperity as well. The theological commitment to the family and the cultural aptitude for market economics lead most Mormon ideology to favor conservative policies in both economic and social arenas. That is the political ideology that seems to best serve the contemporary Church. On the other side of the interaction between Church and state are the benefits the political system receives from the Mormon faith. As loyal citizens, the state is reinforced in its legitimate claim to authority despite a Mormon belief in eventual theocracy. Though Mormons live throughout the United States, the electoral effects are still most powerful in regional politics. States of the American West like Utah, California, and Arizona are the places where Mormon electoral strength is clear. On a national scale, the ever-growing Mormon population should mean increasing influence in national politics for both Congress and the presidency.

The biggest challenge for the Church in coalitional politics is the deep belief of some conservative Christians that Mormonism is not a Christian religion. There are several theological reasons at play that will be discussed later. For the moment, this is important as it relates to the Church's ability to join forces with the other similar religious traditions at work in American politics. The conservative Protestant traditions that make up the Religious Right are natural allies for the Mormon Church in the perceived cultural struggles over American social issues. However, this coalition fails to materialize largely because evangelical Christians claim Mormonism is a cult and not a Christian religion. The Mormon Church has been working diligently to cast itself as a Christian tradition. These efforts have helped to make the Church more mainstream and accessible, but have yet to sway enough evangelicals to make any lasting political coalition. Recent conservative Christian leaders, however, have taken to referring to Mormons as brothers and sisters with shared moral and cultural goals in an effort to get past the theological divisions and unite forces for political causes. The success of these efforts remains to be seen, but given the Mormon Church's purposive actions to become more acceptable to culturally Christian Americans, such coalition electoral politics seems like a good bet for the near future.

The Mormon faith has so far not been much of an asset to individual political candidates. It has been something to downplay or assuage fears about. As the Church has become more mainstream, and as it has grown tremendously, we are fast approaching a time when the potential strengths of such a religious background are likely to benefit candidates. It has become a classically conservative religious tradition with all the moral strength this conveys for a potential officeholder. It is a tightly organized church with demonstrated ability to mobilize its constituents. Mormons are financially better off than most religious traditions and are known to support fellow Mormons in business and in campaign contributions. These are all ingredients for a religious background that will support many successful candidates. However, lingering fears about the secret proceedings of Mormon practice still create an uncomfortable position for candidates. No candidate wants to spend time dodging questions about secret religious acts, but it is a part of the tradition on which the Church works to deflect media attention from and investigative reporting about. The actions of fringe ex-communicated Mormons further threaten the chances that a candidate features his or her status as a Mormon on the national electoral stage. Despite consistent efforts by the Church to dispel notions of ongoing polygamy, much of the American public remains ignorant of the difference between fringe sects and the practices of the Mormon Church.

OUR APPROACH

This book is an effort by two political scientists to summarize how the Mormon religion fits into American politics. In order to do this, we need some historical and cultural background. The story told here is of an evolving church moving into the realm of politics. We also need some theological grounding to be able to understand how ideology fits with religious doctrine. Nevertheless, this work is not intended as a complete history of the Mormon faith. There are many historical works that deal more completely with the development of the Church. There are also many religious works that deal more completely with Mormon theology. Studying Mormonism in general is an interesting endeavor. There are pieces of the faith that are rather straightforward and simple. There are also pieces of Mormon theology that are elaborate and confusing for a newcomer to consider. In any case, this book focuses on how the religion fits into the American political system and what impact the Church has on American politics.

The authors have extensive experience working with and living among Mormon Americans. Neither author, however, is a member of the Mormon Church. The arguments and conclusions put forth in this book are those of two political scientists drawing on existing scholarship, interviews, and related theoretical knowledge. The attempt is to sum up the implications of Mormonism for contemporary politics. In the process we present some substantiated factual data and some level of conjecture based on existing religious and political theory. This is meant to give the reader a fuller understanding of how the Mormon faith has related to political power and what the future will likely hold. The broader story is one of growing influence and power. It is difficult to forecast the exact route this growth will take, but we do our best to capture a snapshot of past, present, and future Mormon political power.

Religious traditions are rarely monolithic. Doctrine and practice tend to bend to local culture and tradition. Mormon believers from different parts of the country have different understandings of the proper interaction with the political world. Mormons around the world have similar variations in belief and practice. The Mormon Church is more successful than most other religious traditions at preserving a unified theological belief and organizational practices. As such we present what the Church does as representative of most Mormons. Certainly, there are those who will not fit into the generalizations presented. Furthermore, it is likely that some of the cultural understanding of what it means to be a Mormon citizen will not be captured in our snapshot of political power. These nuances of identity as they pertain to political power are not the focus of our study, but rather the larger trends of the Church over time.

There is some danger in looking at the history of the Church and early leaders as active parts of the faith. As a church that has adapted and grown, the faith does not draw spiritual guidance from Joseph Smith or Brigham Young, but from the current prophet and president of the Church. It is important to note that while Smith and Young are integral parts of Mormon development in the United States, they are not necessarily active parts of Mormon theological teachings. It would be a mistake to read selections from Joseph Smith's writings and think contemporary Mormons necessarily believe in or behave in a manner consistent with his words. Continued revelation through the president of the Church has guided Mormonism through many substantial changes that make some of the historical edicts of Smith, Young, and other important figures somewhat irrelevant to the life of the Church today. Accounts of these figures are provided primarily to understand the historical development of the Church and not necessarily the theological foundations of the Church.

The Mormon faith is an intricate and textured religion. To understand its place in American politics we need some understanding of its historical development and how it dealt with persecution and political pressure. We also need some understanding of basic theology and how this theology relates to political decision making. The Church of Jesus Christ of Latter-day Saints has emerged from isolation and fused with much of traditional American culture. How this happened is a story in assimilation and accommodation. These are interactive developments. As the political system pressured the Mormon people, the Mormon faith has exerted cultural and political pressures on the larger American population. The political influence of the faith is growing as the Church becomes a more prominent player in the religious landscape. The story begins, however, with a new religious movement in upstate New York. In chapter 2 we discuss how the Church grew from a fledgling movement into a rising power. Joseph Smith is the founding prophet, and his role in the history of the Church is examined with a look at his use of religious and political rhetoric. Using themes of restoration Smith brought about a new and successful religious tradition with a myriad of theological innovations. His use of restoration rhetoric while presenting something radically different is a typical and successful mechanism for presenting change of any kind in the American context. The Church moved out from the periphery of American society and registered on the radar of many politicians and conservative Protestants. As the Church grew larger and larger, so too did the perceived threat of the new religious tradition, and thus began many years of persecution.

The third chapter takes a look at how the religion moved from cultural obscurity to the big stage of Broadway musicals. The process reveals the problems of translating a new religious tradition into the politics of existing dominant religious traditions. The Church traveled from upstate New York, through Ohio and Illinois, and came to rest in the territory of Utah. This journey signifies a continued withdrawal from American society mainly to avoid unceasing persecution. The Broadway musical *The Book of Mormon* is an attempt by mainstream culture to understand Mormonism and symbolizes the Church's transition from a withdrawn and persecuted minority to an established piece of traditional American culture. How the Church is portrayed in popular culture has important effects on the politics of outsiders and believers alike. Continuing misconceptions shade public opinion. From within, Church members still feel threatened at least as it pertains to the potential dangers and social ills of society. There are ways the faith fits into popular culture that facilitate inclusion and ways that lead to exclusion. We examine the Mormon subculture and what that means for American politics.

In the fourth chapter we take a look at the transition of Mormonism from the local and state politics of Utah to the national stage. This ascent is a long process that began with political positions that often put the Church at risk of state military action. In terms of nineteenth-century politics, the Church was against slavery and fairly proactive in securing women's right to vote. These progressive positions likely contributed to fears from majority religious traditions concerning the role of Mormons in political power. A new religious movement with radical, or at least innovative, theology was one thing, but to pair that with radical political action was another. The move from progressive politics to more traditional conservativism accompanies the move of the Church to the national level. The Mormon tradition now represents conservative American values, but recent elections still show lingering concerns regarding the prospect of Mormon candidates.

In the fifth chapter we examine what is known about Mormon political attitudes with special attention paid to Mormon thought about welfare.

There is a rich communal history for the organization, with ample doctrinal support for compassion and the redistribution of resources. Here the Cold War plays an interesting part, along with other social forces, in cementing a Mormon disposition to avoid government assistance. A general mistrust of the government, along with a healthy dose of fears about socialism and communism, broke what ties the Mormon Church had to communal systems of redistribution, especially from the U.S. government. As part of the move into mainstream American cultural and political power, this era is an example of the development of Mormon political thought.

In our sixth chapter we tackle the irony of Mormon opposition to gay marriage. This is not to say that the political position does not align with Church doctrine, for it certainly does. However, for a population that suffered persecution for a form of marriage that deviated from majority norms, it is at least initially ironic to see that tradition target another deviant form of marriage. Explaining this irony requires an understanding of how thorough the break with polygamy was and the lengths to which the Church has gone to distance itself from that legacy. The Church of Jesus Christ of Latter-day Saints has been instrumental in several recent political battles concerning gay marriage including those in Hawaii and California. Aside from the Mormon focus on a traditional family and on childbirth, much of the political motivation comes from the culture war dynamic present in the Mormon subculture.

In the seventh chapter we take a look at how Mormon citizens relate to national political power. Religious faith and nationalism are often loyalties in competition. In many parts of the world, religious violence erupts when these two forces collide. The secular state is not always tenable from a religious nationalist point of view. Mormonism is unique in its American-ness. It fits in seamlessly with the civil religion of the United States and the nation's founding principles. The Church teaches good citizenship to its members around the world, but the American state is of special value and prophetic importance. Service in the U.S. armed forces is a highly regarded practice. Serving the strength of the United States is indirectly a service to the Mormon Church and the future kingdom of Zion. No national service though is more important than service done through the Church in missionary work. The success of the Church is largely due to the widespread missionary work of its members across decades of global reaching. The Church, however, maintains much of its identity as an American church with a special regard for the political principles and structures established during the founding era.

Our eighth chapter takes a look at the remarkable global growth of the Mormon Church. Transnational religions generally develop an authority that supersedes national political authority. As the Mormon Church has grown worldwide, it has become somewhat less nativist in its doctrine. The process of globalization is good and bad for religions. Some minority traditions can be threatened by the homogenation of world economics and culture. For the most part, the Mormon Church has benefited from an increasingly connected world. This is true, in part, because of the attractiveness of American society and the Mormon Church's connection to the United States. Global politics have pressured the Church, though, especially on the issue of race. We take a look at how the Church adapted doctrine that excluded black Americans and the interesting relationship with Native Americans. We argue that the Mormon impact on regional political structures may well facilitate democracy to the extent that it encourages an active civil society. This in turn means some political gains for American foreign policy. Also discussed is the effect the global reach of the Church has on the political power in domestic American politics.

In the ninth and final, conceptual chapter, we discuss the Mormon Church's efforts to become part of mainstream American culture. Some discussion of secularization in general provides a context for understanding how the Church moved from isolated religious tradition to a bastion of conservative and traditional American values. This process involved a fair amount of assimilation and some theological concessions. It is an interactive process with much pressure to assimilate applied from majority political power, but also a good deal of strategic, proactive adjustments on the part of Church leaders. This assimilation is a contemporary and persistent force on the evolution of the Church. That is not to say Mormons are mainstream politically or culturally speaking. Rather, the Mormon Church has closed the gap enough to exist within a moderate spectrum of political thinking and behavior. The role of women is one area that illustrates a balance between adjusting to modern conventions while maintaining traditional values. Mormon women are encouraged to have a voice in Church matters. Church doctrine on home life requires an egalitarian sharing of power between husband and wife. Nevertheless, the voice and role of women is primarily justified by the important role they play as child bearer and mother. The dominant understanding of the woman's place is still found in these two activities.

The Mormon story in American politics is one of persecution and rising power. The Church has experienced the entire spectrum of interaction with the state and the political system. Its history contains a marginalized existence and the threat of violent oppression. There are moments of concerted political action that are undone by the majority political power. There are times of growth and financial success. Those who once were bitter political rivals now are potential political allies. What was once a struggling minority religion is now a thriving church nestled comfortably in conservative political culture. It all began with one man in the state of New York.

2

A Uniquely American Story

THE RISE OF THE SAINTS

The Church of Jesus Christ of Latter-day Saints (LDS) began in 1830 with just six members, under the leadership of Joseph Smith Jr., the founding prophet. Membership grew to over 26,000 people by the time Smith was killed in 1844. Today the church has a global membership of over 14 million, the majority of whom live outside the United States. "Saints" in "Latter-day Saints" refers to a name used for Christ's followers during his life. "Latter-day" refers to the Mormon belief that the Saints are renewing Christ's mission as begun at the outset of the Christian era. "Mormons" developed as a nickname for the Saints because of the Book of Mormon, which is understood as an additional volume of scripture to the Bible. Mormons have become the fourth-largest church in the United States and the country's wealthiest relative to size with approximately $30 billion in assets and $6 billion in annual income.[1]

Joseph Smith Jr. was born in Sharon, Vermont, on December 23, 1805. Smith was a descendant of English Puritans who migrated to Massachusetts in the 1630s. The family grew disinterested in the Congregational Church of their Puritan ancestors and moved to Palmyra, New York, in 1816 as part of an unsuccessful farming venture. Western New York was experiencing a period of religious revival known as the Second Great Awakening. "Evangelical pastors pressed the question of salvation at their weekly meetings" and "itinerant preachers stirred the population in periodic camp meeting revivals,"[2] but "Mormonism stood out by virtue of a number of unorthodox beliefs and practices."[3]

Smith's revelations began in 1820 when the 14-year-old boy prayed in a grove outside his home in Palmyra, seeking guidance on which church was true. Smith recorded two primary accounts of this experience, one in 1832 and the other in 1838. The first account reads like a free-flowing rough draft. The second was more formal and became part of Mormon scripture. The first version stated that the Lord appeared before Smith. The later account stated that God the father and son appeared. Smith wrote that God informed him through a pillar of light from heaven that all religious denominations were incorrect. This moment is understood by Mormons as the greatest event in world history since Christ's resurrection. Richard Bushman explained the significance of Smith's first vision:

> Every major change in doctrine or policy comes by revelation. Reasoned debate may precede the revelation, but communication from heaven decides the issue, just as it did with Smith at age fourteen. Like all strong founding stories, the First Vision governs and authorizes current practice.[4]

Smith faced skepticism after sharing his experience with a Methodist preacher and lost confidence in existing clergy and churches as a result of his early experiences with rejection. The preacher reacted negatively because of the familiarity of Smith's account, not because it was particularly unusual. In 1823, the *Wayne Sentinel* reported a vision of Christ by a man in Amsterdam, New York, in which Christ told him that all Christian denominations were corrupt. In 1826, a preacher at Palmyra Academy claimed to see Christ descend "in a glare of brightness, exceeding ten-fold the brilliancy of the meridian Sun."[5] These are two relevant examples of many divine encounters reported in western New York at the time.

In 1823 Smith testified that he was visited by an angel named Moroni, who spoke of a book written on gold plates that provided an account of the former inhabitants of North America. Moroni was once a mortal and is viewed by Mormons as the last ancient American prophet having authority from God. His image is found today atop Mormon temples. Smith claimed to be visited by several other important prophets during his lifetime, including John the Baptist, who conferred the Aaronic priesthood on him, one of the two forms of priesthood in the Mormon tradition, and Moses, who Smith named a book after in the Pearl of Great Price, part of the Mormon canon.

Smith took possession of the plates four years after his first encounter with Moroni and spent nearly three months transcribing the contents, which Smith believed were written in an ancient language resembling Egyptian. The plates were accompanied by interpreting stones, Urim and Thummim, named after the stones in Aaron's breastplate in the story of Exodus.[6] Seeing stones were a part of mystical folk practices at the time and not unfamiliar to Smith, who had been prosecuted for treasure seeking, examining a stone to help find lost objects. Treasure seeking was illegal in New York because it was often undertaken by swindlers. Some of Smith's former treasure-seeking partners claimed the golden plates were partly theirs.[7]

Smith claimed that he was able to translate the plates because of divine assistance. At the time, Smith "could neither write nor dictate a coherent and well worded letter."[8] Several people assisted Joseph in this process.

The first, Martin Harris, was separated from Smith by a curtain while Smith dictated and Harris recorded what he said. Harris was pressured by his family to show them the plates. Smith reluctantly lent Harris the transcript they were working on after a revelation from God granted permission, but only five specified family members were permitted to view it. The 116-page manuscript disappeared from the Harris house and was never recovered. Harris lost his position and was replaced by Smith's wife, Emma. Emma sat at the same table as Joseph while he looked into the stones, with the plates wrapped in a cloth on the table. Emma was soon replaced by Oliver Cowdery, an early follower of Smith's visions. Cowdery also sat at the table with Smith while he looked into a hat. Smith decided not to rewrite the lost section of the manuscript after a revelation suggested doing so would potentially fuel opposition to his teachings. Eight men, all friends of Smith, provided signed testimony that they saw the plates. Three other men, including Harris and Cowdery, claimed "they had seen an angel and heard a voice commanding that 'we should bear record.' "[9]

Smith's 584-page translation was copyrighted in 1829 and became the Book of Mormon, which is understood by Mormons as the restoration of the gospel of Jesus Christ. Martin Harris mortgaged his farm to serve as security for the publisher from Utica, New York, if the books were not sold. Thousands of phrases from the Book of Mormon are also found in the Bible, including whole chapters, in some cases. This has prompted criticisms, then and now, that the book is fraudulent and blasphemous. Publication of the Book of Mormon elevated Smith "from an obscure money-digger of local fame to full-blown religious impostor" with national notoriety.[10] Sales began slowly through word of mouth, mostly limited to family and friends. They accelerated with efforts to convert natives on the frontier and like-minded Christians, such as Campbellites, a small group of Christians who already subscribed to the doctrine of restoration.

The book is "a thousand-year history of the rise and fall of a religious civilization in the Western Hemisphere beginning about 600 BCE."[11] A shorter history of a second civilization, from the time of the Tower of Babel to a few centuries before Christ's birth, chronicled "a group of Israelites who migrated from Jerusalem and practiced their religion in the New World until internal wars brought them to the verge of extinction in 421 CE, when the record ends." The book reads as an elaborate tale of a succession of prophets sharing their encounters with God. The Nephites and Jaredites are the protagonists who illustrate the primary message: "submission to God is necessary to survive."[12]

The Book of Mormon can be viewed as a nationalist text because it presents a new history of the American continent dating back to pre-Christian times.[13] At the same time, the American Revolution is mentioned briefly in one of Nephi's visions, but American development is not a prominent theme. "American constitutionalism is faintly invoked and then dismissed."[14] Monarchy is the predominant form of government throughout the text. Church and state are typically mixed. Rule was based on who was righteous, not on limited government. "The gathering of lost Israel, not the establishment of liberty, was the great work," so that "the biblical overwhelms the national."[15] The new purpose for the United States was to become the realm of righteousness in contrast to the secular notion of an empire of liberty.

The Book of Mormon, along with the Doctrine and Covenants, a series of revelations experienced by Smith during his ministry, constitute the central teachings of Mormonism. The church is described as "the only true and living church upon the face of the whole earth."[16] Smith viewed his revelations as the basis of his authority, but "he did not treat them as if they were written by the finger of the Lord." "When it came time to publish, he freely edited the words," and "sometimes he would paste together revelations given at different times into a single text" or occasionally insert verses to elaborate on the meaning of the revelation.[17] The mid-Atlantic states, including New York, experienced a unique level of religious freedom during Smith's time. Government establishment of religion had disappeared and created a period of religious fertility that gave birth to Mormonism. Native American archaeological sites, which typically included mounds, abounded in the lands Smith and his followers inhabited. Contemporary thinking among Anglo-Americans was that these mounds were not related to native tribes but to ancient peoples, including Jews, Welshmen, or Vikings who came to North America from the East. The basis of this was racist. "Native Americans, the dark-skinned people, could not do this by themselves," so "it had to be light-skinned people."[18] Parts of the Book of Mormon exhibit the Jacksonian view of Indians, commonplace in the United States in the 1830s. Lamanites, for example, are the precursors to American Indians who were marked with dark skin because of their adherence to false beliefs about the prophet Nephi. The Lamanites were described as "an idle people, full of mischief and subtlety."[19] The Book of Mormon could also be understood as overturning conventional American racism by making American Indians the founders of the civilized New World, granting them historical dominance of God's esteem and future ownership of the American continent. Race was a divisive issue surrounding Mormonism from the outset.

SMITH THE REVELATOR

Smith's family and cultural environment were open to heavenly communication because Smith's father and grandfather had visions as well. Not every child is able to say his parents "'God and Christ have just visited me in a grove of trees' and be believed, but of course, he was."[20] "For Latter-day Saints, the process of getting to know God . . . is similar to that of getting to know an earthly loved one: a process contingent upon a lifetime of experiences that are motivated by devotion, tempered by service, and refined by reflection."[21] In 1830 a revelation informed Smith that he was "a seer, a translator, a prophet, an apostle of Jesus Christ, an elder of the Church through the will of God, the Father, and the grace of your Lord Jesus Christ."[22] Smith was "inspired of the Holy Ghost to lay the foundation" and build "the most holy faith."[23] "Mormons know full well that Joseph Smith's story is hard to accept."[24] According to former LDS president Gordon Hinckley, the revelations of Joseph Smith are either true or false. If the revelations are false, the Mormon Church is "engaged in a great fraud," but if the revelations and teachings are true, "it's the most important thing in the world."[25]

There are several different ways to understand Joseph Smith's revelations and teachings. One way is based on faith. Smith's detailed description of the characteristics of the golden plates sought to draw followers to the physicality of their presence. This has made it very difficult to find a middle ground in regard to the Mormon faith, because people either believed Smith was visited by the angel Moroni, received the plates, became a prophet, and spoke for God, or did not.[26] Devout Mormons take church teaching seriously and literally, similarly to how Muslims believe in the revelations of the prophet Muhammad. In the words of Marlin Jensen, LDS church historian, Mormons "don't deconstruct and feel that what we have is the figment of language or our imagination, or that there is some middle ground. I know that is very polarizing. In a sense, I think the hardest public relations sell we have to make is that this is the only true church."[27]

A second approach to understanding the teachings of Joseph Smith is anthropological. Yale anthropologist Michael Coe has argued that "the Book of Mormon is very explicit about what the Nephites brought with them to this land," such as domestic animals and crops of Old World origin, metallurgy, the compass, yet "nobody has ever found the bones of horses and cattle in these archaeological sites" from the time period in question—that is, from 500 BCE to 200 CE—nor crops of wheat or rye, grown in the Middle East.[28] Coe concluded that Smith was an extraordinary man who composed a religion, likely with many falsehoods, but "eventually came to believe in it so much that he really bought his own story and made it believable to other people." In this regard, Smith was "a lot like a shaman in anthropology," who begins as magicians do, practicing magic, and transforms himself into a religious practitioner.[29]

Some Mormon intellectuals, such as Terryl Givens, professor of literature and religion at the University of Richmond, defended Smith's teachings on the ground that several features exist that "seem inexplicable in any way other than to attribute to the Book of Mormon ancient origins," including "the number of hubric structures and patterns in the Book of Mormon, such as chiasmus." These ornate and extremely elaborate literary structures were unfamiliar to most people in the early nineteenth century and certainly not familiar to Joseph Smith. Certain physical structures constitute evidence for Mormons of the validity of the Book of Mormon as well, including altars in Yemen, one of which is believed to have an inscription of a name found in the Book of Mormon.[30] The stakes of the empirical debate are high, given the relatively brief existence of the Mormon tradition compared to other world religions, and the doctrinal emphasis Mormons place on their church being the one and only true religion. Brigham Young University (BYU) has a foundation, the Foundation for Ancient Research and Mormon Studies (FARMS), that consists of Mormon scholars whose work seeks to connect archaeological discoveries with teachings in the Book of Mormon. FARMS scholars use techniques such as glottochronology, a controversial means of studying language that uses statistical comparison of vocabulary of two or more related languages. Critics such as Coe contend that it is not possible to apply the Book of Mormon to studying the ancient peoples of Mexico and Central America. Indeed, Coe compares the work of FARMS to building an engaging stage set without any actors to play the parts.[31] Daniel Peterson, FARMS member and BYU professor, agreed with Coe that scholars probably do not have archaeological evidence of the ancient civilizations discussed in the Book of Mormon, but the problem for him is that contemporary scholars are not in a position to recognize the evidence, because the appearance of the Nephite artifacts is dependent on the Book of Mormon and unknown.[32] DNA evidence is an emerging area within the empirical debate over the Book of Mormon. Scholars have taken thousands of samples from people in various American Indian tribes throughout different regions. The DNA consistently points to Asian descent, particularly the Mongolian people from Northwest Asia. "This does not seem to match the traditional ideas of the Book of Mormon, which ought to be giving us Hebrew, Semitic DNA."[33]

For many Mormons the truth of Joseph Smith's experiences is beyond question. For many non-Mormons Smith's historical assertions range from unusual to absurd. This disjuncture promotes unity within the Mormon culture and generates a degree of disfavor among the American populace at large. Non-Mormons tend to lump all Mormons into one monolithic caricature, given the intricacies of their beliefs, their predominance in one state, and their relatively small numbers as a segment of the overall population. As with any religious group, there is a spectrum of belief and adherence within the Mormon tradition. Some scholars, including Mormons such as Kathleen Flake, professor of American religious history at Vanderbilt Divinity School, have put forth alternative understandings of Joseph Smith beyond faith and science. Flake observed that several motivations simultaneously inform human behavior, making it difficult to reduce all of Smith's revelations on polygamy to sex drive or the whole Book of Mormon to treasure hunting. In turn, Smith is too complex to understand as God's puppet, doing solely what God wanted, or as a charlatan pretender, who fabricated the entire religion for personal gain.[34]

Along these lines, Jon Butler, professor of American studies, history, and religious studies at Yale University, argued that even those who believe Smith's teachings are a fraud, should understand his work as an act of creation. Nonbelievers can acknowledge that the message and approach were extraordinarily compelling and effective, considering how Mormonism persisted and grew, while many other faiths that emerged at that time and place have perished. For Butler, Smith's genius was his organizational ability. Mormonism redefined how people organized their lives and fanned out across the country and eventually the world. Connections within families and within communities were different from what Protestants and Catholics typically experienced. In this regard "nineteenth-century Mormonism is one of the most astonishing creations ever put forward in American society and certainly ever put forward in American religion."[35] Mormons turned Smith's revelations and "a small, very cult-like sect into a flourishing and worldwide religion."[36] Mormonism is "a living historical religion in a peculiar kind of way," one that "actually emphasizes contemporaneous belief and practice," because its faith is founded "on a history that is in fact difficult to ascertain as what we might say is a scientific fact."[37] Mormonism is more a religion of personal transformation, particularly within the context of family and society, than historically based. The practice of modern faith, one that reconstructs the family, the community, and ultimately society, trumps the lack of archaeological evidence in support of the events of the Book of Mormon in the United States.

Mormons are also awed by the creative aspect of Smith's work, but understand Smith's young age and lack of education as signs of divine intervention. Apostle Jeffrey Holland argued that "the only thing more miraculous than an angel providing Joseph Smith with the golden plates" and "him translating them by divine inspiration would be that he sat down and wrote it with a ball-point pen and a spiral notebook." Smith is mortal, not divine, and Mormons do not worship him, but what Smith witnessed, and his testimony about God, Jesus, and related beliefs, are incredibly important to contemporary Mormons. Holland suggested that the objections some nonbelievers have about the timing of Smith's revelations are unfounded. For Holland, it is "much easier to believe or conceive the traditions of 4,000 years ago, a lot easier than 40 years ago, let alone four weeks ago. It's just easier to have that distance," but "why is the appearance of angels in the Old Testament less satisfying or more threatening than the appearance of an angel in upstate New York in the early part of the nineteenth century or today? The miracles of the Old Testament should not have been startling to people in the time of the New Testament, and New Testament miracles should not be foreign to us today."[38] Smith expressed empathy for his skeptics toward the end of his life. "if I had not experienced what I have, Smith conceded, I should not have believed it myself."[39]

Mormonism split after Smith's death in 1844. Mormons, as commonly referred to today, trace their faith back to the contingent of Mormons under

Brigham Young. Many Mormons stayed behind when Young led his followers to Utah in 1847 and formed the Reorganized Church of Jesus Christ of Latter Day Saints, which was led by Smith's son, Joseph Smith III. This denomination was renamed Community of Christ in 2001 and is headquartered in Independence, Missouri. A second major split centered on the abandonment of plural marriage in 1890. Various denominations, such as the Fundamentalist Church of Jesus Christ of Latter-Day Saints, still participate in the practice and oppose antibigamy laws. An estimated 100,000 polygamists reside in Utah. State and local authorities typically decline to prosecute unless sexual misconduct with minors is suspected. This book is focused on the primary LDS denomination centered in Salt Lake City.

MORMON DOCTRINE

Mormons view their work as the restoration of the gospel, which they believe lost essential aspects since its origin "through distortions and accretions that were thought to have accumulated over the centuries under Roman Catholicism."[40] Smith deviated from other restoration traditions by using his own revelations as the basis of restoration, rather than biblical interpretation and strict adherence, as undertaken by Alexander Campbell, founder of the rival Disciples of Christ. In fact, Smith had little education and did not attend church regularly as a boy. Smith did not debate Christian theologians or contest creeds. Rather, Smith "simply announced new doctrines rather than posing them against the errors in traditional Christian belief" and "pictured his revelations as a flood of knowledge pouring from heaven."[41]

In the early nineteenth century, there was a "burgeoning sense of the boundlessness of the human spirit," which was evident in political life and theory surrounding the Declaration of Independence and the French Revolution. The human being was being depicted with romanticism in the realm of literature and philosophy. People were understood as capable of infinite potential and unconstrained by physical limitations.[42] From its beginnings, Mormon theology was an optimistic and upbeat reaction against New England Calvinism, which denied original sin, stressed individual moral choice, and proclaimed that every man could become a god of his own planet. LDS theology can be described as "a religious version of the American dream: Everyman presented with unlimited potential."[43] Mormons believe that God talks to them thanks to Joseph Smith. Smith's first visions were important to followers in their "finding that by asking a simple question, God responds in a personal, discernable way."[44] Every adherent seeks inspiration and "revelation provides individual Mormons with a 'testimony,' one of the most potent words in the Mormon lexicon." Revelations to Mormons, men and women, rich and poor, young and old, "confirm the truth of the gospel of Christ and the words of the prophets."[45]

There are two distinct elements to Mormon revelation. The first is the expectation that people will receive revelations. The second is that not receiving revelation is a reflection of failure in one's religious life.[46] President Hinckley explained how Mormons believe in continuous revelation and believe the church is guided by revelation. "We pray, we ponder, we think, we ask, and we receive direction as to what to do. I think that's going on all the time."[47] And as Terryl Givens put it, "Henry Ford wanted a car in every home. Joseph Smith was the Henry Ford of revelation. He wanted every home to have one, and the revelation he had in mind was the revelation he'd had, which was seeing God."[48] Yet according to Kathleen Flake, this can be "dangerous in a pluralistic society where various visions of what is right and good are in competition, because Mormons will look to God to tell them what is right and good."[49] There was a sense during the early years that everyone could be a prophet. This was managed by Smith, who established via revelation that there is one prophet at a time, beginning with him. The "prophet went from being a calling to being an office in the church," which established a hierarchy and a precedent that many Americans likened in a negative way to the Catholic pope, because "it seemed anti-American, anti-democratic that we should have one person that is vested so much power and authority to dictate for his followers."[50] At the same time, the priesthood was made available to virtually every white Mormon male, and the ministry was not paid, which mixed democratic components with a rigid authority structure.

Mormons believe that the spirits of all people lived with God prior to being born. The Heavenly Father loves all His children, but believes that souls need time away from Him to progress, similar to parents on earth. The Book of Mormon builds on Genesis's understanding of Adam and Eve in suggesting that the fall was not all bad. Nephi explained that if Adam and Eve never left the Garden of Eden, "they would have had no children; wherefore they would have remained in a state of innocence, having no joy, for they knew no misery; doing no good, for they knew no sin."[51] Spirits are sent to earth to feel joy and pain through physical existence. The basis of God's plan is for people to become more like Him throughout their lives. Leaving the Garden of Eden enabled Adam and Eve to progress and learn in such a manner that they became more like the Heavenly Father.

Mormons believe that procreation is pivotal for souls to move beyond a childlike state of innocence and understanding morality. Leaving the Garden of Eden enabled Adam and Eve to have children and led the way for billions of people to subsequently come to earth, experience physical life, and be tested and proven through daily choices. God does not interfere with people making poor choices, but offers love, divine guidance, and warnings when people open their hearts to Him, particularly in the face of temptations from Satan. If people are obedient to the gospel of Jesus Christ, as Adam and Eve became, they are able to receive God's inspiration, revelation, and visits from heavenly messengers. Mormons believe that the Garden of Eden was a physical place, located near Independence, Missouri, and that God will return there during the Second Coming.

Mormons believe that God the father, his son Jesus Christ, and the Holy Spirit "are blended in heart and mind like extremely close friends but are not one being."[52] God "the Father has a body of flesh and bones as tangible as man's" and "the Son also, but the Holy Ghost has not a body of flesh and bones, but is a personage of Spirit."[53] Smith's most radical teaching was that "God was of the same order being as humans," so that "humans exist in the same ontological realm as the creator" and belong to "the same species." This collapse of sacred distance contributes to the distinctness of the Mormon faith in the realm of Christianity.[54] Mormons believe that the Greeks distorted early Christian teachings by incorporating a belief in God as outside time and space, contrary to the correct interpretation of the Bible.

Mormons believe that marriages form families and that families are the most fundamental unit of societies. Without family, people are unable to experience God's salvation. Families serve an important role as the institution responsible for passing moral strengths, traditions, and values that sustain civilization for future generations. More specifically, families were established to bring happiness to God's children by allowing them to learn "correct" principles in a loving atmosphere in preparation for returning to God in death. According to LDS historian Marlin Jensen, "in a world of shifting values and in some cases no values at all the eternal truths upon which the gospel is based have positioned the Church in the last century to be an anchor in a sea of change. Nowhere is this more apparent than in the Church's efforts throughout the twentieth century to safeguard the institution of family."[55]

The emphasis on family in the Mormon tradition is different in degree than Protestantism, Catholicism, or Judaism. The family is viewed as a coherent unit with a collective sense of moral responsibility and enterprise. Religion is a family matter, rather than just an individual matter. Men serve as the head of the family. This role traces its theological roots to Ephesians. Wives are directed to submit to their husbands as they submit themselves to God. Husbands are instructed to love their wives as themselves. Husbands are considered the head of the wife just as Jesus is considered head of the church. "As the church is subject unto Christ, so let the wives be to their own husbands in everything."[56]

Urban church communities are specially organized to group singles in the hope of facilitating engagements. Some single Mormon women go to college ultimately to find a husband. A high hope of Mormon parents is for their children to get married in a temple. Marrying in a temple suggests that the people being wed have effectively lived the Mormon lifestyle, selected a worthy Mormon partner, and chosen to abide by the covenant of the temple endowment. Gender is eternal in Mormon theology. Mormons view procreation as a gift and privilege from God that will persist for eternity. This creates difficulty situating homosexuality within Mormon theology. The church directs gays and lesbians to be celibate if they are unable to have an honest marriage with a partner of the opposite sex. Many leave the church, which is particularly difficult given the spiritual, familial, and social interconnection of Mormonism.

Mormons have assumed responsibility for baptizing every person who has lived and sealing every heterosexual marriage. This involves a global effort to digitize every genealogical record in existence.[57] The ordinances of dead are performed in proxy by living Mormons. The LDS church has over 2 million rolls of microfilm containing approximately 2 billion names in their storage vaults. Baptizing humankind is ambitious and costly. Smith believed that the gospel will be preached in the afterlife, so dead people will have the opportunity to convert. Still, Mormons are uniquely dedicated to conversion. Mormons and Jehovah's Witnesses are the only two religious groups in the United States today with majorities who believe their religion is the one true faith leading to eternal life. Most Americans believe that many religions can lead to eternal life, including those besides their own. The Mormon afterlife is understood as a physical and active experience. President Hinckley explained that people are not going to float around heaven with wings. The dead will be individuals with personalities and the abilities to talk, work, and be active in every respect.[58] Mormons believe that the spirit leaves the body like a hand in a glove. The glove is buried, but the spirit body lives on. There are gradations of heaven, and people receive a just reward for how they have lived their lives, exercised agency, and made choices.[59]

Discipline is an important part of the Mormon tradition. "Smith constantly engaged in disciplining believers and thrusting some believers out and not accepting others."[60] This was not unusual. All religious groups create mechanisms to establish and maintain their religious authority. Mormon parents today appreciate the difficulties behavioral rules place on their children, such as prohibition of smoking, drinking, and premarital sex, and the expectation to serve on missions. The continued devotion of new generations of Mormons is imperative for survival and growth, particularly given the lack of professional clergy. The church sponsors numerous activities designed "to keep young people within the orbit of the church," including Scouting, dances, youth conferences, service projects, and weekly or daily instructional classes.[61] Sins can be forgiven when transgressions occur. The larger concern is abandonment of the faith. " 'Excommunication' is a word that does and should send a chill down the spine of Mormons," because in the Mormon belief system the repercussions affect the entire eternal structure of one's family.[62] Only a very small percentage of people who are excommunicated return, and often there is a ripple effect, in which other family members leave the church if one member is excommunicated. Direct and public challenges to Mormon leadership and Mormon doctrine are the primary grounds for excommunication.

THE MODERN CHURCH

The Mormon church experienced unprecedented international growth during the 1950s and 1960s. David O. McKay, the first Mormon president with a college degree, presided over the church during this time. McKay "knew the importance of image before the era of professional image makers." Greg Prince explained:

> David O. McKay not only looked modern and looked different; he transformed the church into a modern worldwide church.... We were a church that still was insular. We brought people to Salt Lake.... Rather than saying, "Come to Utah when you're converted," he said, "let's reverse that, stay where you are. Make the church a vital force throughout the world." We've been in the game for more than 100 years. We didn't have an authentic presence outside of the United States.... He made the decision to plant temples internationally. We had never had that before. The number of missionaries multiplied severalfold. The number of convert baptisms multiplied even more so because he injected that new spirit into what they were doing.... McKay said: "Every member of the church needs to be a missionary. Take this message throughout the world, and when you take it, by the way, members, stay where you are. Put the roots down where you're already planted, and let's make this church succeed everywhere."[63]

The growth rate of the church in the second half of the twentieth century was nearly double that of the first half. In 1965 the church published its family home evening manual, which later was designated for Monday nights. In 1971 existing Mormon magazines were consolidated into *Ensign* for adults, *New Era* for youth, and *Friend* for children. The First Quorum of the Seventy was developed in 1976 to help administer the church. Two years later President Spencer Kimball allowed racial minorities to receive priesthood privileges. The current three-hour Sunday meeting was adopted in 1980. Previously, church meetings were held at various times during the week.[64] The purpose of the consolidated meeting was "to reemphasize personal and family responsibility for learning, living, and teaching the gospel" and "to allow Church members more time for personal gospel study, for service to others, and for meaningful activities."[65] From 1900 to 2000 the Mormon community grew from 268,000 to nearly 11 million people.[66] At century's end the religion was gaining 1 million adherents every three and a half years.[67] Five out of six Mormons lived in the western United States in 1901. By 1996, Mormons living outside the United States outnumbered American Mormons. Spanish is on pace to become the predominant language of Mormons by 2025.[68] Contemporary Mormonism is clearly an international force, yet also constitutes a powerful and self-contained American subculture, which still seeks acceptance from the skeptical nation in which their uniquely American tradition was born.

Control and consistency throughout the global Mormon community is a challenge. The Mormon Church operates in "a highly centralized and authoritarian structure" with top-down, "self-perpetuating hierarchy that is ritualistically 'sustained' by unanimous vote at church conferences in Salt Lake City."[69] Global outreach efforts were costly from the outset, and the financial solvency of the church was in question late into the late nineteenth century. Mormons developed a strong financial position by gradually building a collection of church-owned businesses, dating back to the Zion Cooperative Mercantile Institution, one of the first department stores in the United States, established in 1868. The LDS Church went into the broadcasting business during the 1960s and subsequently controlled Bonneville International, a broadcasting empire. The for-profit portion of the church, Deseret Management Corporation, was established in 1966.[70] Estimates of financial worth and land ownership vary. One scholarly estimate suggests that "the church's more than 150 farms and ranches, including America's largest cattle ranch, make it one of the largest landowners in the nation.[71] President Hinckley contended that most of the church's money comes from tithing and that in fact the church's business activity is limited. The holdings and profits of the church are not public knowledge. The net worth of the church is tens of billions of dollars, including ownership of stocks, bonds, and various corporations.[72]

Mormon leadership is patriarchal. The structure was developed by Joseph Smith through revelation and has been described as a "charismatic bureaucracy."[73] The General Authorities constitute the top leadership structure of the church and can serve anywhere in the world. There are five major parts to the hierarchy of General Authorities: (1) First Presidency, (2) the Quorum of Twelve Apostles, (3) Presidency of the Seventy, (4) Quorums of the Seventy, and (5) Presiding Bishopric. The top individual leader of the church is the president and "the prophet." There have been a total of 16 church presidents, as listed in Table 2.1. When a church president dies, it is customary for the most senior apostle to become the next president. The prophet chooses a first counselor and second counselor. These three men serve as The First Presidency. The First Presidency is supplemented by the Quorum of Twelve Apostles, the second-highest governing body of the church. Apostles are considered special witnesses to Jesus Christ, serve for life, and are ranked by seniority.

There are eight Quorums of the Seventy that work under the Quorum of Twelve Apostles. The Quorums of the Seventy consist of up to 70 members per quorum, referred to as "seventies." Their efforts are focused on proclaiming the gospel and building the church. Most seventies work in specific geographic regions, though some undertake administrative functions at the church's headquarters. Seventies and apostles travel frequently in order to

Table 2.1
Presidents of the Church of Jesus Christ of Latter-day Saints

Name	Number	Years of Service
Joseph Smith	First	1830–44
Brigham Young	Second	1847–77
John Taylor	Third	1880–87
Wilford Woodruff	Fourth	1887–98
Lorenzo Snow	Fifth	1898–1901
Joseph F. Smith	Sixth	1901–18
Heber J. Grant	Seventh	1918–45
George Albert Smith	Eighth	1945–51
David O. McKay	Ninth	1951–70
Joseph Fielding Smith	Tenth	1970–72
Harold B. Lee	Eleventh	1972–73
Spencer W. Kimball	Twelve	1973–85
Ezra Taft Benson	Thirteen	1985–94
Howard W. Hunter	Fourteen	1994–95
Gordon B. Hinckley	Fifteen	1995–2008
Thomas S. Monson	Sixteenth	2008–Present

Source: Church History, the Church of Jesus Christ of Latter-day Saints, http://www.lds.org/church history/presidents/leaders.jsp.

visit and counsel various congregations. Members of the First Quorum of the Seventy can serve until the age of 70. Members of the Second Quorum serve for three to five years. Members of the first and second quorums are General Authorities, whereas members in the remaining quorums are called "Area Seventies," whose authority is limited to the territory in which they serve. Seventies are led by the Presidency of Seventy. The Presidency of the Seventy is composed of seven members from the first and second quorums. All seven men serve as presidents. In contrast to the First Presidency, there are no counselors. The seventh and most senior president presides over the other six.

Priesthood holders have the sole authority to baptize Mormons, bless the sacrament, confer priesthood, perform eternal marriages, and anoint the sick.[74] There are two priesthoods in the Mormon faith. The Melchizedek priesthood consists of the highest church leaders who organize and direct the preaching of the gospel around the world. The origins of this priesthood are traced to Adam, who is believed to have been given this authority from God. This authority was taken from earth during the Great Apostasy, which for Mormons refers to the corruption of Christianity after Jesus and the disciples died. The Melchizedek priesthood was reestablished in 1829 when Peter, James, and John conferred this responsibility on Joseph Smith and Oliver Cowdery, one of the witnesses to the golden plates and an early Mormon leader. The Aaronic priesthood is "an appendage to the greater, or the Melchizedek Priesthood."[75] Members of the Aaronic priesthood, who are referred to as "priesthood holders," prepare for the Melchizedek priesthood by receiving the blessings of the temple, serving a mission, and becoming a husband and father.

The Presiding Bishopric serves under the First Presidency and administers the temporal affairs of the church. Specifically, the Presiding Bishopric is the presidency of the Aaronic priesthood. The Aaronic priesthood consists of the offices of bishop, priest, and deacon. Boys can become deacons at the age of 12. Deacons help pass the sacrament, which for Mormons refers to an ordinance, or sacred formal act performed under the authority of the priesthood, in which members consume bread and water in remembrance of the sacrifices Jesus made. The passing of the sacrament is designed to renew the covenants Mormons made with God during baptism. Boys can be ordained as priests at the age of 16. Priests help administer the sacrament and preach the gospel. Bishops are responsible for leading and managing the temporal and spiritual affairs of the ward or congregation.

Smith's revelations spoke little about democracy, Righteousness is the primary value of the priesthood government, which has been compared to eighteenth-century political theory for its emphasis on cultivating virtue among rulers and the citizenry. "Priesthood government sought to redeem people, not just serve their interests."[76] Priests are viewed as godly teachers rather than protectors of rights. Priests are supposed to exercise power in a benevolent fashion, as outlined by revelation, through giving and receiving, not ordering and submitting. The priesthood forms a male hierarchy in congregations premised on age and experience. "Mormon women are keenly aware that that they do not hold the priesthood" and that "their voices are not routinely heard in the leading councils of the church, where power is exclusively male."[77]

SUMMARY

This chapter discussed the origins of the Mormon religion, basic Mormon doctrine, and the structure of the Church of Jesus Christ of Latter-day Saints. Mormonism is commonly understood as a uniquely American religion. The religious freedom afforded Americans beginning in the early nineteenth century created a fertile political climate that enabled creative interpretations of Christianity. From a Mormon perspective, American law and society enabled a theologically paramount correction of Christianity gone astray. This included revealing a lost ancient history of the United States as recorded in the Book of Mormon, reestablishing the important role for prophets and revelation in Christian worship, revealing the prelife experiences of people with the Heavenly Father, understanding life as an enriching test of virtue and righteousness, renewing the spiritual emphasis on individual moral choice, correcting the authority of the priesthood, and reestablishing the central role of families as an eternally bonded unit. Smith once claimed to govern Mormons by a thread. "I teach them correct principles, and they govern themselves."[78] Smith knew that concentrated power in a democratizing society would arouse suspicion, particularly when divine inspiration was the ruling mandate. Unfortunately for Smith, his inclinations proved correct. The following chapter will discuss the historical development of the Mormon community, the extensive persecution experienced by Mormons, and the characteristics of the modern Mormon subculture in the United States.

3

From Temple Square to Broadway

THE MORMON TRAIL

Mormons are among the most persecuted religious groups in American history. As the religion developed, Mormons congregated in large enough numbers "to completely alter the political dynamics in those counties where they settled."[1] Non-Mormon neighbors quickly lost sovereignty over lands they had settled and controlled for years. Mormons regularly differentiated themselves from other Christians, who were labeled Gentiles; proselytized natives; and spoke triumphantly about their beliefs. This offended existing Christians, many of whom viewed Mormon teachings as radical and blasphemous. Mormons did not court persecution, but persecution "brought them exhilaration and conviction [that] what they were doing was the right thing, because God's prophets have never been welcome in their own lands." Persecution experiences were a source of pride to a certain extent and "used as a means of condemning a tyrannical, central government that imposed such pain" and "many wounds on Utah in the nineteenth century."[2] By the end of Smith's life, "Mormons thought of themselves as a persecuted people. Memories of hardship, suffering, and the opposition of a hostile world became a large part of Mormon identity."[3]

Popular portrayals of Mormonism explained conversion as a product of mesmerism or hypnotism conducted by Mormon leaders because it was widely believed that "no one would ever convert to Mormonism of his or her own free will."[4] Mormons were portrayed as villains in popular fiction throughout the nineteenth century and depicted as a physically and linguistically distinct group. This "allayed some of the dread and the anxiety that was provoked by this sense that the Mormons were infiltrating the body politic." People feared neighbors, friends, and relatives "falling victim to these seducing Mormon missionaries" and felt "defenseless because there was no way of identifying them."[5] This imagery was evident in prominent literature, including the first Sherlock Holmes novel, *A Study in Scarlet*, which featured Mormons as the guilty culprits. Mark Twain famously described the Book of Mormon as "chloroform in print." Ironically, Mormons in the twenty-first century are often caricatured in mainstream culture for embodying the center rather than the periphery. Mormons are now "mocked as white-bread, *Ozzie and Harriet,* 1950s families, too good to be true, with boring personalities, and so clean-cut that they're slightly nauseating."[6] In some ways the intense hatred of Mormonism is perplexing. "Mormons were plain old, largely white, English-descended American farmers who were God-fearing, lived in agricultural settlements, and wanted the best for the children, for their wives, for their families."[7] The fear of the unknown surrounding the rise of the Mormons was similar to how American Protestants feared Roman Catholics. Fear was centered on the general lack of transparency surrounding the norms and practices within the Church.

Institutional Mormonism began in 1830 when Joseph Smith organized the Church of Christ. Smith's governing authority was derived from his ability to communicate with God. Smith was directed by revelation to move to Ohio because of secret enemies in New York who sought to kill church leaders.[8] The town of Kirtland existed for 20 years prior to Smith's arrival in 1831. By 1837 over half of the town's population of approximately 2,000 was Mormon.[9] Smith went from the subject of widespread criticism in Palmyra to a religious leader surrounded by thousands of admirers. The practices of Kirtland Mormons were charismatic. Testimony included gyrations, speaking in tongues, and scalping performances.

While in Kirtland, Smith organized a search for the site of Zion in preparation for the Second Coming. The plan was for Zion to become the epicenter of the Mormon community and for Kirtland to become a city stake. Smith originally believed the Second Coming would arrive within six years. Zion would serve as the place where the righteous could find safety during God's wrath. Smith "observed the world through a millennial lens. Mindful of the apocalyptic future, he watched for calamities signaling the end."[10] Independence, Missouri, was selected, a choice later verified through revelation. Missouri's Jackson County was organized just six years prior and the town of Independence had fewer than 20 dwellings. In just two years, 1,200 Mormons settled there. This "remote location in the middle of North America became the place where Mormons from around the globe believed they were to gather, build a temple, live by consecration, have no poor, and be of one heart and one mind."[11] Zion became one of approximately 137 communitarian experiments undertaken between 1787 and 1860.

The Mormons planned to build their first temple in Kirtland in 1833. Cost and public opposition were two major obstacles. The cost of the temple well exceeded what little money the Church had. Smith went deeply into debt and was hounded by creditors for the rest of his life.[12] Mormons lived during a time "when citizen vigilantes considered it their duty to discipline disruptive elements in the community."[13] Mormons first encountered mob violence in 1832. Smith was dragged from his bed in the middle of the night, tarred and feathered, and nearly castrated.[14] Mormons were expelled from Jackson County, and Zion was abolished. "An unanticipated consequence of gathering was the build-up of Mormon political power."[15] Mormons "held 2,400 acres of land in and around Independence and threatened a complete takeover."[16] Jackson County citizens accused Mormons of religious fanaticism and inviting blacks to settle in the county. Mormons were treated like an enemy nation, similar to Native Americans, and were driven away by violence and intimidation.[17]

Experiences in Jackson County prompted Smith to view government with newfound importance as he sought security and protection for Mormons. Revelations had not previously mentioned nations or governments. God was viewed as the only just ruler of heaven and earth. The Mormons framed their political appeals in constitutional terms. A revelation in August of 1833 stated that the rights and privileges of the Constitution belonged to all and were justifiable before God. This was reflected in a letter Smith wrote to Missouri Mormons that asserted "we are all friends of the Constitution yea true friends to that Country for which our fathers bled."[18] Smith was regularly involved in politics from this point on. "For a decade, he sought protection from the government, usually without success, until finally, frustrated by his inability to rally government to the Saints' tide, he ran for president."[19]

Revelation did not clearly instruct Mormons how to respond to violence. Extreme pacifism and vigorous militarism are present in the Book of Mormon. An early revelation instructed Mormons to obtain Zion through purchase, not violence, not to be afraid, but to renounce war, proclaim peace, and avoid retaliation. The same revelation indicated that armed resistance was justified if Mormons were repeatedly injured.[20] A later revelation in 1834 stated that the redemption of Zion needed to come through power. Mormons were instructed to organize hundreds of men to seek restitution from the enemies of Mormons, but fighting was not mentioned by name. Smith typically advocated peace in the face of persecution, but there was a military component to his leadership. The council of elders unanimously appointed Smith commander and chief of the armies of Israel in 1834. The Mormons formed a military group named "Zion's Camp" that consisted of approximately 200 Mormons who hiked 25 miles a day from Kirtland to Jackson County.[21] The group, which included men, women, and children, aspired for military order, but was not strongly disciplined.

The Mormons requested protection from Missouri governor Daniel Dunklin, who assured them that the law would be enforced without using troops. This ignored the fact that members of law enforcement and the courts were actively opposed to Mormons. Dunklin later suggested that the Mormons organize a militia for defense because he could use the state militia only in times of public danger and the Mormon problem did not qualify. This prompted the Mormons to appeal to President Andrew Jackson to use the federal government to suppress insurrection and execute the laws of the land. Jackson also declined to intervene because no federal laws were violated. Mormon pursuit of government protection upset Jackson County residents. Mormon-owned stores and homes were destroyed. Women and children were forced out in search of Mormon men, who were beaten and whipped. Shots were fired and three people were killed, two Missourians and one Mormon.

As Zion's Camp approached, attorneys representing the Mormons met with non-Mormon agitators. Each side sought to buy out the other side. Smith followed the advice of his lawyers, did not engage in violence, and instead sought damages through the court system. The march back to Kirtland was difficult. Members had traveled a great distance for nothing. Missouri Mormons lived as refugees in an adjacent county. A cholera outbreak killed dozens. The failure of the expedition prompted some Mormons to criticize Smith, who was charged with criminal conduct for mismanagement and the use of abusive language, but found innocent by church authorities. Most camp members were closely bonded to Smith as a result of their shared hardships. Several subsequent Mormon leaders were selected from the camp, including 9 of the original 12 Mormon apostles.[22]

Significant internal dissension challenged Smith's leadership in Ohio. Longtime friend and visionary companion Oliver Cowdery accused Joseph of having an affair. Smith never denied having a relationship with the woman in question, Fanny Alger, but insisted their relationship was not adulterous. The nature of their relationship is unclear. Plural marriage may have been the rationale adopted by Smith, but plural marriage was not recorded as a revelation until 1843.[23] Financial troubles were another source of dissension. The Church went deeply in debt building the Kirtland temple. Smith's efforts to recoup these losses were ineffective and embarrassing. He resorted to treasure seeking, which did not work, and opened a bank that failed in under a month. All investors lost their money. "Carried along by the booster spirit that infected virtually every western town in these decades, Joseph promised too much."[24] Smith regularly faced terse questioning and criticism from prominent Mormon leaders[25] Excommunication was used to discipline people who directly questioned church leadership. Over 20 percent of priest-holding converts were excommunicated during Smith's lifetime.[26]

In 1836 residents of Clay County, where Mormons had sought refuge after being forced from Jackson County, also demanded that the Mormons leave. Clay County residents were originally sympathetic to Mormons of little financial means who were violently displaced. But the Mormons wore out their welcome after growing in prosperity, increasing in numbers, and fully displaying their "alien character."[27] The separation was amicable. Citizens raised money for the poorest Mormons and helped them relocate. Mormons were asked to move to neighboring Ray County. After meeting resistance, the state legislature passed a bill to break off a new county from Ray County, called Caldwell County, for the Mormons to settle in. Mormons moved in and planned the construction of a temple. Smith encountered an altar and tower that he believed was used by the Mormon prophet Nephi, then received a revelation that Adam went to the spot after being expelled from the Garden of Eden. Mormons rapidly moved to Caldwell County.

External and internal challenges prompted Smith to flee Kirtland in 1838 with other church leaders.[28] Smith claimed that he left when armed men were within 200 miles of the town. It is not clear if the men were Mormons or angry creditors seeking to collect on their debts. Two months later Smith was greeted warmly by Missouri Mormons. Far West in Caldwell County had become a thriving city.[29] Once again, the growing number of Mormons concerned their non-Mormon neighbors, particularly in Daviess County, the county north of Caldwell County, where Mormons had grown to one-third of the electorate. Tensions arose surrounding a fight that broke out at a local polling booth, when non-Mormons sought to prevent Mormons from voting. Law authorities blamed Smith for the fight even though he was not there. Smith refused to be tried in the county because of concerns regarding lack of impartiality. People throughout the region took up arms against the Mormons.[30] Vigilantes demanded that the Mormons leave. The Mormons appealed to the governor for safety and were told to fight their own battles.

Far West was put under martial law. The Mormons engaged in militant self-defense, led by Danites. The Danites were a secret Mormon society, several hundred in number, originally formed in 1838 to drive out Mormon dissenters, by violence if necessary.[31] Danites consisted of more extreme elements of the Mormon community and were successful in scaring dissenters from Far West. Loyalty to Joseph Smith was the ultimate test of worthiness. The Danites were not led directly by Smith, but he favored evicting dissenters and resisting mobs.[32] This included confiscating property from hostile Daviess citizens and forcing them to move. These efforts fueled vigilantism against Mormons. Daviess County became a war zone. This took a disastrous turn for Mormons when they attacked a contingent of county militia, who were mistakenly thought to be vigilantes. This skirmish at Crooked River in Ray County prompted charges of treason against Joseph Smith. "Resisting a band of vigilantes was justifiable, but attacking a militia company was resistance to the state."[33]

An official decree issued by Missouri governor Lilburn Boggs ordered Mormons to leave under the threat of extermination without regard to age or gender.[34] The decree stated that "the Mormons must be treated as enemies, and must be exterminated or driven from the State if necessary for the public peace—their outrages are beyond description."[35] The Haun's Mill massacre, the climax of the Mormon War, occurred shortly thereafter in October of 1838. A group of Missourians ambushed and killed 17 Mormon men and boys at Haun's Mill, 15 miles east of Far West, as women and children fled into the woods. Smith surrendered with four other Mormon leaders. The men were treated as prisoners of war. The Mormons were expected to give up arms and leave the state. Mormon property was confiscated to reimburse Daviess County residents whose homes were burned by Mormons. Mormon men signed over their property to the state under militia supervision.

Smith was imprisoned and put on trial for treason. Testimony, primarily from Mormons, portrayed Smith as the leader of an independent government who intended to wage war on Missouri.[36] Smith believed Mormons acted in self-defense and failed to sufficiently appreciate that power had slipped into the hands of more militant Mormons with disastrous consequences. Smith and the other Mormon prisoners of war were convinced that vigilantes would kill them even if they were found innocent. The prisoners escaped in April of 1839 and rejoined the Mormon community, who had moved to Illinois. Smith and other Mormon leaders went to Washington, DC, to lobby their cause. Smith met with President Martin Van Buren and members of Congress from Illinois, in the hope of securing reparations for lost property.[37] Missouri representatives opposed these efforts, and the Senate Judiciary Committee ruled that compensation should be attained through Missouri courts. Missouri welcomed Smith's return, so he could be prosecuted, and later unsuccessfully sought to extradite him.

THE CITY OF NAUVOO

Mormons went to Illinois and settled the city of Nauvoo, which became the fastest-growing city in the state, comparable to the size of Chicago. Nauvoo is Hebrew for "a beautiful situation or place."[38] Smith's ambitions for the Mormon community in Nauvoo were typical of the time and place, including population growth, commercial development, prosperity, and "freedom under the law to live and worship as they pleased."[39] "Hundreds of small western American towns aimed to build a 'great Emporium,'" but Nauvoo was the only one that "had a prophet as mayor, uniting religion and the state."[40] Nauvoo was viewed by Mormons as an international religious capital as thousands of English converts arrived, the product of missionary work in England. Earlier predictions of the Second Coming were refined to include a more positive focus on building a spiritual haven on earth. A temple was built and a Masonic lodge was opened. In a few years, Mormon Masons in Nauvoo outnumbered the rest of the Masons in the state. Smith and 11 of the Twelve Apostles became Masons, and Masonic norms were incorporated into Mormon temple rituals.[41]

External tensions resurfaced in 1842 after a potential assassination attempt on Lilburn Boggs, the former Missouri governor who had ordered the Mormon extermination order. Smith was inaccurately rumored to be involved, went into hiding, but was caught in September. He successfully challenged Missouri extradition efforts in the U.S. Circuit Court, a rare political victory for the Mormon leader. Extradition efforts resurfaced in

1843, however, when Illinois governor Thomas Ford agreed to turn Smith over to Missouri to face the charge of treason. Smith and his captors were being transported for legal processing when a band of nearly 200 Mormon men diverted the party to Nauvoo, where Joseph was afforded a hero's welcome. Smith's captors were treated well and offered little resistance, knowing their lives were at risk. The political fallout for Mormons was devastating. Illinois citizens were outraged that Smith had escaped arrest. Nauvoo prepared for war. The city council created a police force and outlawed arresting Joseph Smith on the charges of treason with the penalty of life in prison.[42]

Plural marriage increasingly became a source of tension and criticism for Smith within Nauvoo's Mormon community. Smith's covert practice of plural marriage began with one additional marriage around 1836 and then paused until 1841 when Smith married 30 women over the next two years. Ten of Smith's wives were teenagers and 10 were already married.[43] Smith eventually explained that plural marriage was a revelation from God and encouraged the women he married to seek their own inspiration, so they could know this revelation for themselves. If the revelation was denied, however, they would lose their blessings. "The reaction was almost invariably negative."[44] The husbands were aware of Smith's additional marriage to their wives and consented out of the perceived spiritual benefit of being tied to the prophet. The original secrecy of the practice antagonized divisions over the validity of the doctrine, the perimeters of loyalty to the prophet, and who should be permitted to engage in this practice. Emma Smith, Joseph's wife, "probably knew of plural marriage but had no idea of the extent of her husband's practice."[45] Emma was largely opposed to the practice, but did support some marriages, though later regretted doing so. The couple fought several times about Smith's relationships with other women. A later revelation required men to consult with their wives before taking additional wives, but permitted them to move forward independently if their wives refused.[46]

In addition to plural marriage, Smith's opponents questioned his use of power and new revelations, such as the King Follet sermon, which replaced the notion of God creating the universe with the notion that God learned to become God and organized the universe through extraordinary intelligence.[47] Six of Smith's closest associates publicly denounced him as a fallen prophet by the spring of 1844.[48] Excommunication was becoming a less effective tool for managing internal dissent. A reform Mormon Church emerged. Smith believed his Mormon enemies were trying to kill him, while Smith's enemies believed that secret police were after them. Members challenged Smith in court for malicious and defamatory statements, and in the public by raising awareness of his suspected relationships with various women. Smith's opponents secured a press and began to publish the *Nauvoo Expositor*, a newspaper that was heavily critical of Smith. The paper had printed one edition when the city council, led by Smith, accused the press of libel and creating public danger by rallying a mob spirit against the Mormons. The press was closed, which galvanized Smith's external opposition. Men from surrounding counties gathered outside the city. Smith addressed the Nauvoo legion in full military dress, "declared that he would not give up without a fight," and encouraged his soldiers to "die like men of God and secure a glorious resurrection."[49]

Ironically, Smith initially fled out of concern for his security, then agreed to return and face charges for closing the newspaper. He was imprisoned in Carthage prior to the trial. A group of approximately 100 armed men stormed the jail a few days later. Smith, who possessed a gun, which had been smuggled in to him, emptied the weapon, ran to the window, flashed a Mason sign of distress, and fell to the ground after being shot multiple times.[50] The mob consisted of militia men from surrounding counties who were supposed to prevent violence. Illinois governor Thomas Ford was furious. Ford had worked diligently for a peaceful resolution, albeit unsuccessfully. The Mormons did not counterattack as many feared they would. The leaders of the vigilantes were tried and found innocent. The Mormons decided not to participate in the trial. This enabled the jury to include no Mormons even though Mormons constituted a majority in the county. Religious founders are rarely murdered in the United States. Smith sought an ideal of social order through peace and righteousness, but during "every year of his fourteen years as head of the Church, he faced opposition from within and without."[51]

UTAH SETTLEMENT

Mormons were divided over who the new leader should be. The largest group of Mormons left Nauvoo in 1846 under the leadership of Brigham Young.[52] Young led the Mormons westward after Smith's death. Young's predeparture census indicates that 3,285 families left in 2,508 wagons. The Iowa winter was difficult. The group reached Nebraska in June of 1846, traveled through Wyoming, and arrived in the Salt Lake Valley in July of 1847. Over 300 wagon trains, with a total of 10,000 wagons, traveled west to Utah in the next 20 years.[53] The Perpetual Emigration Fund was developed by the Mormon Church to advance travel costs to poor emigrants unable to afford the trip. The program lasted for nearly 40 years and spent millions of dollars relocating people converting to Mormonism. Many of the loans were later forgiven because of the inability of people to repay them.[54] A transportation system was arranged by Mormon leaders in the 1860s that hauled freight eastward by train and returned west with loads of immigrants. This system relocated over 20,000 people throughout the decade.[55]

Utah settlers quickly sought to transform the desert into farmland. Young planned the urban center of Salt Lake City along the lines of Smith's vision for New Jerusalem. Some Mormons preferred California as the new hub of Mormon life because of the prospects of gold. Young reportedly stated that "you can't eat gold" and insisted on the Salt Lake Valley. The gold rush was highly profitable for Mormons who traded with the gold seekers. An estimated 15,000 westward-bound migrants passed through Utah each year.[56] Mormons established settlements along the Wasatch mountain range and supported those settlements with remote colonies along more distant transportation routes. Young called upon people from Salt Lake to establish these towns. This was done by reading their names aloud at general conference sessions. Followers would then pack up and leave as directed. Nearly 100 settlements were developed in the first decade after the Mormons occupied the Salt Lake Valley and over 500 total throughout the nineteenth century.[57]

Mormons fled the United States, but soon found themselves within its borders once again after the Mexican War. Young was appointed territorial governor in 1854. Mormons lived in a separatist theocracy with political, judicial, and ecclesiastical authority invested in Young and the Mormon hierarchy. The "fusion of religious and secular power ensconced Mormonism as the de-facto state church of the Utah Territory."[58] Young "ran the church and the territory like a single entity, ruling as a benevolent despot."[59] Political officials were drawn from church leadership, most of whom "were nominated by the Mormon hierarchy and 'elected' unopposed."[60] Members of the U.S. government and surrounding businessmen objected to this way of life. This time the federal government, rather than state governments or localities, persecuted Mormons. Federal troops were deployed to invade and control the Utah Territory in 1857. President James Buchanan replaced "the personal despotism of Brigham Young" with Alfred Cumming to restore "the supremacy of the Constitution and laws within its limits."[61] The motivation of Buchanan's move is disputed. Buchanan perhaps sought to make an example of Utah with rumors of secession emerging in the South or, less dramatically, sought to divert attention toward theocracy and away from slavery.

In response, the Nauvoo legion of 3,000 men was mobilized. All Mormon missionaries were recalled. Mormons scouted and harassed the federal troops by "stampeding army animals, setting fire to trains, burning the country before them, blocking roads, destroying river crossings, and waking troops at night."[62] Mormons even burned their own settlements in Wyoming to prevent federal troops from utilizing them. During this time, a group of Mormons engaged in one of the darkest episodes of Mormon history. A group of settlers headed to California claimed that Native Americans had poisoned their food and water. Mormons refused to sell them supplies. "For reasons that have never been fully understood, Mormon leaders in southern Utah proceeded to order the destruction of the company. The Indians and the Mormon settlers therefore killed 120 people, virtually everyone in the company except for a few young children."[63] The Mountain Meadows massacre is a sensitive subject for Mormons given the history of Missouri persecution and this inexplicable use of violence by Mormons.

The federal army increased its military presence in the face of Mormon obstruction. Governor Cumming was allowed to peacefully enter Salt Lake City without military support after negotiations between Young and the U.S. government. Cumming was satisfied with Mormon compliance, and Buchanan issued an amnesty proclamation. Young still evacuated Salt Lake City as a precautionary measure when federal troops marched through during their departure and was prepared to burn the city if the troops attacked. No violence occurred in the standoff. This event, referred to as the Utah War, actually enhanced commerce in the territory. Many troops abandoned their property to Mormons after being called to fight in the Civil War.[64] Mormon theocratic power peaked in the mid-1850s.

The practice of plural marriage garnered mounting criticism for Utah Mormons during the second half of the nineteenth century. Plural marriage was viewed theologically as the reinstitution of patriarchal marriage, so Mormons "understood themselves to have been commanded by God to re-create the marital order of the patriarchs of the Old Testament."[65] Monogamy was viewed as the norm, but on certain occasions God commanded polygamy.[66] Smith informed the Twelve Apostles about his plural-marriage revelation in 1841. Twenty-nine other men took at least one additional wife under Smith's authorization.[67] Smith typically asked permission to marry from a father or uncle of the desired bride. Wives were not gathered in one household. Smith spent occasional nights with different wives and presumably had sexual relations.[68] Richard Bushman suggested that Smith "did not marry women to form a warm, human companionship, but to create a network of related wives, children, and kinsmen that would endure into the eternities."[69] Legally, Mormons were in violation of antibigamy laws in Illinois and later federal laws.

The 1852 public announcement of plural-marriage doctrine was carefully orchestrated. A conference was called by the Church, where the practice was defended religiously, as a divine commandment, and socially, only sanctified men could have multiple wives. Salvation was assured to husbands and wives who followed the practice. The Church defended plural marriage as "the most common form of marriage throughout human history," according to Orson Pratt, an original member of the Quorum of Twelve Apostles.[70] Plural marriage was a "vital symbol of early Mormon sectarian identity" that "allowed Mormons to embody the radical 'peculiarity' of the church's charismatic origins."[71] Maintaining the distinct identity of Mormons became increasingly difficult with the influx of non-Mormons during the construction of the transcontinental railroad in 1860. Mormon entrepreneurs became increasingly prevalent in the world of capitalism beyond the traditional sectarian communal economies Mormons were accustomed to. For many Americans "plural marriage symbolized Mormon depravity and subversion," which prompted non-Mormon politicians and businessmen to draw heavily on this image in seeking to undermine Mormon influence in western territories.[72] In the decades that followed, news of the practice spread and created a strong backlash against the Mormons. Some Republicans likened the practice to slavery.

For Mormons, plural marriage unified sexuality and spirituality. "The idea was that a sanctified man in union with multiple women could bring together male sexual potency and female fertility to create a family that would itself add to his own salvation in the family's status in heaven."[73] Strict rules guided sexual conduct with wives. The idea that men were mirroring God's own sexuality was very important to the early church. Mormon leaders lauded plural marriage as a valuable theological principle and moral duty. Mormon converts raised in monogamous households were often anxious and ambivalent about the practice. An estimated 5 to 20 percent of nineteenth-century Mormons participated in plural marriages.[74]

Smith's application of plural marriage placed him as one of many redefining the notion of marriage in western New York.[75] The Oneida Perfectionist Community, for example, was a group led by John Humphrey Noyes, who had multiple marriage partners. Noyes viewed marriage as the foundation for property and selfishness, both of which were understood as inherently un-Christian. As a result, each community member was covenanted to share himself or herself with all the members in the community. This was done voluntarily, but Noyes was the first sexual partner of young women. The group also practiced stirpiculture, a form of sexual practice in which men pleasure women, but do not have an orgasm themselves. The belief was that proper breeding was necessary to create a new super race of men. Men could ejaculate only when preapproved by community leaders.[76]

Mormons vigorously defended plural marriage until 1890 when faced with highly aggressive federal antipolygamy legislation. Domestic relations were a local concern at the time. The people of Utah favored it and the legislature supported them, which created a firm legal basis until the federal government intervened. Congress first established a series of family laws for residents of Utah, including rules for divorce, adultery, incest, alimony to women who wanted a divorce, and unlawful cohabitation, which prohibited a man from living with more than one woman, even if they were not legally married. These laws essentially applied relevant legal architecture from other states to the Utah Territory. Legal violations resulted in nearly 3,000 separate criminal prosecutions, an extraordinary number at the time. During the 1880s, Congress added political disfranchisement to criminal punishments and imposed a new governing structure on the Utah Territory.

Mormon opposition to plural marriage weakened after Congress attacked the Church's economic power, and went after church property, including temples, which were sacred and private places for Mormons. The attorney general was directed by Congress in 1887 to seize all church property worth more than $50,000. Some of these funds were to be used for a new public education system in the territory. *Late Corporation of the Church of Jesus Christ of Latter-Day Saints v. the United States* (1890) established that the property of the Mormon Church could be taken in this manner, building on previous rulings that stripped away the political and legal rights of Mormons. This decision was instrumental in motivating Mormon centrists, who already thought the cost of preserving plural marriage was too high, to press for abandonment of the practice. There was no public support nationally and declining support within Utah.[77]

The federal marshal informed Mormon leadership that LDS temples were going to be confiscated. In response, the Church issued a public statement that recommended members not engage in plural marriage. This was insufficient for federal agents, so another public statement was made before the general conference. The statement was sustained by vote and became known as the 1890 Manifesto. This was a crucial moment in the Mormon history of plural marriage. LDS president Wilford Woodruff recommended that Mormons refrain from any form of marriage forbidden by law. Church members and leaders continued to engage in plural marriage during this period, which became obvious in the congressional hearings surrounding the seating of Reed Smoot that began in 1903.[78] Still, the 1890 Manifesto was "a very important white flag that finally deflected Congress from going even further" with aggressive antipolygamy efforts. The legal precedent established in the polygamy cases was that "the Constitution protects the freedom to believe but not necessarily the freedom to act."[79]

Six years after the Manifesto, Utah became the 45th state in the union. Public opinion toward Mormons shifted from opposition to neutrality during the subsequent statehood period.[80] "Mormonism itself underwent a period of rapid transformation from a remote, disreputable sect to a more assimilated regional religion."[81] This led to shifts in the Mormon faith. The requirement of Mormons to move to Zion was suspended at the end of the nineteenth century. The impulse to gather as one lessened. Zion was always an expansive concept in the eyes of Joseph Smith, who "dreamed of an array of cities, initially in the United States and then in all of the Americas, extending Zion to the rest of the world."[82] Mormon leaders encouraged new converts to develop the Church in their home areas. Mormonism spread to Latin America in the 1970s, Asia in the 1980s, and Africa in the 1990s.[83] By 1994, the Mormon Church was organized in 149 nations and territories.[84] Over 2 million copies of the Book of Mormon are now published each year in over 50 languages.[85] Calling Mormonism an American religion is increasingly becoming a stereotype as more Mormons reside abroad than in the United States.

MORMON SUBCULTURE

American Mormons are a unique subculture based in Utah. Thomas O'Dea asserted in the *Harvard Encyclopedia of American Ethnic Groups* that Mormons constitute a clear example of the evolution of "a native and indigenously developed ethnic minority."[86] "Common belief establishes trust and a sense of mutual responsibility. Mormons pride themselves on feeling at home with other church members anywhere in the world."[87] Part of this is historical. Smith developed a sense of communal unity by creating complete cities. Mormons develop emotional and spiritual bonds by standing before fellow members of the congregation and expressing their deepest loves, longings, values, and experiences. The vast amount of time Mormons spend together is an important factor as well. Mormons meet as part of church activities several times a week and participate in three hours of worship on Sunday. This contributes to what Greg Prince calls "the Mormon DNA":

> The Mormon DNA, it's the culture; it's the lifestyle. It's much more than the doctrine. Most people who are in the Church would be hard-pressed to write a sentence or two about what the doctrine really is, but they can go on endlessly telling you what their life is within it. That's the real vitality of it. It's not a doctrinal church, regardless of what the strengths or weaknesses of the doctrine itself may be. It's a church that is a very pragmatic church. People come into it not because we can show them a list of theses they agree with; it's because they see [that] for others whom they have known it works, and they get a little bit of a flavor of that themselves and say, "I want some of this."[88]

Conventional accounts of Mormonism in 2011 suggested that "Mormons Rock!" as the nation experienced "a Mormon moment."[89] Politically, Mitt Romney was again seeking the Republican nomination for president, joined by fellow Mormon Jon Huntsman. Harry Reid was the most powerful person in the Senate. On television, political commentator Glenn Beck was a national figure on Fox News. The HBO mini-series *Big Love* held the series finale. *The Book of Mormon* was a popular and critically acclaimed musical. Stephanie Meyer sold millions of copies of the popular *Twilight* series of vampire novels. Still, most Americans viewed Mormons unfavorably. Forty-six percent of Americans held a generally unfavorable view of the Mormon religion compared to 42 percent who held a generally favorable view. Sixteen percent of Americans held a very unfavorable view of the Mormon religion, nearly twice as many as those who held a completely favorable view. As seen in Table 3.1,

Table 3.1
Opinion toward Mormon Religion by Geography

	Favorable	Unfavorable	Net	Do Not Know/ Unsure
West	50%	47%	+3	3%
East	41%	49%	–8	11%
South	40%	46%	–6	14%
Midwest	40%	43%	–3	18%

Source: Newport 2007.

Table 3.2
Opinion toward Mormon Religion by Attendance of Religious Services

	Favorable	Unfavorable	Net	Do Not Know/ Unsure
Weekly	34%	55%	–21	11%
Nearly Weekly or Monthly	41%	47%	–6	12%
Seldom or Never	49%	39%	+10	11%

Source: Newport 2007.

the western portion of the country was the only geographic entity that held a favorable view of the Mormon religion in 2007 when the poll was conducted. The East and South looked most unfavorably toward the religion. As seen in Table 3.2, the more a person attended religious services, the less likely he or she was to look favorably upon the Mormon religion. As seen in Table 3.3, Catholics held the most favorable view of Mormons by far and Protestants held the least favorable view.

There is something about Mormons that bothers Americans at large. As seen in Table 3.4, "polygamy" and "Salt Lake City, Utah" were the two most common responses about what came to mind when respondents thought about the LDS Church. Polygamy, which contributes to their negative image, is a major consideration in how people understand contemporary Mormons, even though the vast majority of Mormons believe polygamy is morally unacceptable. The polygamy charge bothers Mormons because the practice is so outdated. Mormons also point out that "God commanded Abraham, Isaac, and Jacob to practice polygamy at the foundation of Israel." In turn, "plural marriage served the same purpose when the Mormon people were coming into existence."[90] Polygamy is now grounds for excommunication. The vast majority of people who stated that Mormons were good, kind, or caring people with strong morals viewed the Church favorably. Those who viewed the Church unfavorably disagreed with the doctrine, believed LDS

Table 3.3
Opinion toward Mormon Religion by Religion

	Favorable	Unfavorable	Net	Do Not Know/ Unsure
Total Christian	43%	45%	–2	11%
Protestant	36%	52%	–16	13%
Catholic	56%	31%	+25	12%
Non-Christian	36%	46%	–7	15%
None	39%	46%	–7	14%

Source: Newport 2007.

Table 3.4
What Comes to Mind for Non-Mormons in Thinking about the LDS Church

	All Respondents	LDS Favorable	LDS Unfavorable
Polygamy	18%	17%	20%
Salt Lake City/Utah	10%	14%	6%
Good people/kind/ caring/strong morals	7%	13%	3%
Dislike their beliefs/ Do not agree with doctrine/ false teaching	6%	1%	13%
Door-to-door evangelizing	6%	7%	6%
Weird beliefs/strange/cult- like	6%	2%	10%
Big families/family Oriented/ community Family	5%	10%	2%
Just another religion	5%	8%	2%
Secretive/closed society	5%	2%	8%
Devout in their beliefs/ strict/structured	4%	5%	4%

Source: Newport 2007.

teachings are false, and thought Mormons hold beliefs that are weird, strange, or cult-like.

A second point of contention is whether the LDS Church is Christian. According to a 2011 poll nearly all Mormons believe that the LDS faith is a Christian religion. The most common response from Mormons when asked to describe "Mormons" in one word was "Christian" or "Christ centered." In contrast, one-third of non-Mormon adults believe that the LDS faith is not Christian and an additional 17 percent were unsure whether Mormons are Christians.[91] "Cult" was the most prevalent response in an open-ended question that asked what one word best describes the Mormon religion. The LDS faith does include several beliefs that are not part of other Christian traditions. Over 9 in 10 Mormons believe that the LDS president is a prophet, the Book of Mormon was written by ancient Judeo-Christian prophets, families can be eternally bound together in temple ceremonies, and God the father and Jesus Christ are separate physical beings. Mormons deny the assertion that their faith is a cult. "How can a church with nearly thirteen million members, scattered all over the world be considered a cult?" asked Richard Bushman. "By sociological definition, one key feature of a cult is high tension with the surrounding society. Yet Mormons blend with society."[92] Mormons seek political offices, assume leadership positions in business, teach at universities, and work as artists and musicians. "Everything we do is done in the name of Christ," former LDS president Gordon Hinckley explained. "I don't understand why people say we're not Christians."[93]

The 2011 poll found that a majority of Mormons believe that society at large knows little to nothing about the LDS faith and that Mormons are not part of mainstream society. Nearly half stated that Mormons face extensive discrimination. This is much higher than the percentage of blacks and atheists who claimed to face extensive discrimination. A majority of Mormons raised the issues of misperceptions, discrimination, and lack of acceptance when asked to describe in their own words the most important problems facing Mormons in the United States.[94] Most Mormons believe that the way Mormons are portrayed in television and film hurts their image throughout society. Nearly 40 percent believe that news coverage of Mormons is unfair.[95] Still, Mormons are content with their lives and their communities. The poll revealed that nearly 90 percent were satisfied with how their life was going, compared to 75 percent of the general public. Over 90 percent rated their communities as excellent or good places to live. Community satisfaction was particularly high in Utah, where over 70 percent of Mormons believe they live in an excellent community.[96] Most Mormons believe that acceptance of Mormons is on the rise, Mormons will eventually become part of mainstream society, and the United States is ready for a Mormon president. Mormons do not care for the stereotypes applied to them because "they see themselves as a modern people, as integrated into their culture, and are at best puzzled and at worst irritated, aggravated by the stereotypes that would exclude them from the major project that is American culture."[97] A 2011 poll conducted by the Pew Research Center Forum on Religion and Public Life provided comprehensive demographic data about contemporary Mormons. Mormon participation in higher education is on par with national rates. As seen in Table 3.5, the majority of Mormons attended at least some college. Twenty-nine percent were solely high school graduates, 19 percent were solely college graduates, and 12 percent earned postgraduate degrees. These percentages are all similar to national averages. Mormons are more affluent as a whole than the general population. As seen in Table 3.6, 45 percent of individual Mormons earned more than the U.S. median income for a family of four in 2010, which was just under $50,000. Over 1 in 10 Mormons in the United States earned over $100,000 a year. Over 40 percent earned $50,000 plus a year.

Table 3.5
Education Distribution of Mormons

	Percentage of Mormons in the United States
Less than high school	7
High school graduates	29
Attended some college	33
College graduates	19
Postgraduates	12

Source: Pew Research Center Forum on Religion and Public Life, National Survey of Mormons, 2011.

Table 3.6
Income Distribution of Mormons

	Percentage of Mormons in the United States
Less than $30,000	28
$30,000–$39,000	14
$40,000–$49,000	12
$50,000–$74,999	19
$75,000–$99,000	12
$100,000 and over	14

Source: Pew Research Center Forum on Religion and Public Life, National Survey of Mormons, 2011.

According to the 2011 poll, two-thirds of adult Mormons were married, which is much higher than the general public. Eighty-five percent of Mormons were married to other Mormons, which was higher than Protestants generally (81%) and Catholics (78%). Nearly 70 percent of Mormons believe that marriage is more satisfying when the man works to support the family and the wife takes care of the house and children than when husband and wife share both work and domestic responsibilities. Over 70 percent of Mormons stated that having a successful marriage and being a good parent are among the most important goals in life. These ranked higher than having a successful career, having free time, and living a religious life.[98] Utah has the highest fertility rate in the United States. Teenage childbirth is high because Mormon leaders discourage abortion and suggest adoption instead.[99]

"Mormons exhibit higher levels of religious commitment than many other religious groups, including white evangelical Protestants."[100] As seen in Table 3.7, 9 in 10 Mormons believe that the Mormon president is a prophet from God and that the Book of Mormon was written by ancient prophets. Over 8 in 10 Mormons indicated that religion is very important in their lives

Table 3.7
Norms of Mormon Religious Practice in the United States

Believe LDS president is a prophet from God	94%
Believe Book of Mormon was written by ancient prophets	91%
Pray every day	83%
Have supply of food in storage	82%
Stated religion is very important in their life	82%
Believe wholeheartedly in all church teachings	77%
Attend church at least once a week	77%
Possess current temple recommend	65%
Have served a mission	27%

Source: Ferrin 2012.

Table 3.8
Being a Good Mormon

	Essential	Important, Not Essential	Not Important
How important is each of these to being a good Mormon?			
Believing Joseph Smith saw God the father and Holy Spirit	80%	13%	6%
Working to help the poor	73%	24%	3%
Regular family home evening	51%	45%	4%
Not drinking coffee or tea	49%	32%	17%
Not watching R-rated movies	32%	47%	19%

Source: Pew Research Center Forum on Religion and Public Life, National Survey of Mormons, 2011.

and that they pray every day. Over three-quarters of Mormons believe whole-heartedly in all of the Church's teachings and attend church at least once a week. Sixty-five percent of Mormons reported having a current temple recommend, which grants access to LDS temples. Twenty-seven percent of Mormons have served on a mission, 43 percent of men and 11 percent of women. Eighty-two percent keep a supply of food in storage, a majority of whom maintain at least a three-month supply.[101] As seen in Table 3.8, Mormons have various perspectives on what is essential to being a good Mormon. Eighty percent stated it was essential to believe that Joseph Smith saw God the father and Holy Spirit; 73 percent stated it was essential to help the poor; and 51 percent stated it was essential to conduct the regular family home evening. The vast majority of Mormons in the United States were raised in the Church. Converts stated that Mormon beliefs were the most common reason for conversion.[102]

SUMMARY

This chapter discussed Mormon persecution, Mormon settlement in Utah, and the development of a distinct Mormon subculture. The violent persecution of Mormons, which included the assassination of Joseph Smith and relocation of Mormons from New York to Ohio, Missouri, and Illinois, was a crucial element in the development of Mormon history and identity. Mormons made an extraordinary westward migration under the leadership of Brigham Young, fleeing the United States, only to find themselves back under American control, facing condemnation for the practice of plural marriage. Persecution at the hands of state and local governments prompted Mormon leaders to become politically active and pursue protection from the federal government. Disinterest at the federal level shifted to unprecedented political pressure on Mormons to end plural marriage, which occurred in 1890, and enabled Utah to become a state in 1896. Mormon persecution in the nineteenth century was instrumental in the development of a unique American subculture that has struggled to gain national acceptance since its origins. Twenty-first-century Mormons are theologically distinct, religiously committed, well educated, family oriented, and highly content with their communities. The following chapter will discuss the emergence of Mormons in national politics, including Joseph Smith's presidential campaign, Reed Smoot's controversial seating as a Utah senator, Harry Reid's rise to majority leader, and Mitt Romney becoming the 2012 Republican presidential nominee.

4

First a Catholic, Then a Mormon?

THE PROPHET FOR PRESIDENT

The ascendance of Mormons into prominent positions in the federal government was a long process. Early Mormons first looked to the federal government as a means for support in the face of persecution from state governments, local governments, and vigilantes. In 1839 Joseph Smith met with President Martin Van Buren, senators, and U.S. representatives to share the hardships Mormons encountered in being forced from Missouri and lobby for help. These efforts were unsuccessful. When the two met again in 1840, Van Buren said to Smith, "Your cause is just, but I can do nothing for you," because "if I take up for you I shall lose the vote in Missouri."[1] Smith wrote leading presidential candidates during the next presidential election cycle and asked, "What will be your rule of action relative to us as a people should fortune favor your ascension to the chief magistracy?"[2] All three candidates who responded were unsympathetic. Smith called a meeting of Mormon leaders on January 29, 1844, and they decided by unanimous vote that "we will have an independent electoral ticket, and that Joseph Smith be a candidate for the next Presidency; and that we use all honorable means in our power to secure his election."[3]

Smith published a campaign pamphlet entitled *General Smith's Views of the Powers and Policy of the Government of the United States*. Fifteen hundred copies were printed and sent to the president, the cabinet, Supreme Court justices, senators, representatives, prominent newspaper editors, and other influential citizens.[4] Smith's "presidential platform was a secular document couched in the political language of his day."[5] The two most important elements of Smith's campaign were the expansion of presidential power and the elimination of slavery. Smith sought to give the president full power to use the army to suppress mobs without awaiting a formal request from a state governor. A major undercurrent of the platform was "resentment that justice depended in 1844 not so much upon the equal protection of the laws as on the wealth and power of the litigants."[6] Smith's advocacy of equal rights conflicted with states' rights doctrine. The proposed presidential power to suppress mobs inherently posited that the individual rights of American citizens were superior to the rights and powers of state governments. Smith "reserved his deepest scorn for those who asserted that federalism prohibited the federal government from intervening on behalf of citizens who were denied their rights as American citizens." "The state rights doctrines are what feed mobs," Smith recorded in his journal. "They are a dead carcass—a stink and they shall ascend up as a stink offering in the nose of the Almighty."[7] Smith went so far as to suggest in a letter to presidential candidate John Calhoun that the Constitution be amended to use capital punishment on public officials who refuse to assist people denied their constitutional rights. Ironically, twenty-first-century Mormons are among the strongest supporters of the states' rights, particularly in Utah, where the Mormon Church exercises an extraordinary amount of political and social influence.

Smith, who is not traditionally viewed as an advocate of racial equality, discussed the violation of natural rights granted in the Declaration of Independence to millions of black slaves. Smith proposed to free slaves by having Congress sell public lands to raise money and purchase them. Smith's "idealism was always tempered by a deep appreciation of the limits which our imperfect world imposes on the aspirations of men."[8] Other proposed reforms included the reduction of congressional pay, having two House members for every 1 million people, abolishing many prisons, developing a national bank, extending the United States from the East Coast to West Coast if Native Americans consented, and annexing Oregon and Texas.[9]

The General Council took control of the presidential campaign in March of 1844. A formal launch was held at a special conference that April. Brigham Young, as president of the Quorum of the Twelve, called for volunteers "to preach the Gospel and electioneer."[10] Donations and loans were collected. Elders were instructed to return to their states and campaign for Smith by sharing his views and securing voters on his behalf. Smith wanted James Arlington Bennett for his running mate. Bennett was a New York lawyer recently baptized by Brigham Young, but Bennett was ineligible because he was not a native-born citizen. Smith then offered the vice presidential nomination to Solomon Copeland of Tennessee, but the General Council selected longtime Mormon leader Sidney Rigdon instead.[11] This decision speaks to the collective nature of leadership atop the Mormon hierarchy that began to take shape toward the end of Smith's life.

A nominating convention was held on May 17, 1844, in Nauvoo. The convention adhered to the standard norms of organized political parties at the time. All 26 states were represented by counting the places of origin of the delegates, who were mostly Mormon. Two non-Mormons did have prominent speaking roles, which was a tactical move to build political support. Smith and Rigdon received uncontested nominations. Some of the resolutions were unusual for their incongruity with Smith's campaign pamphlet. Scholars have suggested that these resolutions were an overture to Democrats to counter charges made in the press that *General Smith's Views* primarily consisted of Whig doctrine. As a whole, *Views* was a "blend of ante-bellum political rhetoric, Whig economic doctrines, Democratic expansionism, abolitionism, and the original and wide-ranging constitutional and political ideas of Joseph Smith."[12] Mormon missionaries campaigned for Smith despite the opposition he faced from inside and outside of the Church throughout the last year of his life. A parting political commentary from Smith took the form of an editorial published in August of 1844 by *Times and Season*, the Mormon newspaper. The editorial "pledged that the Latter-day Saints would support only candidates who would carry out 'General Smith's program.'"[13] "Among many historical questions left unresolved by the untimely death of Joseph Smith is the question of the Mormon leader's intent and expectations in announcing for the Presidency."[14]

Smith's leadership of the Mormon Church was an interesting mix of authoritarianism and democracy. Smith placed himself at the center of the church structure because of his ability to receive revelations from God. Dissenters were handled with forgiveness if they repented to the satisfaction of the prophet. Those that did not repent were swiftly excommunicated, no matter how close the person was to Smith prior to turning on him. Smith was not a transparent leader by democratic standards, but did subject himself to publicly addressing controversial challenges by malcontents. Furthermore, the priesthood created a highly decentralized aspect of Mormon authority in contrast to the prophet and apostles, who hold extensive power. After Smith's death, Brigham Young assumed the role of Mormon patriarch in the State of Deseret, what became the Utah Territory and later the state of Utah. Young claimed to be inspired by God, and have God's will revealed to him through church administration, but did not claim to speak directly with God or Christian prophets as Smith did.

THE REED SMOOT HEARINGS

Mormon numbers were large enough in Illinois to decide state elections between Whigs and Democrats. Mormon leaders requested that adherents vote in a bloc behind candidates endorsed by church leaders, which was the norm until the Utah settlement. Utah Mormons were politically organized under the People's Party. The Liberal Party was the non-Mormon alternative. The People's Party disbanded in 1891 as part of the effort to pursue statehood, and the Liberal Party followed soon after. Mormons were instructed to join the Democratic and Republican parties. LDS leaders worked closely with Republicans throughout the 1880s and 1890s to establish statehood.[15] After 1896 "Mormons began to hold elected office in the federal government," and "the potential for religious influence on federal LDS-elected officials appeared."[16] "Early allegations of religious influence centered specifically on the notion that Mormon politicians might take direct orders from their ecclesiastical leaders rather than addressing their constituents' interests."[17] In 1903 Reed Smoot was elected a U.S. senator from Utah by a predominantly Mormon legislature. Smoot was the first native-born Utahan to undertake a career in national politics and the only Mormon apostle to serve in the Senate. Smoot's election created controversy because of his position in the church and unease surrounding Mormon religious practices, particularly plural marriage.

Opposition to Smoot's seating from 1903 to 1907 was orchestrated by a co-alition of Protestant churches, directly through their ministers and indirectly through reform organizations. All five of the major Protestant denominations were involved, including Episcopalians, Presbyterians, Congregationalists, Baptists, and Methodists. Mormons were understood as "a glaring example of what America was not and should not be."[18] The Mormons were one of many marginalized non-Protestant religious groups seeking greater legitimacy. Protestants sought to bring marginal Christian groups into the religious mainstream, including Christian Scientists, Adventists, and Mormons. Religious freedom pertained to the powers of the federal government, not state governments, who were able to establish and support religions. Many did to varying degrees. Protestant national hegemony was maintained by casting out unwanted people to the frontier, which was closing by the end of the nineteenth century. At the same time, it was becoming increasingly difficult for one Protestant denomination to claim numerical dominance. Meanwhile, the Catholic population doubled and the Jewish population quadrupled. Smoot's election signaled that religious freedom no longer referred to public officeholders coming from various Protestant denominations.

Smoot's opposition did not accuse him of any legal violation. Smoot was not a polygamist, but did espouse the principle. As late as 1902 Smoot stated in a meeting with apostles that plural marriage "would save the world much sorrow and distress" if universally practiced, and "looked for its restoration."[19] It is not clear why Smoot remained monogamous, given his father practiced polygamy. This was particularly curious after Smoot became an apostle in 1900. Plural marriage was viewed as a duty associated with prestigious leadership, even though the church had publically supported conforming to federal law. Smoot was a "wealthy, influential, and politically active man," when to his surprise he was appointed to the position of apostle.[20] Smoot had drawn some criticism from within the Church for twice declining calls to serve as a missionary. Smoot accepted the third invitation in 1890 and served at the European LDS headquarters. Kathleen Flake has argued that "Smoot was an astute choice to represent modern Mormonism" because he helped replace the Church's reputation of "anarchical fanaticism" with "bourgeois patriotism."[21]

Smoot's perceived ineligibility for the Senate was based on his participation in a religious organization that was in violation of the law, that corrupted family norms, and that exercised disproportionate control over Utah politics and commerce, to the detriment of the nation as a whole. Participants in the hearings thought of themselves as defending Christian America. LDS theology dictated morality for individual Mormons, who understood Mormon teachings as absolute truths that should be spread to save the nation. In contrast, Protestants were united by a Christian way of life, where morality was more of a private matter than a public matter, and civilizing the nation was more the focus than saving it. Mormons were not interested in subordinating the church to the nation in line with the American Protestant tradition.

"Public indignation over Smoot's election was deeply felt and broadly expressed."[22] In 1856 Smoot's own party, the Republicans, believed the federal government should eradicate the "twin relics of barbarism—Polygamy and Slavery." The Democratic platform followed suit in 1904 by calling for "the extermination of polygamy within the jurisdiction of the United States, and the complete separation of Church and State in Political affairs."[23] Protestant activists were previously successful in denying a U.S. House seat to B. H. Roberts, who was a high-ranking church official, but unlike Smoot was a polygamist and a Democrat, and had drawn the ire of Mormon leaders for entering the political arena without church approval. After six weeks of discussion over swearing in Roberts, the 56th Congress voted not to seat him. Mormons believed that " 'free-exercise of religion' could only be preserved by the government's ceasing to criminalize church-sanctioned marriages."[24]

"Unlike the House of Representatives, the Senate had greater concern for state constitutional prerogatives and seated Smoot before trying him on his qualifications."[25] This shifted the terms of debate to why Smoot should keep his seat, not obtain it. Two days after granting Smoot his seat in 1903, the Senate referred the large number of petitions and protests to the Committee on Privileges and Elections, who was tasked with investigating the situation and making a recommendation on whether Smoot should be allowed to serve. The committee organized a public hearing, which did not begin until February of 1904. Smoot used the time to build support among his colleagues and cultivate a more positive public image for Mormons.[26]

Smoot's Senate hearings produced 3,500 pages of testimony by 100 witnesses on various aspects of Mormonism, including polygamy, family structure, ritual, worship, secret oaths, economic communalism, and theocratic politics.[27] One major issue was the dramatic revelation that four of Smoot's fellow apostles took additional wives after the 1890 Manifesto and that at least two apostles continued to perform plural marriages. This blatant disregard for federal law generated animosity nationally and fueled suspicion about other mysterious and illegal activities Mormons might be engaged in.

A second major issue was the loyalty of Mormons to the Church. Concerns surrounding this issue were twofold. First, Smoot's opponents believed that Mormons put the welfare of the Church and their desire to build the kingdom of God ahead of the national interest. Some thought Mormons eventually sought to rule all of the country through the theocratic structure established in the Utah Territory. "Smoot's election forced a deliberation on whether the 'visible' nature of the L.D.S. Church constituted a coercive monopolistic expression that threatened democratic institutions or the legitimate expression of special interests within a political democracy."[28] The second concern was the degree to which the living Mormon prophet would dictate Smoot's political behavior. Mormon president Joseph F. Smith, nephew of Joseph Smith, was repeatedly asked during his Senate testimony if Smoot would be obligated to follow his orders on political matters. Smith consistently replied that Smoot "should follow his own conscience and the obligations he feels to his constituency, not to the president of the church." Smith's testimony was codified by church authorities in the form of an official statement that read "the Church of Jesus Christ of Latter-day Saints holds to the doctrine of the separation of church and state." These were the terms under which Mormons entered the national political scene. The Church would "not interfere in politics or in the action of any politicians who are members of the church."[29]

A third major issue was the hope of Republicans and Democrats to use Smoot's seating for partisan political advantage. Both parties believed that Mormons could influence national politics in the Electoral College and elections of U.S. senators by state legislatures. "Rumors abounded in Washington that the Republicans had promised to defeat any new antipolygamy legislation in return for the previously Democratic Mormon vote."[30] These rumors were supported by Smoot's correspondence during the hearings, particularly with President Theodore Roosevelt. "As requested by his party, Smoot organized a pro-Roosevelt delegation to the Republican convention and delivered Utah's votes in the presidential election of 1904."[31]

Smoot was finally seated in 1907 and became the longest-serving senator from Utah until being surpassed by Orrin Hatch a century later. Smoot's three decades of work in the Senate significantly enhanced the acceptance of Mormons in national politics. The Senate addressed the Mormon problem by pressuring Mormons to conform to Protestant norms of obedience to law, national loyalty, and creedal tolerance, while granting Mormons a representative in the Senate, a form of religious citizenship, which afforded protection for the domestic and international propagation of their faith."[32] Mormon identity "radically changed" as a result of the Smoot hearings because "the nation stated the terms in which it would accept Mormonism, and Mormonism began to conform to those terms."[33] Smoot, rational and soft-spoken, became the embodiment of Mormonism for many Americans, replacing Brigham Young, the bearded patriarch with multiple wives. Smoot became a leading voice of conservative morality and explained Mormonism as a civil religion, in Protestant terms, to the aggravation of some Mormons. Smoot's travel to Europe as an American political representative enabled him to meet with aristocratic, ecclesiastical, and democratic leaders. This work was "a turning point in the internationalization of the Mormon Church."[34]

Opposition to seating territorial delegates was also a problem for Mormons. In 1868, Incumbent William Hooper defeated his opponent 15,068 to 105. A claim was filed with the House a year later that stated Hooper "had taken an oath inconsistent with his duties as an American citizen and as a representative, and also that the Territory of Utah, under the control of the Mormon hierarchy, did not have a republican form of government, and that its institutions were inimical to those of the United States."[35] The House concluded "that 'institutions dominated by such religious ideas as those of Mormonism were necessarily in a sense hostile to those of the United States, and that the evil of polygamy demanded action by Congress,' but refused to set aside the election on the grounds that 'there had been no such overt acts of disloyalty' from Hooper or evidence of 'coercion of voters.'"[36] Apostle George Q. Cannon served as a Utah delegate in the House from 1872 to 1880, and was reelected in 1880 by a landslide, only to have Utah's territorial governor and presidential appointee, Allen Campbell, declare his non-Mormon opponent the victor. "Murray alleged that British-born Cannon was not a properly naturalized U.S. citizen" and that he "was not qualified for citizenship because he practiced polygamy."[37] The seat was left vacant after Cannon protested the decision in the House. The Edmunds Act of 1882 prohibited polygamists from holding federal office, and former delegate and nonpolygamist, John Caine, replaced Cannon.

FROM REED SMOOT TO HARRY REID

An important question in examining Mormons in Congress is the criteria for being considered Mormon. House Member Morris Udall (AZ, 1961–91), for example, was baptized Mormon, and identified himself as a Mormon, but did not engage in church practices or necessarily subscribe to fundamental beliefs. Tom Udall (NM, 1999–present), his nephew, describes himself as a nonpracticing Mormon. The Mormon Church technically defines membership on the basis of baptism and does not keep records of member occupations. Many Mormons differentiate between active and nonactive members, also called "Jack Mormons." The issue of excommunication is an additional consideration. Frank Cannon, the last territorial delegate from Utah and one of Utah's first senators, was excommunicated in 1905 after he blamed church leaders for his failed reelection efforts.[38] Self-identification as a Mormon was used by Robert King and Kay Atchinson King in their comprehensive analysis of Mormons in Congress from 1851 to 2000. Their findings concluded that only 68 of the 11,592 people who have served in Congress were Mormon.[39]

Fifty-seven Mormons have served in the House since 1890, 30 of whom have represented Utah. Eleven Mormons have served in the Senate, 7 of whom have represented Utah. Nevada, Florida, Oregon, and Idaho have also elected Mormon senators. Florida Republican Paula Hawkins (1981–87) was the first Mormon woman to be elected to Congress and the first Mormon member of Congress elected from a state east of Utah. Mormons were three times more prevalent in the House than the Senate. Utah had just one representative in the House until a second representative was granted in 1910, a third in 1980, and a fourth in 2010. There was only one non-Mormon House member in Utah from statehood to 1951. During this time senators from Utah were just about evenly divided in terms of Mormon and non-Mormon members, but the years served by non-Mormon members were a fraction of their Mormon counterparts.[40] Berkley Bunker was the first Mormon from outside of Utah elected to Congress and served one term from 1945 to 1947 in Nevada's only House seat.

From 1951 to 2000 all senators and nearly all House members from Utah were Mormons.[41] "The increasing 'Mormonization' of Utah's congressional delegation reflects the fact that Utah's population has become more Mormon throughout the twentieth century, from 61 percent in 1910 to 70 percent in 1980 and 75 percent by 1995."[42] Aside from Utah, Mormons were elected to the House in the largest numbers from California (10), Idaho (7), Arizona (3), and Nevada (2). Hawaii, New Hampshire, Oklahoma, New Mexico, and the territory of American Samoa each elected 1 Mormon representative.[43] Just over half of these representatives were Democratic in contrast to the dominance of Republican Mormons in the Senate over the same period. Seven of the 10 Mormon representatives from California were Republican, as was Oklahoma's sole Mormon representative. Two of the 3 Arizona Mormon representatives were Democratic. All Mormon representatives in Nevada, Hawaii, New Hampshire, New Mexico, and American Samoa were Democratic.[44]

Six Mormons have served in both the House and Senate.[45] Mormons served approximately 12 years in the Senate on average, 9 years in the House. Four members of Congress were stake presidents prior to having served, and five others went on to become mission presidents. Three bishops have served in Congress, two in the House, Clair Burgener (CA, 1973–83) and Ron Packard (CA, 1983–2001), and one senator, Orrin Hatch (UT, 1977–present).[46] "Since 1951 with the increasing numbers of Mormons in Congress representing non-Mormon constituencies, personal and partisan considerations have become more important."[47] As seen in Table 4.1, Mormons in Congress have shifted significantly from being predominantly Democratic from 1851 to 1951, to being predominantly Republican since. A similar trend is evident throughout Utah statehood as seen in Table 4.2. There is an element of

Table 4.1
Mormons in Congress by Party Affiliation

Era	Years	Percent Democrat	Percent Republican
1851–96	41	98	2
1896–1951	165	61	39
1951–81	258	51	49
1981–99	251	30	70

Source: King 2000, 30.

ideological consistency throughout this partisan shift considering that the Republicans were the progressive party from the Civil War to the New Deal realignment. At the same time, the degree to which Mormons supported the Democratic Party during the New Deal era is often overlooked. Utah was largely Democratic from 1932 to 1948. Contemporary Mormon political ideology began to take shape in the 1950s, but Utah still voted for Kennedy and Johnson in 1960 and 1964 respectively.

Fifteen Mormons served in the 112th Congress, which began in January of 2011. Mormons constituted 2.8 percent of the 112th Congress, which was up slightly from 2.6 percent of the 111th Congress.[48] These percentages were higher than the 1.7 percent of the national adult population that Mormons constituted. Harry Reid is the first Mormon to lead the Senate, a post he has held since 1996. Reid is from Searchlight, Nevada, a small, old mining town that still has the two-room cinderblock schoolhouse that Reid attended. Harry Reid Sr. was a gold miner with an elementary school education. Harry's mother, Inez, did laundry for local bordellos, the town's primary business. Reid grew up in a house built from railroad ties without an indoor toilet or hot water. Harry Sr. developed miner's cough and committed suicide at the age of 58.[49] Reid hitchhiked 40 miles to Henderson to attend high school because schooling in Searchlight only went through eighth grade. Reid was an athletic young man, who learned to box from his high school government professor, Mike O'Callaghan, who became Reid's best friend and mentor. Reid earned a partial athletic scholarship to a junior college in Utah for his athletic prowess in baseball and football. He converted to

Table 4.2
Partisan Identity of Utah Mormons in Congress

Era	Years	Percent Democrat	Percent Republican
1896–1951	161	60	40
1951–81	120	37	63
1981–2000	86	14	86

Source: King 2000, 31.

Mormonism while in college. Reid completed his undergraduate studies at Utah State University and then earned a law degree from George Washington University.

Reid returned to Henderson after finishing law school and worked as the city attorney. A doctor asked Reid to attend an administrative hearing with him. The chairman of the board of trustees told Reid that lawyers were not necessary or welcome at the hearing. This struck Reid as incredibly rude and inspired him to run the for the hospital board. He was elected in 1966 and the administrator in question was fired shortly thereafter.[50] Reid was elected to the Nevada State Assembly in 1968 at the age of 28 and became the youngest lieutenant governor in Nevada history. O'Callaghan appointed Reid chairman of the Nevada Gaming Commission in 1977 after an unsuccessful Senate bid. Reid was elected to the House of Representatives in 1983, the Senate in 1986, and was chosen as Democratic whip in 1998, minority leader in 2004, and majority leader in 2006.[51]

Orrin Hatch, the senior senator on the other side of the aisle, is a Mormon from Utah. He was elected in 1976 and served on the Judiciary Committee, the Finance Committee, and the Health, Education, Labor, and Pensions Committee in the 112th Congress. Mormon Mike Lee was elected to the House from Utah in 2010. Lee was a Tea Party favorite with no previous political experience who defeated three-term incumbent Bob Bennett in the Republican primary. Bennett's support of the Troubled Asset Relief Program was a major factor in his defeat. All three Utah House Representatives in the 112th Congress are Mormon. Two representatives are Republican, Rob Bishop, elected in 2002, and Jason Chaffetz, elected in 2008. Democrat Jim Matheson, the longest serving of the three, was elected in 2000. Two of the remaining seven representatives are from California and Idaho respectively. Arizona, Nevada, and American Samoa are each represented by one Mormon representative. Eni Faleomavaega, serving his 13th term from America Samoa, is the only other Mormon Democrat in the House.

There is little scholarship on the political behavior of Mormons. A notable exception is Damon Cann's study of voting cohesion among Mormons in Congress. Cann examined roll-call voting in the House for all nonunanimous votes in the 109th Congress. There were 11 Mormons in Congress, 10 of whom were active. Eight were Republicans and 2 were Democrats. Most represented districts in the Mountain West. There were sufficient differences among these Representatives and their districts to reasonably expect diverse voting patterns under normal circumstances. Cann found that the Rice cohesion score, a common method of measuring voting cohesion, was no different for congressional Mormons than the scores of 10 randomly selected representatives with a similar ratio of party affiliation.[52] Cann also compared cohesion scores according to votes separated into the categories of social issues, economic issues, and foreign policy issues. Once again, the votes of Mormon representatives fell "within the range of cohesion scores one would expect to observe by chance."[53] Cohesion scores were higher for Mormons on social issues than economic or foreign policy issues, but the same was true for the randomly selected sets. Cann concluded that the effect of personal religious identification on Mormons in Congress was muted. The results found "no empirical support for allegations that Mormon elected officials are beholden to ecclesiastical authorities" and suggested that "religious identity of individual representatives does not seem to affect their ability to represent different constituencies well."[54]

THE CHOSEN SON

Mitt Romney is the most prolific Mormon politician of the twenty-first century. Romney family history has deep roots within the Mormon tradition. Miles Romney, an Englishman, converted to Mormonism in 1837 after encountering a missionary and moved to Nauvoo, Illinois, where Mitt Romney's great grandfather, Miles Park Romney, was born six years later. The Romneys headed west after Smith's assassination, and Miles helped to settle towns in Utah and Arizona, prior to fleeing to Mexico after being pursued by local authorities for being a polygamist. Whereas American law prohibited polygamy, Mexican law did not. Mitt stated that his ancestors took additional wives to help build the church as they were ordered to do and described the practice as "awful." George Romney, Mitt's father, was born in Mexico to Anna and Gaskall Romney, who deviated from precedent and did not engage in plural marriage. The Romneys left Mexico to escape the 1912 revolution and eventually settled in Salt Lake City.[55]

George Romney worked as CEO of General Motors, served three terms as Republican governor of Michigan in the 1960s, and unsuccessfully sought the Republican presidential nomination in 1968. George's presidential campaign was hindered by his position on the Vietnam War, which shifted from support to criticism, explained by the "brainwashing" he received from American generals during his 1965 visit to Vietnam. George was a civil rights advocate, which generated some criticism among Mormon leaders.[56] Implementing the Fair Housing Act of 1968 was George's primary focus as secretary of housing and urban development under Richard Nixon.

Mitt Romney is the first Mormon to receive a party nomination for the presidency. From birth, Romney was viewed as a miracle baby by his mother, Lenore, whose doctor believed she was unable to get pregnant again. Mitt was raised in an affluent suburb of the 1950s. One aspect of his family life was unique:

> The Romneys were one of the Mormon faith's leading families. In fact, the clan's journey from the fringes to the mainstream symbolized the transformation of the church itself. For nearly a century, the Church of Jesus Christ of Latter-day Saints was the most vilified religion in America, its dusty, bearded

adherents derided as polygamous outlaws. Born in a Mexican colony that his grandfather had co-founded to preserve polygamy, George Romney was a product of that outsider status. But by the turn of the century, George's father, like the Mormon Church itself, had broken with that past in exchange for acceptance.[57]

Romney enrolled at Stanford in 1965 and lived in the San Francisco Bay area during the height of the counterculture movement. Romney was exempt from the draft because he was considered "a minister of religion" after accepting a call to serve a two-year mission in France.[58] In France, Romney experienced a deadly automobile accident and sustained serious injuries, including fractured ribs, a broken arm, and a concussion. Romney recovered quickly and assumed significant leadership responsibilities in the French mission when the director returned to the United States to bury his wife, who died in the accident. The mission's goal of baptizing 200 people was reached in 1968, the first time in nearly a decade. Romney returned to the United States with a newfound confidence after a life-changing experience on multiple levels.

Romney completed his undergraduate studies at Brigham Young University to be closer to his wife, Ann, whom he married in 1969. Romney then earned a dual graduate degree from Harvard Law School and Harvard Business School. Mitt and Ann raised five sons in Belmont, Massachusetts, where Mitt served as bishop, and was later promoted to stake president, responsible for approximately 12 congregations. In 1984 Romney was enticed by his mentor and eventual boss, Bill Bain, to run Bain Capital, a new venture capital company. Venture capital is typically a high-risk business, but Romney negotiated a deal with Bain that returned him to his previous position at Bain and Company if Bain Capital went under. Bain Capital launched and reshaped hundreds of companies, including Staples and Domino's Pizza. Romney made millions of dollars and had accumulated an estimated net worth of over $250 million when he launched his first presidential candidacy in 2008.[59]

Romney entered politics in 1994 when he sought to defeat incumbent Senator Ted Kennedy, who Romney mistakenly believed was vulnerable. Romney supported some traditional Republican policies while staking out more moderate positions in a state where GOP candidates had success being fiscally conservative and socially liberal. Romney's campaign was similar to his mother's only campaign for public office in 1970, an unsuccessful Senate bid in Michigan against Democratic incumbent Phillip Hart. Romney was more guarded and calculating than his father, George, who "admonished Mitt to loosen up, stop listening to consultants, and trust his gut."[60] Romney easily won the Republican primary, was competitive with Kennedy at the outset of the general election, but lost badly. Romney told his brother after the loss that "I never want to run for something again unless I can win."[61]

Romney ran for governor of Massachusetts in 2002 after Republican incumbent Jane Swift was accused of ethical transgressions and subsequently withdrew from the race. Romney sought to model himself after Bill Weld, the moderate Massachusetts Republican who served as governor during the 1990s. Romney defeated Shannon O'Brien, the former state legislator and treasurer, by five points. At the time, Democrats outnumbered Republicans by nearly three to one. Romney portrayed himself as an agent of change who would reform Beacon Hill by courting independent voters and rarely referred to himself as a Republican. The party retained their small base in Massachusetts, swept wealthier towns in the Interstate 495 crescent, and limited Democratic margins in urban areas. Mitt won his first election 40 years after his father won his first election as governor of Michigan. Both men were 55 years old.

After one term of governor, Romney sought the Republican nomination for president. Romney was a "telegenic, bright, independently wealthy, articulate, a proven businessman, and by most accounts, a successful governor," who " 'saved' the Salt Lake Olympics and in so doing had become the favorite son of the business and government elites within the Republican Party."[62] The two major obstacles of Romney's candidacy were his Mormon faith and his propensity to switch policy views on controversial issues. No Mormon had ever gained a party nomination for president. Over half of the electorate had little to no knowledge about Mormons, and nearly 40 percent of evangelical Christians, a crucial contingent of the Republican primary, had negative perceptions of Mormons.[63] Romney appealed to religious conservatives by casting himself as a typical Christian, who accepted Jesus as his savior and believed that the Bible is the word of God. Romney denounced polygamy and emphasized his commitment to separation of church and state. Romney deferred to church leaders when faced with specific theology questions, such as the practices of baptizing the dead and wearing holy undergarments. Romney struggled to develop support from evangelicals. The broad perception of Romney was that of a politician willing to reposition his politics depending on the context. This irked the more ideological and enthusiastic Republican primary voters.[64]

Several polls were conducted during Romney's 2008 presidential campaign. A 2007 Washington Post-ABC News poll found that 29 percent of Americans would be less likely to vote for a Mormon presidential candidate.[65] A 2007 Gallup poll found that 17 percent of Americans would not vote for a well-qualified presidential candidate who was Mormon.[66] As seen in Table 4.3,

Table 4.3
Views toward Mormons by Party

	Republican	Democrat	Independent
Total favorable	42%	43%	43%
Total unfavorable	52%	47%	40%
Net favorable	−10%	−4%	3%
Do not know/no opinion	5%	11%	18%

Source: Newport 2007.

Table 4.4
Views toward Mormons by Ideology

	Conservative	Liberal	Moderate
Total favorable	44%	28%	48%
Total unfavorable	45%	61%	40%
Net favorable	–1%	–33%	+8%
Do not know/no opinion	10%	11%	13%

Source: Newport 2007.

Republicans viewed Mormons more unfavorably than Democrats, but liberals viewed the Mormon religion more unfavorably than conservatives. As seen in Table 4.4, 61 percent of liberals viewed the Mormon religion unfavorably, 16 points higher than Republicans. Just 28 percent of liberals viewed the Mormon religion favorably compared to 44 percent of conservatives. Moderates viewed the Mormon religion slightly more favorably than unfavorably. This data suggested that in a general election Romney's religion could lessen his overall support, possibly up to one-third of the electorate as a whole. Evangelical Republicans could be more difficult to turn out, which is a major problem in a two-party system where electoral turnout of partisans is essential to winning elections. Liberal Democrats would likely not support him, which would not have been expected anyway, and importantly, moderates would be very much in play.

Mike Huckabee's rise in Iowa posed an unexpected challenge for Romney. Huckabee climbed the Iowa polls in October of 2007, particularly among evangelical Christians, approximately half of Republican voters in the state. Romney and Huckabee were virtually tied in the polls by December. The campaign "had long planned to give a speech on Romney's faith, but they had not planned to give it in this kind of situation, with a strong evangelical challenger about to overtake the acknowledged frontrunner."[67] The campaign decided that a major speech on faith would be necessary "to normalize Mormonism as a legitimate expression of American religious values, thus establishing a sort of rhetorical benchmark that could guard against the expected use of unfounded rumor and innuendo."[68]

FAITH IN AMERICA

In December of 2007 Romney delivered his "Faith in America" speech, which sought to address concern about his religious beliefs. The speech was given at the George Bush Presidential Library in College Station, Texas. Romney framed the explanation of how his faith would inform his presidency in terms of religious liberty. America's "grand tradition of religious tolerance and liberty" leads some to "wonder whether there are any questions regarding an aspiring candidate's religion that are appropriate."[69] Romney sought to connect his candidacy with John F. Kennedy, in both the location of the speech and selected content. Kennedy addressed the issue of his religion before the Greater Houston Ministerial Association in 1960. Like Kennedy, Romney stated that he did not define his candidacy by his religion and believed that "a person should not be elected because of his faith nor should he be rejected because of his faith." Romney also asserted that every faith draws its adherents closer to God and that Americans "share a common creed of moral convictions," even though theological differences exist between churches. "No candidate should become the spokesman for his faith" because "if he becomes President he will need the prayers of the people of all faiths."[70]

Scholars have identified several important differences between Romney's speech and Kennedy's speech. First, Romney gave his speech during the primary, whereas Kennedy delivered his speech before the general election. Kennedy's Catholicism posed a greater challenge among the general electorate than primary voters. The situation was reversed for Romney who was trying to convince fellow Republicans he was worthy of the opportunity to compete in the general election. Second, Romney's audience consisted of political supporters who were not able to ask questions, while Kennedy's audience consisted of Protestant ministers who were allowed to ask questions. Third, Romney discussed his religious viewpoints in the speech, whereas Kennedy did not because religion was viewed as a private matter. "Kennedy hoped to persuade Americans not to vote against him simply because of his faith," while "Romney appeared to be trying to gain votes because of his faith."[71] For example, Romney used the occasion to advocate social conservative viewpoints, including criticism of a perceived overreach of secularism in American society. Romney argued that separation of church and state recently had been taken "well beyond its original meaning," because some "seek to remove from the public domain any acknowledgment of God."[72] Romney would "take care to separate the affairs of government from any religion," but not separate Americans from "the God who gave us liberty" or America's religious heritage.[73]

Other aspects of the speech clearly sought to address concerns about the influence of the LDS Church on Romney's political behavior. Romney assured Americans that "no authorities of my church, or of any other church for that matter, will ever exert influence on presidential decisions" because "their authority is theirs, within the province of church affairs, and it ends where the affairs of the nation begin."[74] Romney's governorship was put forth as evidence of his ability to serve as a chief executive in a manner that did not confuse church teachings and professional obligations. Still, Romney acknowledged that his word and experiences would not be sufficient for some Americans who would prefer him to distance himself from his religion. "That

I will not do," Romney stated, because "I believe in my Mormon faith and I endeavor to live by it. My faith is the faith of my fathers—I will be true to them and to my beliefs." Romney explained that others "believe that such a confession of my faith will sink my candidacy." This perspective underestimated the American people because "Americans do not respect believers of convenience" and "tire of those who would jettison their beliefs, even to gain the world."[75] Romney addressed concerns about his beliefs in regard to Jesus Christ and understood his candidacy as a test of religious tolerance. He stated that:

> I believe that Jesus Christ is the Son of God and the Savior of mankind. My church's beliefs about Christ may not all be the same as those of other faiths. Each religion has its own unique doctrines and history. These are not bases for criticism but rather a test of our tolerance. Religious tolerance would be a shallow principle indeed if it were reserved only for faiths with which we agree.[76]

Romney climbed two to five points in the polls immediately after the speech. Sixty-two percent of Americans were aware of the speech, 49 percent held a favorable view, and 39 percent held a negative view.[77] Still, nearly 20 percent of Americans would not vote for a well-qualified presidential candidate who was Mormon. In essence, American views toward a Mormon president have changed little since this type of polling began with George Romney, Mitt's father, during his 1967 presidential bid. Over 70 percent of Americans stated that being Mormon did not matter in regard to evaluating a potential presidential candidate, but over 20 percent viewed being Mormon as an undesirable characteristic for a presidential candidate.[78]

Defenders of Romney's speech stated that no serious person of faith could in good conscience completely reject religious influence on governance.[79] As a result, Romney's speech more closely resembled the rhetoric of Mike Huckabee, George W. Bush, and Jimmy Carter than John F. Kennedy.[80] The comparison of Romney to Kennedy "is more complicated for Latter-Day Saints" because Kennedy was a lay member of the Catholic Church, whereas "most Mormon men serve in Church leadership positions, and many of those in Congress have also served at one level or another in the Mormon hierarchy."[81] Jesuit priest and former House representative Robert Drinan, the only Roman Catholic priest to serve in Congress, was put forth by Mormon scholars as a more appropriate comparison. Pope John Paul II prohibited priests from holding public office out of concern that Drinan advocated liberal social positions that conflicted with Catholic doctrine.

A 2011 Gallup poll found that unwillingness to vote for a qualified Mormon candidate held steady into the 2012 election cycle. Education is the main cleavage among American voters in regard to voting for a Mormon presidential candidate. People without a college education are more resistant

Table 4.5
Comfort Levels of American Voters in Regard to Faith of Presidential Candidates

	Entirely Comfortable	Somewhat Comfortable	Somewhat Comfortable	Entirely Comfortable
Catholic	60	23	8	5
Jewish	55	25	9	6
Evangelical Christian	43	24	14	12
Mormon	35	25	19	17
Atheist	24	13	16	44
Muslim	21	17	23	36

Source: Quinnipiac University 2011.

to voting for a Mormon. Twelve percent of people with a college education would not vote for a qualified Mormon presidential candidate, compared to 20 percent of people with some college and 31 percent of people with no college.[82] A 2011 Pew poll found that 68 percent of Americans stated that someone being Mormon would make no difference in terms of voting for a presidential candidate. This is comparable to the number of people who would be less likely to vote for a candidate with a past history of using marijuana.[83] A 2012 Quinnipiac University poll found that American voters are much less comfortable with a Mormon presidential candidate compared to all other religious groups except Muslims. As seen in Table 4.5, 19 percent of voters were "somewhat uncomfortable" with Mormonism as a faith of a presidential candidate and 17 percent were "entirely uncomfortable." Only 35 percent were "entirely comfortable" with a presidential candidate who is a Mormon. This is much lower than comfort levels with Catholics and Jews, and slightly higher than atheists and Muslims. This data suggest that Romney must contend with a sizeable portion of the American electorate who views him with discomfort or disfavor regardless of qualifications.

A central question surrounding Mormons and presidential politics in 2012 was whether Mitt Romney, if elected president, would face politically related requests from the Mormon prophet Thomas Monson, and if so, what Romney would do. Much of this concern emerges from the logic of revelation. Nonbelievers tend to think that believing in a prophet who speaks for God requires unquestioning submission. Not all believers follow this logic, however, similar to Catholics who do not follow all directives of the pope.[84] Historically, "this issue is particularly sensitive for Mormons since one of the crucial issues that delayed statehood was the widely held (and not accurate) perception that Latter-day Saints were intensely loyal to the Church and considerably less loyal to the United States."[85] This issue created internal division as well, evident in Moses Thatcher being removed from the Quorum of Twelve in 1896 for not signing a document that required him to obtain the permission of the First Presidency prior to becoming a candidate for public office.

The Mormon Church is heavily withdrawn from politics in the twenty-first century compared to its roots in the nineteenth century, though Mormons remain deeply entangled in Utah politics. The Church occasionally takes positions on issues viewed as central to Mormon doctrine, such as same-sex marriage, but bishops do not typically excommunicate Mormons for holding political positions contrary to predominant Mormon views. Excommunication is most common in cases where Mormons publicly and directly criticize LDS leaders or doctrine. It is highly unlikely that President Monson would make direct and specific policy requests to Romney if he were president of the United States because the Mormon Church is more interested in national acceptance, given their long and violent history of persecution, than immediate political gains. LDS leaders are well aware that a politically active prophet would be very damaging for public relations, a major focus of the contemporary church.

The historic policy of political neutrality was represented in 2012 with a relevant statement provided by the LDS Newsroom on the church's website. This statement began with the assertion that "the Church's mission is to preach the gospel of Jesus Christ, not to elect politicians" and that the Church is "neutral in matters of party politics" in all nations where the Church exists. The Mormon Church does not: (1) "endorse, promote, or oppose political parties, candidates or platforms"; (2) "allow its church buildings, membership lists or other resources to be used for partisan political purposes"; (3) "attempt to direct its members as to which candidate or party they should give their votes to"; or (4) "attempt to direct or dictate to a government leader." The Church does: (1) "encourage its members to play a role as responsible citizens in their communities including becoming informed about issues and voting in elections"; (2) "expect its members to engage in the political process in an informed and civil manner"; (3) "request candidates for office not to imply that their candidacy or platforms are endorsed by the Church"; and (4) "reserve the right as an institution to address, in a nonpartisan way, issues that it believes have significant community or moral consequences or that directly affect the interests of the Church."

Prior to national elections Mormon authorities typically issue a letter to be read aloud to each American congregation that encourages members to vote and emphasizes the Church's neutrality in regard to partisanship and electoral outcomes. The First Presidency also issues guidelines for political participation among church leaders and did so in June of 2011 in preparation for the 2012 election cycle. General Authorities and general officers, as well as their spouses, are restricted from personally participating in political campaigns. Part-time church officers, such as area seventies, stake presidents, and bishops, can participate in political campaigns provided they do not speak for the Church, use church resources, or engage in fund-raising efforts that specifically target fellow Mormons.

SUMMARY

This chapter discussed the emergence of Mormons in federal politics and the rise of Mitt Romney as a serious presidential contender in the 2012 election. Nineteenth-century Mormons shifted from disinterest in politics to running for federal office in the hopes of securing greater protection. Twentieth-century Mormons increasingly viewed participation in federal politics as a means to enhance legitimacy and acceptance of Mormonism. The LDS Church of the twenty-first century promotes the notion of an active and informed citizenry, but is not involved in political campaigns and gets involved in political issues only when a major doctrinal or moral perspective is at stake. Romney's campaign illuminates lingering concern regarding the prospect of a Mormon in the White House, even though the violent persecution of Mormons is long past and Mormons have held several prominent positions in American government since the creation of the LDS Church. The following chapter will examine Mormon political thought with specific focus on predominant understandings of the Constitution and welfare policy.

5

Mormon Understandings of the Constitution and Welfare

MORMON POLITICAL ATTITUDES

The political ideology of Mormons became a topic of public interest with the church's consistent opposition to same-sex marriage, beginning with Hawaii state politics in the early 1990s, and intensifying most recently with Proposition 8 in California. Empirical study of Mormon political attitudes is challenging. Mormons in government are reluctant to discuss their religious beliefs. In 2011, for example, *Newsweek* contacted all 15 Mormons in Congress to request an interview about Mormons in politics. Only 4 members of Congress agreed to be interviewed and these members represented constituencies with significant Mormon populations. Mormons in society constitute fewer than 2 percent of Americans who are 18 or over. Jeffrey Fox explains:

> Mormons are a political force in the western United States and are one of the largest single denominations in the United States. They are theoretically interesting because the authoritative interpretation of doctrine through church leaders creates a unified doctrinal "stimulus" that allows a unique test of religious effects. Nevertheless, relatively little research has fully examined LDS political views or the degree to which religion shapes those views. There seems to be a conventional wisdom that there is little variance to study—Mormons are assumed to be ideological conservatives.[1]

Fox's research in 2003 and 2006 found that Mormons share several similar political views and values, including economic self-sufficiency, morality, family, citizen involvement, and a preferred role for the United States in the world, but the political attitudes of Mormons vary more greatly than conventional wisdom suggests. These differences include various perspectives on the appropriate role of government, levels of trust in government, views toward affirmative action, and interpretations of the Constitution.[2] A 2010

Table 5.1
Mormon Ideology Sorted by Church Attendance

	Conservative	Moderate	Liberal
Active Mormons[*]	65%	29%	5%
Lapsed Mormons[+]	36%	41%	20%
All other Americans	38%	37%	21%

[*]"Active Mormon" refers to someone who attends church weekly, near weekly, or monthly.
[+]"Lapsed Mormon" refers to someone who attends church less than weekly, near weekly, or monthly.
Source: Newport 2010.

Gallup poll found that nearly 60 percent of Mormons identified themselves as conservative. Sixteen percent of Mormons identified themselves as "very conservative" and just 1 percent as "very liberal." This constituted the largest number of conservatives and strong conservatives among any major religious group and the smallest number of strong liberals.[3] Religious activity appeared to be more influential for Mormons than geographic location. As seen in Tables 5.1 and 5.2, 56 percent of Mormons who attended religious services weekly, nearly every week, or monthly identified themselves as conservative Republican, compared to just 4 percent who identified themselves as liberal Democrats. Mormons living in Utah, approximately 34 percent of the adult Mormon population, did not have significantly different political ideologies than Mormons who lived outside of the Utah.

A 2011 poll conducted by the Pew Research Center Forum on Religion and Public Life found that over 65 percent of Mormons described themselves as politically conservative and 74 percent of Mormons identified or leaned

Table 5.2
Party Identification and Ideology among Mormons by Church Attendance

	Liberal Democrat	Moderate Democrat	Conservative Democrat
Active Mormon[*]	4%	10%	5%
Lapsed Mormon[+]	12%	19%	8%
All other Americans	17%	21%	10%

	Independent	Liberal/Moderate Republican	Conservative Republican
Active Mormons[*]	9%	15%	56%
Lapsed Mormons[+]	18%	18%	23%
All other Americans	12%	12%	24%

[*]"Active Mormon" refers to someone who attends church weekly, near weekly, or monthly.
[+]"Lapsed Mormon" refers to someone who attends church less than weekly, near weekly, or monthly.
Source: Newport 2010.

toward the Republican Party. Republican identification was double that of adults at large.[4] Furthermore, over twice as many Mormons believed the Republican Party (39%) was friendly to Mormons than believed the Democratic Party was friendly to Mormons (17%). Mormon Democrats and leaning Democrats were split on this issue. Thirty-three percent of Democratic Mormons, either full Democrat or leaning, stated the Democratic Party was friendly to Mormons. Similarly, 30 percent of Democratic Mormons, either full Democrat or leaning, stated the Republican Party was friendly to Mormons.[5] This split is remarkable. One would reasonably expect Mormon partisans to identify with a party, the Democrats in this case, that at minimum is friendly to their religion.

Not surprisingly, Republicans are viewed more favorably by Mormons than Democrats. Less than one-quarter of Mormons approved of Barack Obama's presidency in July of 2010. This was the lowest approval rating among any religious group at that point in time.[6] In 2011, Obama's favorability rating among Mormon voters was half as strong as the electorate as a whole.[7] Mormons hold small-government conservative views and socially conservative views to a much greater degree than the general public. Seventy five percent Mormons preferred a smaller government that provided fewer services to a bigger government that provided more services compared to 48 percent of Americans at large. Support for discouraging homosexuality was twice as strong among Mormons (66%) than the general public. Just one-quarter of Mormons believed homosexuality should be accepted compared to 58 percent of Americans at large.[8] As seen in Table 5.3, Mormons were more socially conservative than the population at large in regard to viewing sex between unmarried adults, abortion, and drinking alcohol as morally wrong.

In 2011, Mitt Romney received high favorability ratings from Mormons across the political spectrum. Romney was viewed much more favorably by Mormon voters as a whole (86%) than the general public and even higher among Republican or Republican-leaning Mormons (94%). In fact, Romney's favorability among Mormon Democrats was approximately as high

Table 5.3
Moral Views of Mormons

	Morally Acceptable	Morally Wrong	Not Moral Issue
Polygamy	2%	86%	11%
Sex between unmarried adults	7%	79%	13%
Having an abortion	4%	74%	9%
Drinking alcohol	6%	54%	38%
Divorce	16%	25%	46%

Source: Pew Research Center Forum on Religion and Public Life, National Survey of Mormons, 2011.

as his favorability among Republicans in the general population.[9] John Huntsman, the other Mormon candidate in the 2012 Republican primary, was viewed less favorably than Romney, as was Harry Reid, the Democratic Senate majority leader. Half of Mormon voters viewed Huntsman favorably compared to 24 percent who held an unfavorable view. Not surprisingly, Huntsman, the former governor of Utah, was viewed more favorably in Utah (70%) than nationally. Half of Mormon voters viewed Reid unfavorably, while 22 percent viewed him favorably.[10]

MORMON POLITICAL THOUGHT

Mormon understanding of the coming of God's kingdom serves as a cornerstone for understanding Mormon perspectives on government and governance. Mormons believe that earthly governments will eventually pass away. The Mormon priesthood will then administer the government of the kingdom of God during the apocalypse that precedes Christ's Second Coming. The nucleus of this political organization was developed by Joseph Smith prior to his death. The Council of Fifty was formed to create a theocratic political order among Mormons and direct Mormon activity in political affairs that interested the church.[11]

Brigham Young vigorously pursued Mormon nation building till his death in 1877. Toward the end of his life Young "saw gloom ahead for the United States, whose class conflict, political corruption, and persecution of Mormons seemed to foreshadow 'the breakup of our present form of government' and millennial catastrophe."[12] Young believed a revolution was on the horizon. The body politic was too corrupt, only fit for burning, unless a complete and extraordinary change in the hearts and lives of people occurred in obedience to God's plan. "Despite this pessimism, and even because of it, Mormons continued to build the kingdom of God in their promised land, gathering converts, expanding settlements, experimenting with radically cooperative economics, and working desperately to ward off the seductions and corruptions of the outside world."[13]

The notion of God's kingdom in Mormon thought was gradually connected to the political values of the Founding Fathers. Mormons believed that the political genius of these men enabled the creation of the United States, the only country that granted sufficient religious freedom for the Mormon restoration process to unfold. Praise for the founders became more commonplace as Mormons experienced greater acceptance and ability to thrive socially and economically. Persecution was explained by flaws in implementing the political system, not its design or theoretical underpinnings. Whereas nineteenth-century Mormons sought "to create a society where they could live and grow in pure Christian fellowship without the obstructions of a secular and perverse world," twentieth-century Mormons sought to preserve the Constitution and the political values it contained, particularly individual liberty and limited government.[14] In turn, Mormon political philosophy enlarged the philosophy of the Founding Fathers "into a concept of a world government based upon the freedom and dignity of man."[15]

Constitutional reverence in the Mormon tradition has a theological component dating back to Joseph Smith. Several early revelations explicitly mentioned the Constitution. In 1833, Smith revealed that the Heavenly Father said "I, the Lord, justify you, and your brethren of my church, in befriending that law which is the constitutional law of the land."[16] God stated that He suffered to establish the Constitution, which "should be maintained for the rights and protection of all flesh, according to just and holy principles." Popular sovereignty is particularly important to Mormons. Mormon doctrine states that no one should be oppressed so that all people can act freely in the moral agency granted by God. "For this purpose have I established the Constitution of this land, by the hands of wise men."[17] "May those principles, which were so honorably and nobly defended namely, the Constitution of our land, by our fathers, be established forever."[18]

In addition to these explicit teachings, there is a unique Mormon mythology surrounding the founders and their role in Mormonism that few non-Mormons are aware of. Two relevant examples are particularly noteworthy. The first has to do with a strand of myths and prophecies that suggest Mormons will save the Constitution. Joseph Smith and Brigham Young spoke of a future time when the Constitution would be in great danger. During that time, it is believed that Mormon elders will rise up and defend the Constitution. This rhetoric dates back to the White Horse Prophecy, which was derived from a conversation between Smith and two church members, Edwin Rushton and Theodore Turley. The prophecy was recorded 10 years after Smith's death, and its authenticity remains in question. Smith supposedly discussed a future time where the Constitution will be in danger as the United States experiences an end-of-days type revolution where the government falls and a group of Constitution-loving people restore order. Subsequent prophets adopted this narrative in teaching the importance of defending the constitutional order and emphasizing the role Mormons will play in that process. Brigham Young's statements on defending the Constitution are recorded in the *Journal of Discourses*, an important collection of Mormon sermons from the early years of the church. Young stated:

> Brethren and sisters, our friends wish to know our feelings towards the Government. I answer, they are first rate, and we will prove it too, as you will see if you only live long enough, for we shall live to prove it as certain; and when the Constitution of the United States hangs, as it were, upon a single thread, they will have to call for the "Mormon" Elders to save it from utter destruction; and they will step forth to do it.[19]

Regardless of whether Smith really issued the prophecy or not, the myth thrived over subsequent generations. Various church leaders and politicians have incorporated the notion of an endangered Constitution into religious and political rhetoric. Even contemporary Mormon officeholders, such as Orrin Hatch, frequently use general language that portrays the Constitution in danger and occasionally the specific phrase that the Constitution is hanging by a thread. Interestingly, what appears to simply be a metaphor to non-Mormons is actually a deeply rooted theological appeal to Mormons.

The second particularly noteworthy aspect of Mormon theology is a famous account within the Mormon tradition of the American founders appearing to church leaders from the afterlife and asking to be baptized. Former LDS president Wilford Woodruff claimed to be visited by the signers of the Declaration of Independence in 1877 as an LDS apostle and president of the Mormon temple in St. George, Utah. The founders waited on Woodruff for two days. "The spirits of the dead gathered around me," Woodruff explained, "wanting to know why we did not redeem them. Said they, 'You have had the use of the Endowment House for a number of years, and yet nothing has ever been done for us. We laid the foundation of the government you now enjoy, and we never apostatized from it, but we remained true to it and were faithful to God.'"[20] Mormon leaders decided to baptize "the signers of the Declaration of Independence, and fifty other eminent men, making one hundred in all, including John Wesley, Columbus, and others."[21] Mormon baptism of the dead is a controversial practice, but an important one to Mormons, given the prominent role that family plays in the afterlife, and the prominent role missionary work plays in converting others to the Mormon faith. This experience, real or imagined, is a vivid example of the fusion of religion and the Constitution in the Mormon tradition.

From a practical perspective, Smith's lauding of the Constitution could be understood as an effort to secure protection for Mormons from vigilante and state-sponsored violence by positioning Mormons as patriotic constitutionalists who wanted nothing more than the government to live up to its laws and ideals. The strong shift of Mormons to conservatism after World War II and anti-Communist efforts surrounding the Cold War gave birth to a large body of Mormon political thought, still prominent today, that understands the Constitution as divinely inspired. Ezra Taft Benson was among the most outspoken politically conservative Mormon leaders in this era. Benson was an apostle when he served as secretary of agriculture under President Eisenhower and went on to become the LDS president from 1985 to 1994. Benson is one of a handful of Mormon leaders who authored books providing a religious interpretation of the Constitution. "It would be erroneous for people to conclude that the Constitution is the sole genius of the Founding Fathers," Benson argued, because "theirs was a combined wisdom derived from heavenly inspiration, knowledge of political government from ages past, and the crucible of their own experience."[22] According to Benson, "every true American and true friend of liberty should love our inspired

Constitution" for "its creation was a miracle."[23] Benson's theological understanding of the Constitution was summarized this way:

> History is not an accident. Events are foreknown to God. His superintending influence is behind the actions of His righteous children. Long before America was even discovered, the Lord was moving and shaping events that would lead to the coming forth of the remarkable form of government established by the Constitution. America had to be free and independent to fulfill this destiny.[24]

Apostle Dallin Oaks, former University of Chicago law professor, president of Brigham Young University, and Utah Supreme Court justice, cited George Washington as the first to use the term "miracle" in describing the creation of the Constitution. Washington wrote in 1788 that "it appears to me, then, little short of a miracle, that the delegates from so many different states (which states you know are also different from each other in their manners, circumstances, and prejudices) should unite in forming a system of national Government, so little liable to well-founded objections."[25] Oaks emphasized the extraordinary influence of the U.S. Constitution in defending the notion of a divinely inspired constitution. Two centuries after the United States adopted the first written constitution in the world nearly all countries subsequently adopted a written constitution, many of which follow the American model. Thus the "miracle" of the Constitution was twofold, the fact that it was created and its remarkable impact on world history.

In Mormon political thought the miraculous creation of the Constitution is separated from the supposed divinity of the text itself. For example, Oaks "never considered it necessary to defend every line of the Constitution as scriptural," in particular, the compromise on slavery or citizenship requirements.[26] This position was echoed by apostle Reuben Clark, former ambassador to Mexico and the namesake of the law school at Brigham Young University. Clark viewed the Constitution as part of his religion, but argued that LDS doctrine does not understand the Constitution as a "fully grown document." Rather, doctrine holds that the principles of the Constitution must grow and develop to address needs in an advancing world.[27]

Mormon constitutional scholarship has sought to identify the core elements of the Constitution that establish its greatness. These elements have been referred to by different names, including "great fundamentals" and "basic and eternal principles." Clark, for example, identified three great fundamentals of the Constitution: (1) separation of powers, (2) protection of essential freedoms, and (3) equality before the law. Separation of powers and individual freedoms were not new at the founding, but "the Constitution's closest approach to scriptural stature" was found in "the phrasing of our Bill of Rights." "Without the free exercise of religion," Clark explained, "America could not have served as the host nation for the restoration of the gospel."[28] The final fundamental, equality before the law, served as the foundation of liberty and ensures that Mormon allegiance to the Constitution is based on its principles, not individuals.

Oaks supplemented Clark's great fundamentals with two additional fundamentals, federalism and popular sovereignty. Federalism was unprecedented in theory and practice at the time of the founding. For Oaks, federalism was crucial in reserving powers for the states as a systematic limitation on the federal government and further protection of individual liberty. For Mormons, Oaks explained, popular sovereignty implies personal responsibility. Citizens share the burden of governing and cannot blame a sovereign for their troubles. Personal responsibility is an important element of Mormon doctrine as taught in the Book of Mormon, which states "burden should come upon all the people, that every man might bear his part."[29]

Benson identified five basic and eternal principles of the Constitution: (1) political liberty, (2) the proper role of government, (3) understanding God as the source of human rights, (4) believing people are superior to government, and (5) believing that government should have only limited powers. Benson explicitly connected political liberty with Mormon theology. Political liberty, as codified in the Constitution, is so important to Mormon thought because it permits the exercise of individual agency and allows humans to complete their earthly test. God's plan requires "all people to obtain moral bodies, be tried and proven in all things, and have opportunity to choose by their own free will to obey the laws and ordinances essential to their exaltation."[30] The first and best form of worldly government was theocracy, but Adam and his descendants degenerated from this perfect order into different political systems that resulted in human misery and centuries of oppression. Americans "live in one of history's most exceptional moments—in a nation and a time of unprecedented freedom."[31]

Governments were instituted by God for the benefit of man, and "He holds men accountable for their acts in relation to them." The single most important function of governments "is to secure the rights and freedoms of individual citizens."[32] According to Benson, there are two types of rights, those given by God as part of the divine plan and those granted by governments as part of the political plan. "Reason, necessity, tradition, and religious conviction" lead Benson to accept the divine origin of rights.[33] If people view rights as granted by government, then people must be willing to accept the corollary that they can be denied by government as well. People are superior to government because government is essentially a small group of citizens hired by society to discharge certain responsibilities authorized by society. In turn, government has no innate power or privilege to do anything. The governed are the only source of political authority. Government is primarily a mechanism for defense against bodily harm and "cannot claim the power to redistribute money or property nor to force reluctant citizens to perform acts of charity against their will."[34]

The teachings of Smith, Young, Woodruff, Benson, Clark, Oaks, and other various other church leaders over the past century have produced a powerful strand of contemporary Mormon political thought in which the Constitution is viewed by Mormons to various degrees as an important spiritual document in the American political tradition. This is a striking contrast to conventional views of the Constitution that understand the document as a secular contract between the government and the governed. Typically, the Declaration of Independence is understood as the more spiritually influenced founding document within scholarship on American political thought because of its reliance on deism and natural-rights theory. Furthermore, the conservatism of contemporary Mormons is slightly different from typical small-government conservatism, which calls for a return of classic liberalism and free-market economic principles out of the belief that freedom is inherently valuable. Freedom is valuable to Mormons because of what it has enabled as part of Mormon theology, past, present, and future. Its significance extends beyond the notion of a secular political value. This is evident from the development of the religion, to the judgment day all Mormons believe they will experience, to the Second Coming Mormons continually prepare for.

THE MORMON WELFARE SYSTEM

The notion of social welfare is important to Mormons even though Mormons are heavily conservative and prioritize individual freedom. Compassion for the poor is prominent in Mormon doctrine. Nephi wrote that God invited all people to partake in his goodness, "black and white, bond and free, male and female," because "all are alike unto God."[35] Mormon revelations have cautioned "woe unto you rich men, that will not give your substance to the poor, for your riches will canker your souls"[36] and "remember the poor, and consecrate of thy properties for their support that which thou hast to impart unto them, with a covenant and a deed which cannot be broken."[37] Mormon doctrine states that in temporal things Mormons should be equal and "the Saints were to be organized to be equal in all things."[38] Smith's experiences growing up in poverty likely influenced his thinking toward social policy. Smith "displayed an unceasing interest in social reform" and issued a range of related recommendations that included the emancipation of slaves, penal reform, enhancing public education, and developing a sophisticated system of urban planning.[39]

Concern for the poor was the driving force behind the law of consecration developed by Smith. This law was presented as a divine principle "whereby men and women voluntarily dedicate their time, talents, and material wealth to the establishment and building up of God's kingdom."[40] Early Mormon settlements practiced what was called "united order," where Mormons shared all property, goods, and profits according to their needs and wants. The order was managed by LDS leaders and gradually eroded in the face of public resistance. Early communal experiences undertaken by Mormons sharply contrast with contemporary Mormon attitudes toward individual freedom and the protection of private property. Since the 1960s Mormons have increasingly viewed government with skepticism, if not disdain. Ironically, early teachings and practices emphasized a form of collectivism and systematic poverty reduction that more closely resembled Marxist thought than modern conservatism.

During the Great Depression, Mormon leaders sought to create a system by which Mormons were able to take care of their own, rather than relying on the government for assistance. The modern welfare program was formally organized in April of 1936. According to LDS president Heber Grant, the objective was to develop "a system under which the curse of idleness would be done away with, the evils of a dole abolished and independence, industry, thrift and self-respect be once more established among our people." This fit with the aim of the Church, to "help the people to help themselves," as work was "re-enthroned as the ruling principle of the lives of our Church membership."[41] This was more of an ideal than a reality. Utah received among the highest proportions of public assistance during the 1930s.

State-sponsored welfare programs grew unpopular within the Mormon community as Mormons as a whole became increasingly conservative during the 1950s and 1960s. Government efforts toward poverty alleviation were increasingly viewed as a form of Communist penetration. This led to divisions between conservative Mormon politicians and the liberal Mormon minority. Debates ensued behind closed doors about doctrinal interpretation and the relation of doctrine to public-policy making. Occasionally, conservative Mormons questioned the faith and religious motivations of their liberal Mormon colleagues.[42] Liberal Mormons argued that social welfare programs enhanced, rather than diminished, one's individual agency. Conservative Mormons argued that government involvement in social welfare programs was antithetical to preserving the political freedom necessary for one to exercise individual agency. A common sentiment among conservative Mormons was that "my great-great grandfather didn't get any help from the government, and yet he succeeded in establishing himself out West as a prosperous farmer. Why can't you do the same thing? What you need is more backbone and initiative."[43] A second commonly held conservative position was that voluntary organizations and local governments were better at addressing social and economic ills than the federal government. The appeal of this position, still prominent among contemporary Mormons, is understandable considering the communal history of Mormon settlements and the unique legacy of Mormon control in Utah.

The contemporary LDS Church has identified several basic principles that inform their work in promoting Mormon welfare and providing humanitarian assistance to peoples of all faiths. Mormons cite Matthew in expressing their desire to follow Christ's teachings to feed the hungry, give drink to the thirsty, take in a stranger, clothe the naked, and visit those who are sick or imprisoned.[44] Similar to popular sovereignty, mentioned earlier, Mormons view general welfare from the perspective of personal responsibility. "The responsibility for each person's spiritual and temporal well-being rests first upon himself, second upon his family, and third upon the Church."[45]

The LDS website has a large section devoted to "provident living."[46] Provident living is the suggested means by which Mormons care for themselves. This begins with becoming self-reliant. Preparing for adversity is understood as central to self-reliance. The Mormon Church suggests that members compose a family emergency plan that should consider the accumulation of a typical three-month food supply, drinking water, medication, first aid, clothing, important documents, and means to communicate with family following a disaster. The accumulation of food through the process of home storage is a unique and largely unknown aspect of Mormon life. Mormons believe that God "lovingly commanded" them to "prepare for every needful thing" in order to overcome danger and adversity.[47] The motivation for home storage is threefold. First, Mormon history has taught that anticipating and preparing for hardship is helpful in overcoming adversity, which can arise from a multitude of causes. Second, there is a practical benefit to working, planning, and saving as it relates to building self-reliance and avoiding debt. Third, there is the theological element of the Second Coming of Christ and the prominent role Mormons believe they will play in leading Christ's followers through the end of days. The Mormon Church provides several resources for members storing food, including lists of food that can last more than 30 years, product and packaging recommendations, and advice on ideal storage conditions.[48]

Proper financial conduct is the second component of provident living. The LDS Church urges Mormons to create a budget, spend modestly, and avoid debt. Separating need from want is emphasized in avoiding debt. Mormons have an instruction manual for marriage and family relations. Lesson 8 is devoted to managing family finances. All Mormons are expected to honestly tithe 10 percent of their belongings. The process of determining what to include in measuring one's tithing amount is not standardized, which is remarkable considering how many procedures are standardized within the Mormon tradition. The teachings of Malachi in the Book of Mormon are cited as the scriptural basis for tithing: "Bring ye all the tithes into the storehouse, that there may be meat in mine house, and prove me now herewith, saith the Lord of hosts, if I will not open you the windows of heaven, and pour you out a blessing, that there shall not be room enough to receive it."[49] The Mormon Church asserts that fulfilling the tithing obligation reduces the likelihood of financial mismanagement.

Mormons are also expected to make a "fast offering," which refers to forgoing two meals a month and donating the cost of the food to a local church fund for those in need. Members are encouraged be generous and give as much as possible more than the cost of the meals. These relatively modest contributions of individual Mormons quickly add up. Each congregation has approximately $50,000 a year to spend at the bishop's discretion. Mormons may seek out temporary assistance from their bishops "when members and their families are doing all they can to provide for themselves and still cannot meet their basic needs."[50] The bishop is perceived as the best person to determine what help is required because of his position as a local minister who regularly interacts with members of the congregation. "Recipients of these resources are given the opportunity to work, to the extent of their ability, for the assistance they receive."[51] Utah has 3,600 Mormon congregations alone, which annually produces nearly $200 million in welfare funding. This equals approximately one-fifth of what the state of Utah spends on welfare and nearly mirrors state spending on health. According to Bob Bennett, former bishop and U.S. senator, the system works well because the money remains localized. Bishops have extensive latitude to use the money to help those in need and "everyone trusts the bishops."[52]

Nationally, the LDS Church operates storehouses, thrift stores, employment centers, and family services offices to promote self-reliance and provide benefits. The tradition of bishop storehouses dates back to 1830, when Mormon leaders began developing places where donated grains and commodities could be stored and distributed. Modern storehouses are like supermarkets without tills. Goods are distributed to Mormons on the basis of written requisitions composed and signed by bishops. There were a total of 143 storehouses in 2011. Mormons dedicated a new Bishops' Central Storehouse in Salt Lake City in January of 2012, a 570,391-square-foot facility on 35 acres. Don Johnson, director of production and distribution for LDS Welfare Services, described the facility as " 'the hub of a wheel' of the church's vast welfare efforts."[53] Seventy percent of the food is produced by Mormons. The rest is purchased at large wholesale discounts. Food is distributed to Mormons in need as part of the LDS welfare program and distributed to people in need of all faiths as part of the LDS humanitarian program. Deseret Transportation, an LDS transport company, is housed in the building. The company uses 43 tractors to haul church goods in 98 trailers over 3 million miles per year delivering goods to 110 LDS storehouses throughout the United States and Canada. LDS Welfare Services holds a two-year supply of food. The network of LDS storehouses and transportation capabilities enables the church to quickly respond to natural disasters, evident in the speed with which supplies were deployed to New Orleans after Hurricane Katrina in 2005 and Haiti after the 2010 earthquake.[54]

Deseret Industries is a nonprofit thrift store that accepts tax-deductible donations of household goods and clothing, and provides temporary employment and vocational training. There are 43 Deseret Industries stores in seven western states. Nearly half are in Utah.[55] The stores are engaged in various community partnerships and house LDS Employment Resource Centers and LDS Family Service Centers. Employment centers are operated by local missionaries and aid Mormons through job placement services and training in career development and small-business management. Two thousand Mormons are served annually by employment centers through an estimated 7,800 hours of volunteer service. Family Service Centers provide consultation, counseling, and adoption services. These centers are operated by licensed professional therapists. Each center has a board-certified psychiatrist.[56]

The Relief Society is the primary women's organization in Mormonism. The group was organized by Joseph Smith in 1842. Smith wanted the society to work for the relief of the poor, the destitute, widows, and orphans. His conception of relief included saving souls as well as helping those in need. The Relief Society is tasked with looking after the spiritual welfare and salvation of all female Mormons. Mormons believe that the society was divinely made, authorized, instituted, and ordained. The Relief Society is administered by the dictates of Handbook 2. The LDS Church has composed two handbooks. Handbook 1 is for stake presidents and bishops. Handbook 2 is for administering the Church. Chapter 9 of Handbook 2 is devoted to the Relief Society. According to Handbook 2, the purpose of the Relief Society is to prepare "women for the blessings of eternal life by helping them increase their faith and personal righteousness, strengthen families and homes, and help those in need." The society pursues these objectives "through Sunday gospel instruction, other Relief Society meetings, visiting teaching, and welfare and compassionate service."[57] The motto of the Relief Society is "charity never faileth."[58] Membership is open to Mormon women 18 years of age and older. The group is understood by Mormons as an auxiliary to the priesthood and beholden to priesthood leaders. The LDS Church claims the society is one of the largest women's organizations in the world with over 5 million global members.

The LDS Church keeps detailed records of their welfare services and produces public fact sheets. As seen in Table 5.4, the 2011 fact sheet reported that 872,721 days of labor were donated at Mormon welfare facilities and 9,832 missionaries served in the realm of welfare services. Missionary assignments included managing employment centers, teaching English as a second language, teaching marriage and parental skills, improving agricultural and medical practices, distributing clothing, and supervising welfare projects and missionaries. A total of 147,855 Mormons were placed in training or employment opportunities.

Table 5.4
2011 LDS Statistics of Welfare Services

Days of labor donated to church welfare facilities	872,721
Employment and training placements	147,855
Total number of:	
Storehouses	143
Home storage centers	101
Production projects	54
Processing facilities	19
Storage and distribution facilities	36
Employment resource centers	327
Deseret Industries thrift stores	43
LDS Family Services offices	85
Number of missionaries serving in Welfare Services	9,832
Examples of missionary assignments	
Managing employment centers	
Teaching English as a second language	
Teaching marriage and parenting skills	
Improving agricultural and medical practices	
Distributing clothing	
Supervising welfare projects and missionaries	
Number of major disaster assistance efforts (1985–2011)	202
Recent examples	
Japan earthquake and tsunami relief 2011	
Haiti earthquake relief 2010	
Chile earthquake relief 2010	
Pakistan flooding relief 2010	
Samoa tsunami relief 2009	
Philippines typhoon relief 2009	
Indonesia earthquake relief 2009	
Ethiopia famine relief 2008	
Peru earthquake relief 2007–9	
Humanitarian assistance rendered (1985–2011)	$1.4 billion
Countries and territories served	179

Source: Welfare Services Fact Sheet 2011, http://www.lds.org/bc/content/shared/ content/ english/pdf/ welfare/2011-welfare-services-fact-sheet.pdf.

SUMMARY

Mormon political thought tends to hold heavily conservative perspectives and provide strong support for the Republican Party. The Mormon theological tradition has influenced political thinking. This is evident in Mormon thought regarding constitutional interpretation and welfare policy. Mormons view the Constitution as a divinely inspired document and believe that public assistance is better undertaken through their private welfare system than public social programs. Understanding specific political attitudes of Mormons and the larger theoretical underpinnings of their political thought is important in understanding the political behavior of Mormons in and out of government. The following chapter will examine the efforts of the Mormon Church to oppose the legal recognition of same-sex marriage at the state and federal levels of government.

6

Now It's Okay to Redefine Marriage?

MINORITY RELIGION

Despite its remarkable growth in recent decades, the Church of Jesus Christ of Latter-day Saints is, and always has been, a minority population. As such it has been subject to the pressures of majority politics and sensitive to the position of minority rights within American politics. There are several fears that are common to all minority religions as they seek to survive within their respective nations. In general, they must prepare for some level of preferential treatment for those other religions that constitute the majority. This leads to worries ranging from sheer organizational failure to simple competitive disadvantage in a pluralist marketplace of religion. A minority religion must develop a response to this disadvantage that somehow offsets the negative consequences of joining such a population. A second fear involves the risk that legislative authority might subject members to laws that are untenable. Naturally, a minority voice has rare opportunities to affect the governing laws of society. In such a position, religious sects either choose to excuse members from breaking religious law in order to obey secular law or choose to consistently break the law appealing to the potentially higher authority of fundamental rights. A third fear is the more apocalyptic fear that they will be driven from their homes, persecuted, or killed if they remain in the majority population. In many cases, this paranoia is rather warranted.

Mormons have faced all three of these fears since the birth of the religion. Many times the church faced organizational challenges in the face of majority power. As Protestantism provided the backdrop for majority moral politics for much of American history, Mormons faced constant pressure through the political system in the particular ways in which Protestants responded to their fears of the new religion. Although such pressure was a challenge for a minority religion like Mormonism, in many ways the distinct minority status is what generated the initial novelty to draw in new converts. As a minority religion, it drew strength from the otherness proscribed by the majority population. Legislative action was a constant majority force working against the Mormon Church. The strategic use of party politics and, when necessary, the physical withdrawal from spheres of legislative authority were needed to keep the church afloat. Mormons fought back against the pressures of majority power as they could, but eventually retreated west to diminish the choice between religious and secular law. This retreat succeeded only in delaying the inevitable acquiescence to the larger majority politics of Protestant-infused American laws.

Majority populations often respond to the tenuous position of minority religions by providing a separate status or separate state for their community. This allows the majority to ignore the perceived affront to majority moral constraints and allows the community to deal with fears of persecution within the safety of its own sphere of authority. The other option for the majority population is to accommodate the community within the prevailing ideology. In these cases the dominant religious ideology is viewed as a general cultural phenomenon to which a variety of religious communities are sub-groups allowed their particular divergent views.[1] The separate-status solution is usually a problem for majority power in that it requires finding cultural and political space for such a status. No less problematic is the need for a separate physical space. The issue of land use in such cases is quite often significant. Efforts by majorities to solve the problems that arise from clashes with minority religions through removal are often failures because some compromise is eventually necessary when the land matters. The scarcity of resources for most nations allows for only a temporary solution through separation. When land use becomes an issue, so too does the original tension.

Compared to many other nations, the United States had quite a bit of extra physical space to deal with Mormonism through removal—namely the Territory of Utah. This relative abundance of space allowed more time for the religion to exist in a separate sphere of authority and for the majority to deal with its existence from afar. Nevertheless, the Mormon faith was eventually forced to compromise its beliefs when the land mattered. The second option of accommodation allows more flexibility for the conflict to resolve itself gradually. Aside from the issue of polygamy, this is the path more often chosen by the American majority. The physical separation aided in a general accommodation to what the majority considered a strange and perhaps dangerous new religious movement. Mormon citizens as individuals were addressed according to these two approaches. Insofar as the separation or accommodation provided for their ability to express needs and concerns, the political tension could be resolved. However, when these approaches led to oppression and ostracism, the political problem was that of any minority population struggling under the potential tyranny of a majority population.[2] Majority legislation is then countered with some claims of fundamental or constitutional rights.

This is not an easy struggle for most religions because the classic liberalism that supports these claims to constitutional rights rests on assumptions of individualism that run counter to many theological positions. Protecting religious minorities under the banner of rights can actually undermine some of the theological authority inherent in those religions. Many religions feel that a definition of rights held by individuals, rather than by groups, requires the acceptance of a society composed of persons with authority and independence. This individual authority is seen as existing at the expense of the integrity of the communal whole.[3] Rather than use the concept of individual rights, most religions would choose to describe the relationship of the individual to the whole as one of moral responsibility. They prefer the concepts of duty and obligation to that of rights. When secular forces cite religion as being out of step with modernity, it is more or less in reference to this inability to regard individualism as the ultimate value. This inability to embrace rights, and individualism more generally, leads minority religions to take on the majority power as a defiant whole—which requires the kind of separation evident in the westward travels of the Mormon Church.

This resistance to individualism does not necessarily lead to conflict with the modern secular state. The nation as a whole needs a homogenous social identity to facilitate governance. In a very real sense, religion helps to provide the sense of community that allows for easier governance. Thus religion can be inherently useful in reinforcing the unit of nation-state.[4] However, the nation also controls the violence of social coercion. It is in this balance between the state drawing strength from religion and using violence to coerce religion that religious minorities struggle. Those religions and religious movements that exist and grow within the majority cultures of modern religions provide a synthesis between religious identity and national identity. Those that exist outside of the majority culture are pulled between accommodation to the homogeneity of the nation and the separation that is natural when violent coercion is used. As the majority power adjusts to the minority religion, so does that religion adjust to the majority power. This interaction continues until some equilibrium can be reached or the minority religion extinguished or exiled.

Although the modern nation represents a monopoly of violent authority and the underlying logic of individualism, many leaders of minority religious communities are eager to embrace secular nationalism because of the protections provided against the majority religious powers.[5] It is often the unit of nation-state that provides the individual rights necessary to allow a minority population to survive. This irony is not easily resolved as these minority religions struggle with the implications of individualism while practicing more communal understandings of rights. The only way the nation-state protects minority religions from majority religions is with an authority invested by the larger population. For this authority to exist, the modern nation must provide something to believe in that is somehow as compelling as religious belief—otherwise authority will ultimately rest with the religious leaders of society. There must exist some faith in the secular order that is as compelling as faith in the sacred teachings of religion. This is essentially the role of civil religion.[6] Civil religion, though, inevitably draws on the moral and cultural power of existing majority religion. Thus, minority religions are caught in the legitimizing cycle that exists between nation-state and majority religion. As such, they are protected from the majority religious culture by the state, while the state is legitimized by the same majority. This protection succeeds only as long as the constitutional rights are interpreted in a way that favors the minority religion. When those basic rights are seen through the lens of majority power, the protection fails.

MORMONS AND POLYGAMY

No piece of Mormon faith illustrates the struggle of a minority religion within a majority culture better than the practice of plural marriage. Polygamy distinguished the Mormon faith within the American context for many years and played a role in its early vitality. Marriage within any faith brings kinship and reinforces relationships and communal bonds. Within Mormonism it also reinforced ritual secrecy and business relationships. In the early years of the Mormon faith, American society was still profoundly structured by ties of family, and in this respect, plural marriage was an extension of this pattern of affiliation.[7] American society and economics were built on the networks of familial relationships, and the Mormon practice of plural marriage provided a very stable, interwoven social structure on which to build a community. Although the taking of multiple wives was scandalous, the use of familial bonds to build and reinforce community was completely in keeping with the larger American society.

Aside from the practical benefits in community structure, plural marriage fulfilled a deeper spiritual calling. Polygamy was considered divine revelation and a sacrament. In the early years of the church, it was seen as central to the restoration of biblical truth. As with any central teaching, change in the practice of plural marriage would be seen as a violation of scripture and would require extensive measures to shore up the confidence of the faithful in the Church's authority to mediate eternal truth.[8] From the beginnings of the Church, this practice was a focal point of tension with the majority religious culture. It distinguished the Church in important theological ways, but also made it a primary target for majority opinion. Plural marriage was central to the worldview of Mormonism and meaningful as a symbol of separateness and innovation.[9] Religious minorities must harness the uniqueness evident in the divergence from majority culture to justify the spiritual superiority. It is in the magnitude of difference from majority culture that a religion derives its claims to righteousness, and in this way polygamy was Mormonism's innovation with the greatest magnitude of difference.

This innovation was not seen as invention, but as revelation. Mormon interpretations of the Bible suggested the existence of polygamy in the New

Testament and even suggested the plural marriage of Jesus Christ to both Mary and Martha.[10] Most of the concept of plural marriage, though, lay in Joseph Smith's early efforts to translate the Old Testament. The priestly control over marriage and the defiance of civil authority required by the practice were considered at length by Smith[11]—considered both from the spiritual point of view of revelation and from the organizational needs of a young church. The spiritual meaning of plural marriage served to fulfill an eternal desire for each Mormon to seek a higher order of being. Children are very important in the spiritual progression of Mormonhood. Each Mormon male needs spiritual offspring. The more spiritual offspring, the higher one is elevated up the eternal ladder of gods in the universe.[12] Great theological emphasis was placed on the importance of the home and the role of women in rearing children.

Plural marriage provided additional wives through whom men could continue eternal progression.[13] A plurality of wives, and their many children born on earth and in heaven, would increase the familial kingdom. As this kingdom increased, the Mormon patriarch was elevated to higher degrees of glory.[14] The spiritual purpose of plural marriage was a grand vision of the eternal elevation of an individual to the level of the gods. While much of the attention of the majority population was focused on the oddity of multiple wives, Mormon converts were concerned with an eternal vision of glory. Outsiders balked at the day-to-day realities of what plural marriage would mean for average households, while Mormons accepted a sacred obligation and challenge to produce many children and create eternal bonds of family.

As plural marriage evolved, it became more than just a spiritual commandment. Polygamy became integral to the social structure of the church. It became a necessary functional strategy in achieving higher social status. Thus, as in many aspects of the Mormon faith, the temporal world mirrored the vision of the spiritual world. Plural marriage became the primary means of gaining status in the church as an organization. Some accounts characterize the effects of polygamy as fostering an atmosphere wherein men had to take more wives or suffer the consequences of perpetual low status.[15] Such accounts tend to exaggerate the extent to which plural wives were taken within one household. Most Mormon males took fewer than three wives. The number of households with four wives was less than 10 percent.[16] Those households that did have more numerous wives, however, were elevated in status in the Church. In a practical sense, those households able to support more wives were naturally more integrated into the social and economic structure of the given community. The largest families came to dominate the church structure as familial bonds spread and business relations strengthened through such bonds.

An exact picture of the practice of polygamy is somewhat difficult to draw, however. As a young religion, Mormonism had a limited amount of time to practice plural marriage before the state's persecution of the practice drove it underground. Most historical accounts of the details of the social realities of polygamy are profiles of particular families working out for themselves how to function as a plural household. There are not many accounts from outside observers that describe stable patterns of polygamous behavior is it concerned the status among wives, rules of residency, priority of children, and the other norms of daily life.[17] As the practice was driven into secrecy by the national government's persecution, so too were many of the details of the cultural and familial norms. Plural marriage as it is still practiced by excommunicated fringe Mormon sects may or may not resemble the early years of the Church when the practice was central to the theological and social identity of Mormons.

U.S. GOVERNMENT AND POLYGAMY

The practice of polygamy brought many years of strife to the Mormon faith as the U.S. government rose to challenge and eliminate the practice. A half century of intense conflict between the Church and the federal government forever changed the faith. Perhaps no other religious minority in the nineteenth century was so relentlessly pursued by the government by means of legislation and prosecution.[18] The nuts and bolts of the government's eventual success came with the Morrill Bigamy Act of 1862 and the Supreme Court decision of *Reynolds v. United States* in 1870. The political power, however, came from the majority cultural and religious authority of mainline American Protestantism. Mormonism was one of many minority religions practicing unconventional doctrines, but the Mormon practice of plural marriage hit the majority population in the proverbial gut. Public reaction was fierce and persistent. The practice deeply upset the majority's sensibilities about the proper moral structure for an American family. Not only was it out of the ordinary, but it was seen as a practice that was deeply wrong. It was such an affront to the basic morality of the majority that simply separating the immorality from the rest of society was not enough—it was necessary to root it out and end it.

Aside from the moral outrage, there was fear in the majority population that polygamy might spread. Were it perhaps simply an immoral practice removed from society, it might be something the majority could bear. But the possibility of its spread stoked the fires of panic and outrage. The issue of slavery came to play a role in the fears about polygamy's spread. As the nation attempted to resolve the issue of slavery state by state, the practice was left up to popular sovereignty. Before the Civil War, this method of deciding a moral issue provided the possibility that states might willingly choose other potentially immoral practices. Despite the fact that the Mormon Church opposed slavery, the way in which slavery was dealt on a national level actually contributed to fears about the spread of plural marriage. If states could choose slavery, then they might be able to choose polygamy.[19] The democratic process was deemed untrustworthy for determining the moral worth of certain practices.

The tension between democracy and constitutional rights was evident in the entire Mormon struggle over plural marriage. The U.S. government tried for years to destroy polygamy. The relentless pursuit included various statutes including the Wade Bill (1866), the Cragin Bill (1867), the Ashley Bill (1869), the Cullom Bill 1870, the Voorhees Bill (1872), and the Logan Bill (1872).[20] These bills all failed to pass both the Senate and the House to become law, but show how serious and persistent the government was in pursuing the practice. The congressional act that finally outlawed the practice was naturally challenged in the courts as to its violations of constitutional rights. The *Reynolds* decision upheld the federal law outlawing polygamy. In the decision the Supreme Court argued that the belief was a right, but the practice of the belief was not. In other words, Mormons were free to believe in polygamy, but if they practiced it they were ordinary lawbreakers.[21] In a legal sense, this put the pressure of majority power on the Church to change its practices or to make them secret. The law would be enforced and the power of the state brought to bear on any Mormon breaking that secular law. The real political pressures, though, did not end with the law. Mormons were legally permitted to believe in polygamy, but in any practical political setting this belief would remain unpalatable for the American majority even to today—so unpalatable, in fact, that the mere historical existence of polygamy still affects the political standing of the Church.

Implementing this policy and enforcing the law was somewhat of a challenge. Polygamy, as a practice, was very difficult to prove beyond a reasonable doubt in the average court proceeding. This difficulty usually resulted in suspects being tried for other crimes related to the practice. Between 1884 and 1893 there were 31 convictions for the actual crime of polygamy. During that same time, however, 1,004 suspects were successfully convicted for the crime of unlawful cohabitation.[22] The ability to punish citizens for unlawful cohabitation came from the Edmunds Act of 1882, whose sole purpose was to put teeth into the previous antipolygamy legislation.[23] It was a much easier crime to prove in court. The fact that legislation persisted following the *Reynolds* decision is further evidence of how widely supported the battle against Mormon polygamy was in public opinion. The language of the law was especially restrictive, requiring punishment for living with or lending material support to a woman. Even talking with a woman could be used as legal evidence of cohabitation. The Edmunds-Tucker Act of 1887 went a step further and mandated an antipolygamy test oath for any Mormon wanting to hold public office, serve on a jury, or vote.[24] Public opinion was strongly opposed to plural marriage, and the political pressure to convict was strong. This political pressure was not simply secular worries about the power of the Church, but also other religious sects worried about the competition and inroads Mormon practices might make within their spheres of influence. Congregationalists, Methodists, Presbyterians, and other mainline Protestant churches all considered Mormonism a threat to American morals. Perhaps this threat to morality was enough in and of itself to account for the level of animosity thrust at the problem of polygamy. Adding to this moral outrage the potential competition the Mormon Church might create in the American religious landscape helps explain how the doctrine of an isolated minority religion could receive such vitriolic attention from the majority culture and the majority power of the U.S. government.[25]

Following the move to the Salt Lake Valley, the Church of Jesus Christ of Latter-day Saints lived the practice of polygamy openly in their isolation. It was announced publicly in 1852, and the subsequent years of oppression and persecution took a slow but steady toll on the practice. Nevertheless, it was practiced until 1890 when the Church finally capitulated to the pressure of the U.S. government.[26] In a document known as the Manifesto, the Church announced the discontinuance of the practice of plural marriage. Ending polygamy was not an easy task for the Mormon Church. Spiritually speaking, the Church could rely on the authority of continued revelation to guide the theological development. God had given the Church further guidance and a new understanding of the importance of worldly polygamy. Among the faithful, though, there were those who saw the change as a matter of political and social opportunism and not a matter of theology. Some of these members were lost to the Church forever as they carried on the practice in schismatic churches of their own.[27] The Mormon Church had been faced with the political problem of polygamy for decades and now faced the practical organizational problem of discontinuing and banning its practice. There was substantial resistance from within.[28] Nevertheless, the Church discontinued the practice and excommunicated those who were not willing to adapt to the newly revealed doctrine.

Within the body of the Church, the organization took some significant steps to appease the political majority of the nation that the change was legitimate. The Church publicly disciplined apostles for the practice of plural marriage. It then reconstituted its quorum with monogamous men. Based on bold actions like these, church leaders were able to convince the majority that Mormons would subject themselves to the laws of the land, even at the expense of the law of their God.[29] This complete acquiescence to the pressure of the majority was possible because of the active revelation of the Mormon prophet. The flexibility afforded the organization and theology by continued revelation allowed for a vital transformation of the minority religion. The push and pull between the Mormon faith and majority culture in American religion covered most of the possible interactions. There were times of accommodation, years of persecution, and plenty of separation attempted. The showdown over polygamy provided an opportunity for the Mormon Church to make a bold statement of accommodation to the larger American culture. It was a difficult and painful process, but the grand scale of this particular battle and the persecution endured lend credibility to the faith as it relates to the other American religions. The lost battle over polygamy is a victory in terms of securing a spot in the American religious context that is shrouded in the theological sacrifice. There may be many other aspects of Mormon practice that are not especially palatable to the majority, but given the sacrifice of plural marriage, they are small in comparison.

Polygamy, today, is banned. The huge Mormon clans that resulted from previous generations of polygamy, however, still dominate church leadership and life in Utah. Descendants are generally proud of their forebears who grew the religion and family through the practice of plural marriage.[30] That pride is evident in the slow transition the culture of the Church made following the Manifesto. A follow-up manifesto of sorts was needed 14 years later in 1904, and even then plural marriages continued among those who felt that the proclamation was only a public exercise.[31] The practical dangers of excommunication varied depending on local traditions. The trauma of the struggle with the U.S. government produced a host of splinter groups. Some splinter groups represented those who had been caught continuing the practice. Others formed as a more purposeful political response to the change. Nevertheless, the vast majority of Mormons adapted to the new church doctrine. Mormonism has accommodated its teachings to the dominant monogamous mores. In fact, so important has conformity to the laws of the state and nation become that the Church has, at times, been rather harsh in its proceedings against those who revert to the plurality of wives.[32]

Some of the vigor with which the Church pursues lawbreakers is simply due to the nature of the organization, which is a rigid and demanding church for members. It is likely, however, that some of the Mormon cultural values of conformity and loyalty to the nation are due to this violent and difficult struggle with the U.S. government. This is not to say that the Church spends much time dwelling on this historical struggle with polygamy. In fact, it spends very little time discussing it, and many of contemporary Mormon religious materials simply omit the entire history, making no mention of polygamy at all. As a testament to the adaptability of a religious tradition with an active prophet, it is almost as if plural marriage was never an early church doctrine at all.[33] And so, polygamy has largely disappeared from the theological language surrounding the Mormon faith, and what remains is a strong persistent cultural commitment to the family as the center of life. Plural marriage is gone, but the emphasis on family and the bearing of children is as strong as ever.[34]

The effects of the struggle over polygamy, however, reach far beyond the nineteenth century. The legacy of plural marriage hung like a cloud over the Mormon Church for four decades after the resolution with the U.S. government. The practice was such a morally outrageous issue to many Americans that the cultural memory far outlasted the practice. One of the first things that helped to break down this residual prejudice was how involved the Mormon Church was in World War I. The Church pledged well above the quota of financial support to the war effort through its purchase of government bonds.[35] This Mormon support for the American cause was the first breakthrough for the Church in dispelling the lingering suspicions of polygamy. These suspicions were never completely dispelled, though. And while the Church has been free from plural marriage for many decades, the contemporary political culture still finds it difficult to move past the very idea of polygamy and its association with the Mormon Church. The persistence of the practice among rogue sects continually piques the majority's attention and does little to aid in the Church's efforts to distance itself from the past.

HOMOSEXUALITY

Many American churches emphasize the importance of strong traditional family structures and traditional family relationships. No American church does so with as deep a theological significance as the Church of Jesus Christ of Latter-day Saints.[36] This position is clearly outlined in several church documents including the *Proclamation on the Family*.[37] This document proclaims that families are not just good, but are essential to human progress. Married couples are sealed through the priesthood for all time and eternity. The importance of children to the spiritual development of Mormons is hard to overestimate. It is largely from this emphasis on the traditional family structure that the contemporary Mormon Church opposes homosexuality. To be sure, the Church also uses the same biblical passages and references used by Protestants and Catholics to denounce homosexuality as sinful. However, the official LDS position has more to do with the eternal structure of the Church than with the individual behavior. It is considered sinful, but more importantly, it is not supporting the all-important traditional family structure—at least as far as the mainstream Mormon Church is concerned.

Homosexuality is one of the sins for which a person can be excommunicated from the Mormon Church.[38] Given the relative social weight of this issue, it is interesting to note how relatively recent this position of excommunication is, although perhaps the acknowledgment of homosexuality among church doctrine in general is relatively recent. The Church made homosexuality an excommunicative sin in 1968. Since then church leaders have made an effort to distinguish between homosexual feelings and homosexual activity. This is an interesting distinction, with an obvious parallel to the historical battle with polygamy. There the U.S. government deemed it acceptable for a Mormon citizen to believe in and have the desire for plural marriage, but to act on this desire would be unlawful. So it is with the Church's position on homosexuality. It is acknowledged that some Mormons, and humans more broadly, will experience feelings of homosexuality, but to act on those feelings is a sin. Because of this struggle, the Church spends a fair amount of organizational resources dealing with homosexual church members.

Gay Mormons are instructed to remain both chaste and celibate.[39] Homosexuality is considered a condition induced by something especially temporal and so not found in the eternal realm. Thus, the hope extended to gay Mormons is that after death they may be properly sealed and so have an opportunity for exaltation. Mormon singles are assured that they will be married eventually if they stick it out through their mortal life and allow the Church to fulfill the hope in the next life. This is possible because of the Mormon doctrine allowing for the seals of marriage to occur posthumously. Like other conservative religious denominations, the Church of Jesus Christ of Latter-day Saints counsels its gay members to counteract and resist the homosexual urges through prayer and discipline. The Church contends that homosexual orientation is a choice rather than an inborn trait. Because it is a choice subject to the free will of members, the Church expends considerable energy and expense on social services programs. These programs seek to train individual members into making the correct choices and thus ridding themselves of the propensity to give in to homosexual desires.[40]

The Church does not limit its activity to the passive counseling of gay members. There are numerous examples of the Church's actions attempting to disrupt organizations that support gay-straight alliances. The Church is actively engaged in strenuous efforts to get rid of gay-straight high school student clubs and other similar organizations in Utah.[41] The Church's activism is notable because it does not have a long history of political action within specific public policies. However, sex and gender in all their variety form a crucial nexus in Latter-day Saint thinking.[42] Sex and gender are powerful issues for any religion, but the spiritual connection to children and the eternal family is central to all of Mormon theology and is thus a central concern in the Church's interactions with the political world. In recent years, current events have sparked an even higher level of awareness within the Church regarding homosexuality. The Church has strong connections to the Boy Scouts of America, for example. There have been numerous accounts of the Church dealing with the issue of homosexuality as it relates to this organization and its interaction with children that illustrate how the issue of homosexuality connects directly with the most central tenets of Mormon belief.

GAY MARRIAGE

The Mormon Church is strongly opposed to gay marriage. Its opposition is more than just a belief in the deleterious effects on society, or the sinfulness of the individual behavior. Gay marriage is seen as the utter destruction of God's plan for humanity.[43] It is possible that were the issue one of individual sin, the Church may not be involved much at all. Such has been the case in plenty of other policies that are typically hot buttons for culturally conservative religions. The fact that the perceived behavior challenges the entire eternal order of the universe motivates the Church to intervene as it can. And so, the Church lobbies against the legalization of gay marriage in every possible political arena. Mormon efforts to fight gay marriage are evident in courts, legislatures, and public referenda across the United States. These efforts are usually chalked up to the typical motivations of protecting traditional family values and fighting sexual immorality. There is, however, a larger theological scope at work that leads the Church to strongly oppose homosexual unions.[44]

The Church has opposed any recognition of same-sex marriages in several states. Mormon leaders solicit financial contributions and the labor of local members.[45] Between 2004 and 2008, defense-of-marriage amendments passed in 26 states.[46] It is worth pausing to consider what that means for the political process. Majorities desired some legal standing for the moral position against gay marriage. The constitutional issues that arise in such legal language are substantial enough to challenge the existence of such laws. Under the threat of court interference, or in some cases the actual overturning of laws, the majority then seeks to amend the Constitution and change the basic rights afforded to minorities. The fact that the Mormon Church is on the side of the majority in this particular case is interesting. To describe the Church as part of the majority in many cases would be underestimating the impact that it has had in certain states. When the gay-marriage issue came to popular vote in California, for instance, Mormons were integral to the successful efforts of Proposition 8, the California Marriage Protection Act. There Mormons joined Hispanic clergy, evangelicals, and conservative Catholics to back the proposition in November of 2008.

The battle was very close, and at times the proposition looked likely to fail by some narrow margin. Frank Schubert, one of the leading political strategists backing the effort, commented to leaders of Protect Marriage, "We're going to lose this campaign if we don't get more money."[47] The campaign issued an urgent appeal, and in a matter of days had raised more than $5 million, including $1 million from the grandson of a former president of the Mormon Church (Alan C. Ashton). Although Mormons made up only 2 percent of California's population, they volunteered and contributed more than $20 million to the campaign fund. They also offered hours of hard campaigning. The extra support allowed the campaign to drive a sharp advertising campaign. The proposition ultimately won with 52 percent of the vote. Mormons were credited as a major cause for its passage.[48] The 2008 campaign was only one of several examples of Mormon political support and mobilization against gay marriage. Earlier in the same state the Church had supported the Knight initiative preventing the recognition of same-sex marriages that might be performed in other states.[49] Members of the Mormon Church have felt intense pressure to support and fight for this cause.[50]

For a church that picks its political battles rather sparingly, it has been front and center in the cultural battles over gay marriage. These efforts have brought intense media scrutiny to bear on the Church of Jesus Christ of Latter-day Saints. There is enough historical memory within the Church to prevent all-out mobilization over each and every issue that violates LDS doctrine, but the efforts against gay marriage have been full and public. Aside from supporting constitutional amendments, the Church has issued public statements declaring support for a federal amendment to the Constitution prohibiting gay marriage. In 2006, the Church went so far as to have read from every pulpit a letter encouraging members to contact the Senate in support of the constitutional amendment.[51] Many churches encourage the cultural knowledge in members that leads to particular mobilizations or electoral outcomes, but rarely in a religious organization so specifically policy oriented as a unified body as is the Mormon Church in regard to gay marriage. It has consistently played a significant role both financially and organizationally in the fight against homosexual marriage.[52]

For the most part, the Church of Jesus Christ of Latter-day Saints has presented a unified front on this policy issue. Mormon opposition to the acceptance of homosexuality in general is starkly stronger than the average American's.[53] When more specifically applied to the bonds of marriage, that opposition increases dramatically. Much of the ubiquity within the Church has to do with the recognition of the authority of its president as a prophet. This gives a great deal of organizational strength to the Church and maintains a potent electoral resource. This same kind of political authority was seen in the Equal Rights Amendment battle of the 1970s as Mormon leaders mobilized members effectively toward a political objective.[54] This political mobilization has not been common, but it is common in contemporary gay-marriage politics. Having described Mormons as rather cohesive on this policy matter, it is worth noting that not all Mormons oppose gay marriage. A prominent U.S. senator (Gordon Smith) from Oregon is a member of the Latter-day Saints and a known supporter of gay and lesbian political organizations. He, like other Mormons, distinguishes between the civil rights of his constituents and the policies of the Church.[55] Nevertheless, there are few contemporary political issues that mobilize Mormons more monolithically than gay marriage.

There are a number of factors that account for the Mormon opposition to gay marriage. Some are obvious, and some are less obvious. Since banning polygamy, the Church has remolded and reshaped its place in the American culture. It is now a bastion of conservative and traditional family values. All that the cultural imagery can convey with those topics is central to contemporary Mormon culture. This is the obvious source of the kind of motivation shared by all conservative American religions to save or rescue the traditional family values of some perceived American traditional nuclear structure. The second source of motivation for the strong opposition to gay marriage is the clear message sent from the prophet as to the severity of the sins involved. Since 1968 it is such a sin that a member can be excommunicated for taking part in homosexual activity. Sins that carry the punishment of excommunication are eternal sins, and that message is not lost on members. A third motivation is that provided by the historical memory of the Church as it has adapted and learned how to survive and thrive in the American context. After years of intense struggle with the majority, the Church eventually assimilated. It altered the minority behavior of plural marriage and adjusted to the norms of the majority. Since then the Church has experienced unparalleled success. For many years the Church was on the losing side of a battle that pitted minority behavior against majority norms. Now aligned with majority norms, the Church is taking advantage of being on the winning side for a change.

In contrast, there have been some interesting coalitions that formed from the legacy of polygamy. In many states, polygamist Mormon sects have teamed up with the ACLU and gay-rights advocates to keep the government out of their bedrooms. It has made for some especially curious and uncomfortable coalitions.[56] Uncomfortable as they may be, there is an undeniable logic at work when polygamists join forces with gay-marriage advocates. Both are minority populations struggling against the moral authority of the majority power. The Church of Jesus Christ of Latter-day Saints is on the exact opposite side of this political battle. The legacy of polygamy is still a cloud that hangs over the Mormon faith, but there is no will remaining to fight for any sexual behavior that deviates from the norms of the majority. In fact, the theological conversion is so complete, that the Church fights with an intense moral obligation to oppose sexual behavior that violates traditional familial structures.

CULTURE WAR

The Mormon Church is no longer locked in battle with the American government. In fact, as discussed in the next chapter, the Church is rather supportive of the national government in general. However, Mormons do feel themselves engaged in a larger cultural battle. This fight is analogous to that of other religious traditions that see themselves as the protectors of traditional values in the face of declining morals and modern relativism. The degradation of traditional values that surrounds conservative religious rhetoric is common to the Mormon sense of self. Mormons reject modern sexual immorality, including premarital or extramarital sex and pornography. Church leaders condemn the content of television, movies, and the Internet because they believe these media contribute to the moral decay of society.[57] Although at one point the Church was the focus of other majoritarian moralists' outrage of the degradation of sexual morality, the Mormon faith has become one of the most conservative in this area of cultural and social politics. There are other conservative American religions that share this outlook on modern society. Southern Baptists, evangelicals more broadly, and conservative Catholics all describe the moral world around them as in decay. Only the Church of Jesus Christ of Latter-day Saints, however, has become more culturally conservative relative to the rest of the nation since the 1970s.[58] In other words, those other American religions have always occupied the spot on the ideological spectrum that denotes a conservative worldview as locked in cultural battle with modernity. The Mormon Church did not always view its place in the nation in the same way. It now rests firmly with those traditions who take it upon themselves to protect society from the perceived moral decay.

This cultural worldview has implications for the preferred professional and intellectual pursuits of modern Mormons. There has always been a classical ambivalence toward scholarship and intellectualism within the Mormon Church. This is typical of religions that rely on revelation and especially true for Mormonism, which has only lay clergy and theologians.[59] This ambivalence is now shaped by a particular ideological disposition as it relates to issues of cultural values like gay marriage, abortion, violence in media, sexuality, and pornography. "We are at war . . . in the media today . . . Lucifer's influence has a far more dominant influence than has the Lord's."[60] This statement from apostle M. Russell Ballard illustrates the Church's understanding of the world and state of the nation. Locked in a cultural battle between Lucifer and the Lord, active Latter-day Saints tend to agree on the necessity of traditional family values and the need to oppose gay marriage, abortion, and gambling. They also agree that the media causes moral deterioration and thus external sources of information (the media) are not to be trusted.

This cultural battle is only occasionally evidenced in political efforts. The Church once faced constant political pressure over polygamy, but now enjoys a complementary role in the traditional norms of American political culture. As such it can strategically choose which political causes to engage in. Because of the widespread belief among Mormons that they are locked in a cultural battle, it should be expected that these chosen causes would reflect a rather socially conservative agenda. The Church once faced the U.S. government as its primary political enemy. Now the various political opinions among Mormons focus on the proper role of government. There are far fewer antigovernment opinions than the history of the Church might suggest. In fact, often what defines the partisan divisions among Mormons is this debate over the proper role and use of government.[61]

MINORITY RELIGION AGAINST MINORITY POPULATION

Glancing at the history of persecution Latter-day Saints have suffered, the political efforts against a minority population might seem out of place. Mormonism was a religion that suffered many years of political pressure to assimilate. The theology of plural marriage was central to the uniqueness of the religion in its infancy. And to whatever extent it contributed to the religion's alternative culture, polygamy was responsible for some of its early successes as a growing religious movement. The majority of Americans refused to allow this central theological practice to continue. Through sustained political support over decades of the nineteenth century, the U.S. government chased the polygamist Mormons to Utah and eventually convinced the religion to assimilate. This assimilation caused serious tensions within the religion, led to several schisms in the organization, and required some bold public gestures. Nevertheless, the Church adapted. Not only did it adapt, it evolved into a traditional conservative religion that now seeks to fight against a minority population that refuses to assimilate in the majority culture. In the context of majority versus minority power, the Mormon religion was shielded initially by the constitutional rights afforded all citizens with regard to personal religion. The dominant force in the history of Mormonism, though, is that of the majority power that did not yield until the Church assimilated. This majority power indirectly drew its strength from the majority religious traditions of the day. As a minority religion, the choices for the Church were to separate or assimilate. After first attempting to separate, the Church eventually assimilated.

Despite its impressive growth, the Mormon Church is still a minority religion in the context of American politics. And yet, on the issue of gay marriage the Church has pursued decidedly majoritarian tactics. This embrace of the process of majority rule has some grounding in the theology of Mormonism. The conception of government in the Book of Mormon is democratic. At least among the elect, rule is by the voice of the people with a strong emphasis on the intention of the penitent to keep the commandments.[62] This may aid in understanding the transition from persecuted minority religion to a church that embraces the kind of majoritarian processes represented by Proposition 8. In that particular battle, Mormons contributed half of the $40 million war chest. A spokesman for the Church of Jesus Christ of Latter-day Saints, Michael Otterson, called it "a moment of emergence."[63] If so, the Church emerged through the kind of political process that produced the laws against polygamy. At the time it may have been the high-water mark of Mormon political advocacy, but it came with some costs. It sparked a vicious backlash from gay-rights activists, with claims of bigotry and blind religious obedience. These claims came laced with insinuations about the Mormon Church's history with unconventional marriage. The Church's response to these claims, as to all claims related to polygamy, is revealed truth. Polygamy was once practiced, but through active revelation it was discontinued. From an outsider's perspective political action against unconventional marriage through democratic politics seems contradictory. However, the constitutional rights as defended by the Supreme Court could not avail the Mormon cause either (see the *Reynolds* decision), so perhaps it should not be surprising to find the Church more comfortable with the majoritarian processes found in its own sacred text.

The Mormon Church contends that it is not political, at least to the extent that it is not partisan. In a practical sense, though, the Mormon Church is very political. It works carefully within the American political system as any minority religion must. It is political in a couple of ways. The Church encourages involvement in politics. Citizenship is a virtue, and active engagement with the American political system is part of that citizenship. On occasion, the Church mobilizes thousands of members and millions of dollars to advocate specific political outcomes. The Church has created a setting where conservative values and politics are a way of life.[64] In Utah and some surrounding areas, it is political suicide to clash with the Mormon Church. Mormons are a small faith, but unlike most small faiths, they are adequately represented as a proportion of the nation's legislative bodies. This is largely due to the heavy concentration of the religion in Utah and neighboring states that secures Mormons positions of power within the American government. While still technically a minority religion, this presence provides a modicum of security compared to other minority religions, which are vastly underrepresented.[65]

Latter-day Saints have not been extremely active in the history of American politics, but in recent years this trend has been changing. The Church has enjoyed tremendous growth and some level of insulation from its vantage point in Utah. Despite claims of nonpartisanship, the Church is a political force to be reckoned with. The political advocacy evident in the struggle for homosexual marriage is a prime example of this political force. The opposition to homosexual marriage is possible because of the financial resources and membership of the Church. The opposition is grounded in the sinfulness of the act of homosexuality in general, but more importantly, in the threat posed to the larger eternal plan of God. In this particular political battle, the Church is intimately aware of the political forces at work. Centuries after assimilating and giving up its unconventional plural marriage, the Church still has to work hard to dispel the myth that it supports polygamy today. This makes it all the more likely for Mormons to seek outlets that demonstrate conventional traditional family values. Gay marriage provides just such an opportunity. At first glance it appears ironic that a minority religious tradition would seek to fight against a minority population. The lessons of the Church's battle with the U.S. government and the evolution of the faith since that time, though, compel Mormons to fight against a minority population seeking protection for an unconventional state of marriage.

7

Mormon Patriotism

RELIGIOUS AND SECULAR NATIONALISM

The idea of a people voluntarily attaching themselves to a political order separate from culture, race, or religion is a relatively new idea. Historical bonds between different groups of people, and the governing structures that emerged, were largely based on these primal forces. It is not until the eighteenth century that nation-states emerged and quickly became the only viable unit of political power in the world. Individuals now naturally associate their identities and political obedience with a place of birth, an economic system, a political system, or simply a set of shared ideals. This shift from cultural and religious definitions of community to the more conceptual political unit of the secular nation is the origin of nationalism and patriotism. Asking an American citizen about his or her patriotism yields some affirmation of the constitutional government created in the 1700s, or, more often, an affinity for the American regime more generally described in the Declaration of Independence. This is true for many of the secular nations found across the globe. Religious nationalism, however, has not disappeared. There are many areas of the world dominated by this earlier form of cultural identity. Generally, these two forms of nationalism (secular and religious) are in competition with each other. Rarely do the two coexist as easily as with contemporary Mormonism.

Nationalism is the expression of a justification for the state's existence. There are extreme displays of patriotism, and more subtle expressions of identity based on shared assumptions regarding the legitimacy of the state. The state does not need to be secular for nationalism to exist, but that is the dominant condition in the world today. Religious people and organizations are often able to accept the idea of a nation-state, even though they may reject the idea of secular nationalism.[1] The unit of order provided by the state comes to represent a buffer for religious institutions from the sordid dealings of worldly matters. Often, though, there is a resignation to comply with the state for the moment given some eventuality of godly rule. For Christianity, the Second Coming is this eventuality. It is a time when the secular state will give way to the rule of God. Thus the church tolerates an inferior position to the state for two reasons. First, there is a willingness to let the state deal with worldly matters that are somehow beneath the more lofty matters of the soul. And second, it is but a temporary subjugation to the state given the eventual Second Coming that will sweep aside the secular state.

The eventual superiority of a given religion's position in society is described in different terms for different traditions. For many Christian sects the Second Coming initiates some version of the kingdom of heaven taking root on earth. The Mormon theological tradition follows a line of thought similar to the Social Gospel movement and other millenialists. The Lord's Prayer is seen as a literal prediction of a future state of glorious rule on earth. God will descend and rule justly and a time of heaven on earth shall unfold. In many religious movements in the United States over the past two centuries, such a millenarian impulse produced a collective moral project, established a new social order, and stressed the moral authority of the collective.[2] This collective authority is often embodied in two ways: in the state and in a charismatic leader. The history of the Mormon faith is a prime example of this shared collective authority. The state is not an impediment to the coming rule of God, but rather an eventual tool that can aid in the transition to heavenly rule. The Social Gospel movement and other progressive strains of Christianity embraced the state in the early twentieth century with much of this same theological thinking. These traditions, however, fell victim in many ways to the success of the state as it took over many of the social services the church once provided. Mormons, on the other hand, had active revelation and authority in the supreme church leader to avoid becoming replaced by the state.

Much in the same way the Social Gospel movement recognized the state as one step along the path to the kingdom of heaven on earth, so too did the Mormon faith embrace the American state as part of an eventuality. The events leading up to this eventuality, for the Mormon Church, are more specifically tied to the American state than most religious traditions. In fact, the founding documents are considered to be influenced, if not guided, by God. The Constitution is an original document of statehood provided by God. The tenets of living revelation (that God still speaks and guides the Church through the prophet) allow the Mormon faith to avoid some of the pitfalls of legalism with regard to the founding documents. Much like the Bible or the Book of Mormon, the Constitution is open to revision. All three documents are connected to God, but still up for amending. The Mormon Church is, in this way, rather flexible in adapting to the state.

Secular nationalism does not easily accommodate religion and religion does not accept the ideology of secular nationalism. However, religion can sometimes be hospitable to the institution of the nation-state, albeit usually on religion's terms.[3] For Mormons, not only is the secular nature of American order temporary, it is not quite as secular in nature as it might seem. The heavenly guidance given to the founding documents creates a connection between the Church and the state. It is not an especially overt connection; nevertheless, the patriotism expressed by Mormons is shaped by this connection between the founding documents of statehood and God's eventual reign.

CIVIL RELIGION

Religions in the United States exist amidst a civil religion that ties political culture to religious tradition. Citizens in modern secular nation-states attempt to imbue their nations with transcendent value. This effort defines the concept of civil religion—the idea that a nation can be understood as a historical experience nestled in the context of eternal truths provided by religion. More than just history, civil religion provides citizens with a national purpose defined in religious terms.[4] In the United States, civil religion is a commonly held view that a long Judeo-Christian tradition defines the religious significance of the entire nation and the government. This is not so much an active political force as it is the result of a passive cultural legacy.[5]

For the most part, Americans hold this civil religion loosely and retain a commitment to a division between church and state. Some sects, however, are less casual about the importance of civil religion. Many of the more legalistic and fundamentalist strains of Christianity seek to more firmly establish civil religion (as is typical of the more legalistic and fundamentalist strains of any religion). These sects believe that a generalized, nondenominational Judeo-Christian tradition should predominate and even break through the wall of separation. The state and its republican institutions would thus be saturated with such civil religious virtue.[6] The Mormon position on civil religion is similar to this legalistic Christian understanding of civil religion. There is no need for a wall of separation, per se, since the founding documents already tie the fate of the state to the fate of the Church. The active role of the prophet in receiving God's word does tip the scales toward theology in many cases. However, the history of the Mormon faith has taught the Church to value the separation of church and state, at least in terms of the Establishment Clause, which allows for new religious movements to flourish.

The United States is often noted for being significantly more religious than other modern, industrialized nations. Much of this continued religiosity is attributed to the separation of church and state itself. That separation, perhaps more than anything else, has preserved religion as a vigorous force in American life. Not only does the structure of the secular state prevent one religion from dominating the political order, it also forces churches into a realm of market forces. A religious movement must compete with other existing movements. This competition compels any church to continue reenergizing the spiritual and administrative parts of the organization. The Mormon religious tradition made strategic decisions, like moving westward in the nineteenth century, in order to more successfully compete.[7] The space provided by the American religious marketplace, and perhaps the physical space of the move west, allowed Mormonism to develop, adjust, and change into the most competitive version of itself. It became a religion that can mesh with contemporary American society just enough. It is connected enough to coexist and thrive alongside the secular state, but not so much that it is pulled into the day-to-day sordid details of contemporary political life. It can embrace the state as part of the eventual reign of God, but also offer a rebuttal of the disappointing spiritual residue of conventional, material life.

It is not just the separation of church and state that benefited the Mormon Church as part of the structural foundations of the United States, but also federalism. Part of the United States' patriotic legacy is derived from the space provided by a large federal republic. Americans have often been held together by their ability to live apart. The segmentation of society facilitated tolerance for others—so long as those others could live at a reasonable distance. Here the benefit was not just in the space for a religious movement to develop and adapt, but also in the space for any aberrant minority population, such as the Mormon population, to survive in the United States. The United States was a diverse nation from the beginning and lacked many of the natural bases of cultural solidarity and commonality that most nations have drawn on in founding eras. Thus the federal Constitution itself has often served as the United States' civil religious scripture. It is an attempt at a scientific, logical solution to the problems of popular sovereignty that soon became elevated to religious and cultural significance.[8] The elevation of a political document to the realm of cultural and religious meaning is in part due to the original lack of natural solidarity, but also to the development and influence of religious sects like Mormonism. Civil religion requires reinforcement, mobilization, and organizational buy-in; otherwise it fades and becomes rhetorical, nostalgic, and void of power.[9]

The Mormon faith fulfills these roles and serves to reinforce the United States' civil religion in a more targeted way than other faiths by imbuing the Constitution with heavenly authority. In other ways, Mormon theology can be seen as potentially more dangerous to the state of civil religion than other traditions. This is largely due to the implications of active revelation and what that can mean for the secular state. When Joseph Smith ran for president in 1844, he proclaimed God to be the judge of all men and the source of all law. For most observers this appears to be a mainstream statement of guiding principles for personal decision making. Keeping in mind the radical nature of the politics of his religion's ongoing revelation though, the statement is more indicative of a preference for theocracy. The sovereignty of the people was not entirely paramount for a charismatic leader, such as Smith, who believed the Mormon Church would one day have to rescue the American institutions of government from ruin.[10] Despite the eventuality of a Mormon theocracy in the United States, the faith has had a mutually beneficial relationship with American civil religion. It reinforces the quasi-worship of the founding documents, while drawing unique strength from its connection to the secular state.

CHURCH AND STATE

The proper connection of the Church to the state has been a difficult proposition for the Mormon faith to deal with. There is no other problem in the history of Mormonism that is more complicated and varied.[11] At times the Church considered dissipating the power and structure of the faith. Eventually though, the Church chose to centralize power and this centralization shapes much of the church-state relationship. The Second Coming provides for a theocracy, but until then the church government decided it would also be theocratic—drawing on the divine authority that flows through the prophet-president. The concept of the Second Coming as a theocracy is a commonly held understanding of the end of days among virtually every monotheistic religion. However, the theocratic tendencies of the Mormon Church are somewhat different from other religious traditions. Most Protestant faiths, for example, see the role of the church as primarily dealing with spiritual matters and not directly involved in the machinations of political power. Those Protestant sects that sought a deeper connection to political power (like the Social Gospel movement) declined as the state co-opted services once fulfilled by the churches. This left the churches, once again, to deal solely with spiritual matters.

Much of the Protestant United States' understanding of the end of days is flavored by a shared heritage of Puritan thought. The purification of religion and society was brought to fruition through obedience and purity of purpose. The primal Mormon impulse for the restoration of a spiritual kingdom of God, however, lies somewhat outside this tradition.[12] A kingdom in which men hold supernatural powers on earth is a rather different kind of kingdom than envisioned by puritan orthodoxy. Ultimately, the Mormon establishment of the Kingdom of God on earth is an explicitly political process.[13] It is the establishment of a theocratic world government. Thus the secular state is merely a stepping-stone, albeit one imbued with some heavenly guidance. As a stepping-stone, it is not to be reviled as inherently ungodly, but it is not to be taken for anything more than a temporary order of power. Politics, in general, is in the same category—a worldly creation that, while prone to ungodliness, is not necessarily unrelated to the future of the Church. Obviously, the practical effects of political decision making have had dramatic effects on the Church's chances for survival. But also in a larger sense, political processes are part of the eventual theocracy and so not without intrinsic value.

Exactly where the nation is on this timeline of eventual theocracy is hard to pin down. The rhetorical flourish of Joseph Smith, while candidate for president, seems to suggest the possibility of some midpoint between secular nation-state and a kingdom of heaven on earth. "I go emphatically, virtuously, and humanely for a Theo-Democracy, where God and the people hold the power to conduct the affairs of men in righteousness."[14] Here the language of sovereignty is muddied a bit with the combination of theocracy and democracy. Nevertheless, the ideal is not to retreat from the world (ostensibly to Utah) and wait for the Second Coming. The ideal is somehow to progress to a state of "Theo-Democracy" that might usher in the kingdom of heaven on earth. The Mormon Church does not see the coming reign of God as centered in Utah or any other especially Mormon-specific location, but rather in the United States as a whole. As Smith declared when asked about the future kingdom, "The whole of America is Zion itself from north to south."[15] The Mormon temple was to be built in Utah not just because of the proximity to its people, but also because it should be situated in the center of the land of Zion. Mormons shall not isolate themselves and simply purify their own community (as many other traditions do), but rather embrace the entire nation as the future kingdom. The state of American political power and virtue is of interest to the Church.

Ever since the days of Joseph Smith, Mormonism has pushed the boundaries of the separation of church and state. Not shy about upsetting one of the most deeply rooted mores of the republic, the Church has, on occasion, introduced entire slates of Mormon candidates for local office.[16] Such moves have often met with backlash as Americans generally expect ministers of religion to abstain from politics. However, Mormon theology does not place as much importance on the division between heaven and the world as many other traditions. The earthly church, in fact, participates in both the eternal and temporal worlds. This fusion leads to three further principles.[17] First of all, there is no need for a real distinction between temporal (meaning secular or worldly) and spiritual government. This principle does not value the separation of church and state much, and clearly allows for a predilection toward theocratic government. The second derived principle is that temporal property and labor are dedicated to spiritual purpose. The understanding of this principle has evolved over time. The initial interpretation led to some experimentation with a structure of property not unlike communism. It has since changed into the more common obligation of dedicated tithing. Mormons overall are rather comfortable succeeding as capitalists, so long as their financial support of the Church and each other is significantly demonstrating spiritual purpose. Mormons are loyal to Mormon businesses and tithe heavily. This is an indirect contribution to the building of the kingdom of God on earth. The third principle is that agreements consecrated by the Church are not merely temporal, but eternal as well. This is why Mormon marriages are seen as eternal bonds between two people, and the importance of family is elevated past the temporal world as well. The division between temporal and spiritual worlds is, in many ways, a false construct for Mormons. What boundary that does exist will, in their eyes, eventually be reduced and the boundary between purity and danger reestablished as the more lasting boundary.[18]

The history of church and state relations has been a checkered one for Mormons. At times, the state has been quite hostile to the Church and vice versa. On July 18, 1957, President Buchanan sent 2,500 federal troops to establish and maintain law and order in the Utah Territory. The troops were to put down what the president claimed was a "substantial rebellion against the laws and authority of the United States."[19] The president further characterized the territory as being under the personal despotism of Brigham Young. The incident resulted in no bloodshed. The troops were under orders not to act in any manner of violence unless absolutely requiring self-defense. Nevertheless, the incident is an example of the American government's animosity toward the monolithic power growing in the Mormon Church (primarily in historical terms over the issue of polygamy). Brigham Young, for his part, claimed on many occasions that the U.S. government was controlled by "ignorance, folly, and weakness."[20] Young personally hated a number of American presidents, including Abraham Lincoln. He once described Lincoln as having so little strength of character and political resolve that he was as "weak as water."[21] Despite the checkered past in church-state relations, several factors have kept the Mormon faith tied to the American republic and nation as a whole—perhaps no factor more clearly than the theological connection to founding documents.

It is a common belief among Mormons, and a prediction of Joseph Smith, that the Constitution will one day falter and the Mormon Church will save it. In its hour of need, as the republic hangs by a thread, the Mormon Church will rescue the United States from doom.[22] This belief is, at times, seen by outsiders as somehow a conspiratorial desire to overthrow the government. The LDS leadership is characterized as having a long-held dream of taking over the U.S. government, should the opportunity present itself.[23] A more accurate theological interpretation sees the Church stepping in at an hour of need and as part of the overall transition to the eventual reign of God. The connection to founding documents goes even deeper than the Constitution, in fact. The Declaration of Independence is woven into Mormon theology through the baptizing of the signers. The Church baptized "the signers of the Declaration of Independence, and fifty other eminent men, making one hundred in all, including John Wesley, Columbus, and others."[24] The notion of a divinely inspired set of founding documents is central to the church-state relations of Mormons. In the twentieth century they have sought to protect and preserve the Constitution and the political values it contains—such as individual liberty and limited government.[25] "Every true American and true friend of liberty should love our inspired

Constitution . . . its creation was a miracle."[26] There is some range of opinion within the Mormon faith as to how miraculous or direct God's involvement in the documents was, but some level of divine influence is undisputed.

Insofar as the coming kingdom of heaven on earth is an eventuality for Mormons, it is not a daily reality. And so, there does exist a practical separation between overtly political matters and matters of faith. For the most part, Mormon leaders publically espouse support for the separation of church and state favored by most Americans. Church leaders sometimes go so far as to insist on the distinction between strictly political issues, in which the Church should not intervene, and moral issues, in which intervention is justified.[27] This represents a strain of Mormon thinking that remembers the long history of struggles with the state. However, for the most part Mormons have forgotten part of their history with theocracy. The 40-year battle between the church and the U.S. government in the nineteenth century seems at odds with the enthusiastic patriotism of the Mormon heartland today.[28] Much of the long political struggle is ignored. But it is somewhat incorrect to frame Mormon patriotism as somehow ignorant about its history. More accurately, the Church is willing to overlook those historical struggles in the larger context of the coming theocracy. And until that theocracy arrives in the form of God's reign, the Mormon Church is tied to the United States as a nation and has always recognized the legitimacy of its civil government.

MORMONS IN PARTY POLITICS

The push and pull of church-state relations is further illustrated through the history of Mormon involvement in American party politics. In the 1800s, the Mormon use of party politics was extremely pragmatic and utilitarian. Joseph Smith, as prophet, issued edicts about who to vote for as a bloc of voters. It was a very cohesive bloc of voters and a powerful strategic weapon—strategic in the short-term repayment of political debts. For example, the election of November 1840 saw the Mormon vote go straight ticket to the Whig Party, except for one candidate who had done some favors for Smith. There was but one Whig candidate not to receive the support, and that candidate happened to be Abraham Lincoln.[29] Smith made it clear that the Mormon vote could be swung on a moment's notice.[30] While this created many short-term opportunities for political favor, it did little to endear the population to the political elite. At times the outright command of the Mormon vote embarrassed the very party in whose favor Smith turned the vote. Accusations of despotism followed, not to mention the dubious nature of collaboration with the Mormons as seen by the general public. Nevertheless, the sheer cohesiveness of the Mormon vote secured power within both parties in the politics of Illinois in the 1800s.[31]

Later in the 1800s, the Mormon vote became a powerful player on the national stage. In a time when electoral colleges determined the presidency, and state legislators elected senators, it was widely feared that the Mormon vote could actually make the difference in national elections.[32] Smith argued that party politics was the way to secure rights for the Mormon people. As he entered the presidential election of 1844, he proclaimed the necessary use of party politics and electoral politics in general. "We have as good a right to make a political party to gain power to defend ourselves . . . as for demagogues to make use of our religion to get power to destroy us."[33] Despite the use of party power, the Mormon vote was never tied to one specific political party. This was true even when the Church wholeheartedly believed in a specific cause—such as opposition to slavery. The Church still did not declare specific party support and often bounced between parties. This pragmatic, short-term style in party politics has given way to a more consistent Republican vote in contemporary elections.

Since its founding in 1830, the Mormon Church has grown to over 4 million members, making it now the sixth-largest religious body in the United States. In the 1990s, the Church grew faster than any other denomination at approximately 19.2 percent.[34] Aside from the sheer size of the Church, the relative concentration of population in western states creates a formidable electoral bloc in Utah, Idaho, Wyoming, Nevada, and Arizona. Many contemporary national surveys have failed to gather much in the way of Mormon data and so there are few reliable statistical analyses of Mormon voting behavior. Nevertheless, Mormon voting behavior has become nearly as reliably Republican as African American voting is Democratic. The history of the faith is one divided between the two political parties. At statehood, Utah voters divided themselves into Democrats and Republicans, though Republican candidates have generally predominated. Despite the division of voters, many American political elites still had suspicions about church political influence and were still likely to paint the region as not far removed from the taint of polygamy.

Mormons are cohesive and conservative voters.[35] There is some irony in the contemporary voting behavior of Mormons given that the initial aim of the Republican Party was the elimination of the "twin relics of barbarism"—slavery and polygamy. The bias toward Republican Party politics is mainly due to ideological concerns on social matters, rather than economic values. Mormons are more socially conservative than the average American. For instance, Mormon positions on the role of women have remained markedly conservative, while most Americans' views have moderated or become more liberal. The national average on the National Election Survey question of whether women should stay in the home dropped from about 30 percent affirmatives in the 1970s to less than 12 percent today. Mormon respondents, however, remain at 1970 levels with about 30 percent affirmative responses.[36] Having political views that are disproportionately aligned with the Republican Party makes for a fairly partisan group of voters, despite the nonpartisan nature of the Church as a whole. Not only are Mormon voters reliably conservative, they are reliable in terms of turnout and overall political participation. In terms of civil society, Mormon populations have a large amount of social capital due to the amount of time required attending meetings, tithing, and other organizational responsibilities. This makes them a good source of political resources in general.[37]

Although the Church's political predilections are known to politicians and members, it is very nonpartisan in its message. The Church maintains strict political neutrality. This is confirmed by National Election Survey data that show that very few political cues occur in Mormon services. Only 1 percent of Mormon respondents cite any instance of cue giving.[38] In other words, it is rare for a Mormon leader to give the impression that one candidate is better than another. Furthermore, support for any political party is voluntary and compliance is not a condition of membership or of good standing.[39] There are other interesting indications of neutrality in partisan politics, like the Church's unwillingness to ally with the Christian Coalition. In fact, the Mormons are the one important religious group in the United States with a conservative voting record and conservative views on almost all moral issues that has been notably indifferent to any alliance with the Christian Coalition.[40] This is probably due to a long history of being the target of religious laws throughout the nineteenth century. Some reticence is natural given the way in which particular religious politics forced them to renounce a central tenet of Joseph Smith's. Mormons vote for Mormon candidates, but recognize that in the matter of religious politics they have easily been victims in the past and could conceivably in the future as well. Since the 1890s, Mormons have been reluctant to team up with other religious groups, while proudly proclaiming their faith in increasingly modern terms. The Mormon Church may be staying out of overt party politics, and there may still be many Democratic Mormons in the United States, but overall, Mormons have become a cohesive part of the Republican electorate.

MISSIONS IN THE MORMON FAITH

The Mormon Church has engineered an organization of proselytizing virtually unmatched by any other group. There are now more Mormons living outside American borders than within. Each year more than 20,000 young men leave on missions to maintain a missionary labor force of about 50,000 in the field.[41] In the early days of mission work, men would set off even when poor, hungry, and sick. Often they had no money and were leaving behind families, frequently for years at a time. Wives stayed behind and supported the children through farming, teaching, and whatever other work could be found.[42] For the most part, today's Mormon young men are obligated to enter mission fieldwork at the age of 19. For two years they, or their families, pay the cost of missionary work.[43] Mission work is both a rite of passage and a test of faith. Each missionary must choose for him or herself whether to reenter the faith newly committed. The hardships of missionary work basically function as a form of adult initiation into the Church.

About one-fourth of Mormon adults have served in such a mission at some point in their lives. This number is significantly higher for men than women (43% compared to 11%).[44] Because of the age when missionary work is most often undertaken, the numbers are higher for those under age 50 and among those raised Mormon compared with converts. Missionary work represents the Church's goal to serve and convert. The nature of missionary work since the turn of the century has changed, with more emphasis on humanitarian efforts. This increased focus on human works and endeavors, though, has been hedged with an increasingly authoritarian organizational structure. Individuals are to seek their own salvation and exaltation, but with increasingly narrow channels of church-sanctioned missionary activity.[45]

In some ways, the theology behind mission work mirrors that of legalistic Protestantism. Such theology teaches a few core things about faith that apply to proselytizing and mission work in general. Jesus's death was a transaction in which he paid for the sins of believers and won them eternal life. Thus, there are transactions in the physical realm that mirror this act and are heavenly in nature. Jesus's chief purpose was to carry out an act of atonement. Heavenly life after death for those who are saved is a tangible reward. This is especially true for Mormons, who see the temporal and spiritual realms as intertwined and church covenants as eternal (marriage/family). The rewards of conversion, from a missionary's point of view, are tangible and of material value. Individuals should be wary of trusting their own minds, emotions, and aesthetic value. Fortunately, for Mormon missionaries the active revelation of the prophet is continually providing updated church policy for the concerns of potential converts. Truth is established in the Bible and the Book of Mormon. Unlike legalistic Protestantism, however, the inerrancy of the Bible or Book of Mormon is not a central theological tenet because, just as the Constitution can be amended, so can scripture through the active revelation of the prophet.

THE VALUE OF MISSIONS

Missionaries receive special training before embarking on their two years of service. There are training centers in South America, Europe, Asia, and elsewhere—14 centers all around the world.[46] Mormon youths are prepared for mission work from childhood. Bishops of the Church enlist and judge qualification for the rigors of mission life. The Church president sends letters with the time and place for reporting to missionary training. The two years are trying years. Missionaries live in cheap housing. They do not do much in the way of entertainment. No dance, romance, or pop music is allowed. The letter may send a young Mormon abroad, or it may send him or her to New Jersey. It can be anywhere, and often personal preferences are ignored.[47] Some will become disillusioned and demoralized. Roughly 2 percent will return home early, unable to complete their service.[48] For those who complete the mission, they return with a new challenge to reintegrate and reinvest in their faith.

The value of missionary work to the Mormon faith is immeasurable. The spread of American Mormonism after the 1830s would have been unthinkable without the proselytizing skills developed by the Latter-day Saints.[49] The timing of the Mormon faith was fortuitous given how strong revivalism was as a cultural phenomenon across the United States in the nineteenth century. The ability to convert and proselytize is integral to the success of any religion, especially in the marketplace of American religion. The Mormon Church placed even more emphasis on proselytizing than most. Growth outside the boundaries of Utah lent crucial credibility to the story of Mormon legitimacy and power. The extent of Mormon influence now reaches far beyond the state politics of Utah and into the realm of international power and politics.

SERVICE IN THE ARMED FORCES

There are many ways in which service as a missionary parallels that of military service. As the social scientists Gordon and Shepherd have argued, missionary religions have a military mind-set with individual interests subordinated to a transcendent cause. Solidarity requires stereotyping the virtues and objections of one's community against a common enemy. Discipline is encouraged and individual dissent discouraged.[50] Thus, military service provides a similar experience for those who choose to enlist. Many Mormons must choose between mission work and military service. Service in the American armed forces does not take the place of actual mission work. It is, however, seen as a viable and honorable alternative. The fact that it is viewed in this light speaks to the nature of Mormon patriotism. Mormon theology is clear in its opposition to war. War is referred to as evidence of Satan in the world, and when Mormons are asked foreign policy questions, they often do not support increases in military spending. This is a church position as taken from a national and structural point of view. For an individual to serve in the military, however, is viewed very favorably. To serve the nation that is the future home of Zion is a worthwhile endeavor and, though not overt, there are religious overtones to Mormon service in the military. President Gordon B. Hinckley of the Mormon Church discusses this in somewhat veiled terms that hint at American foreign policy as contesting with forces of evil and repression.

> This places us in the position of those who long for peace, who teach peace, who work for peace, but who also are citizens of nations and are subject to the laws of our governments. Furthermore, we are a freedom-loving people,

committed to the defense of liberty wherever it is in jeopardy. I believe that God will not hold men and women in uniform responsible as agents of their government in carrying forward that which they are legally obligated to do. It may even be that He will hold us responsible if we try to impede or hedge up the way of those who are involved in a contest with forces of evil and repression.[51]

Much like the Mormon experience with the state, the relationship with the U.S. armed forces has a mixed history. One of the earliest and most notable pieces of Mormon military history is the so-called Mormon Battalion, which served from July 1846 to 1847. It is one of the only religiously based units in American military history. The battalion helped the United States secure much of the American Southwest in the Mexican-American War—an interesting contribution to a nation that was not ready to even recognize statehood for the homeland of the soldiers. Then there was the strange incursion by the U.S. government into Utah in 1858. The bloodless confrontation, discussed briefly earlier, was quite a different interaction with military personnel. Naturally, though, citizenship and service were complicated by the question of statehood. The turning point for Mormons serving in the U.S. military was the Spanish-American War of 1898. This was the first war in which large numbers of Mormons served. From this point until the present day, Mormonism has encouraged and supported military service.

Often Mormon soldiers have found ways to spread their faith while serving in the military. While technically against the regulations of the armed services, there are numerous accounts of such proselytizing. One well-known account traces occupation troops in Japan following World War II who were tasked with evaluating damage and rebuilding. Two such troops, LDS Army servicemen Elliott Richards and Boyd Packer, used their military service as missions, dedicating themselves to teaching and testifying to Japanese citizens.[52] The missionary successes in countries such as Japan and Korea have gained momentum from the work of servicemen and women.[53]

The missionary opportunities in the stresses of military life have proven to be significant on both a personal and national basis. The membership of the Mormon Church commonly prays for service people as a group, much as it does for the missionaries. Servicemen's conferences are held in Europe and Asia, providing members with a full program of the Church and access to missionary resources. Military service may not be the same thing as missionary service, but often the two overlap. And in a more general sense, the honor and resources given to LDS service members convey a similar sense of initiation and spiritual meaning. Mormons, on the whole, have become decidedly promilitary and interventionist in foreign policy. From the Church's point of view, this is to promote safe conditions for proselytizing in the long run. Church leaders are interested in foreign affairs in order to retain the Church's ability to preach the gospel to every nation, kindred, tongue, and people.[54] This is a natural strategic concern for a tradition whose survival often depended on spreading the word. Aside from strategic concerns, and the ability to spread the gospel, support for the military is a cultural value. The service rendered in the American military may not replace that of missionary work, but it is treated with equal respect and admiration.

The Mormon Church provides preservice orientation for its members. This process is directed by stake presidents and usually employs a current active-duty Mormon solder for the actual orientation proceedings. These sessions are designed to ensure that Mormons remain strong in their faith while serving the nation, but also that they are prepared to spread the gospel when the opportunity presents itself. There are sessions designed to teach resistance to peer pressure, the importance of setting a good example, the importance of attending church, and the importance of writing uplifting letters home to parents and family. This last feature of the preorientation training is an indication of the Church's commitment to armed service in the U.S. military. Sending encouraging letters home to family is meant to reinforce an image of valid service in the name of God and country. It is also intended to reassure family that the faith is maintaining and not at risk in the face of a competing institutional culture. The military requires loyalties of its own, but those Mormons who serve are better prepared to balance the competing institutional pressures of the Church and the state.

Many Mormons seek to serve as chaplains in the military. The U.S. government has some basic requirements for service as a chaplain that include a bachelor's degree and a graduate degree in a related field such as theology and religious philosophy.[55] These are the basic requirements, to which the Mormon Church adds some of its own. A Mormon soldier must be married in the temple and have at least two years of practical ministerial experience. Although it is not required, the Church prefers its chaplain applicants to be those who have already completed their missionary work. The extra requirements are seen as a necessary step in qualifying members to serve the dual role of representing church and state. Whether or not the Church happens to embrace a particular military campaign, chaplains and other Mormon service members see themselves as defending more than just the nation. They are involved in a larger struggle to defend the freedom that ensures the survival of the Church. By defeating previous threats like the Axis powers and the Soviet Union, the U.S. military has created incredible worldwide opportunities for the Church of Jesus Christ of Latter-day Saints to spread the gospel to millions. The mission of the American military is a complement to the Mormon faith. Securing freedom and peace further supports the fulfillment of the Church in proselytizing to the world. Defending freedom is even more valuable for the land Mormons believe to be the future seat of God's reign. There is a special responsibility for those Mormons who live in the nations of North America to live righteously and do all they can to defend the land itself.

PATRIOTIC RELIGION

The patriotism of Mormon Americans has been challenged throughout history. This, however, is primarily due to the contentious early relationship between the Church and the mainstream political establishment. Following various degrees of persecution, Mormons did experience a phase of antiestablishment sentiment. In fact, some went so far as to swear an oath of vengeance against the U.S. government in the name of avenging the blood of Joseph Smith.[56] The entire religion pulled away from the nation as dramatically as the reaches of the U.S. frontier would allow. A fortress of isolation was sought in the Territory of Utah—a place to escape the power of the state. However, following the granting of statehood, this fortress mentality dissolved. Mormons became avid citizens and adopted national economic and political patterns.[57] This transition after statehood ushered in the modern Mormon citizen. Once isolated and nonideological, church members grew more integrated and more consistent in their political conservatism. Mormons overall found it easy to adapt to the marketplace of American capitalism and became pro-American individualists.[58]

Contemporary Mormons are quick to point out their church is loyal to the American government and seeks to contribute to the nation's social welfare. Love of country and devotion to the republic are central teachings of the Mormon faith. Church members cite numerous historical examples of this love and devotion. Utah residents were among the first to volunteer in many wars as far back as those against Spain and the Philippines.[59] Even in the ritual celebrations of the Church, national pride and patriotism mix with religious teachings. Mormon celebrations often blend Mormon history and American nationalism.[60] Mormons are taught to be good Americans and adopt the political and cultural values of the nation.[61] This is not unique to the United States, nor is it necessary for Mormons around the world to feel patriotic toward the United States. Citizens of each country are taught to be loyal, patriotic, law-abiding citizens. There is no mistaking, however, the special pride and righteousness expressed by American Mormons. The nation is physically and spiritually linked with the particulars of Mormon theology. Thus, much as the temporal and spiritual realms are intertwined for LDS believers, so are the Mormon faith and the United States of America.

8

Going Global

TRANSNATIONAL RELIGION

Most religions of the world are transnational in the sense that they are not created specific to the borders of a given nation. Depending on the historical era, religions align themselves with political systems of different order and size as the politics of the day dictate. The arbitrary borders of nation-states rarely have any meaning for religious traditions, aside from those married to the state. In these cases, the cultural identity of the nation is shaped by the establishment of a preferred religion. More often, though, borders of the state dissect natural religious identity and ethnicity. Finding authority in a higher power than national political structures, religions work within national borders as it suits the organizational survival of the tradition, but rarely because the nation is theologically relevant. The Mormon Church, as discussed in previous chapters, is inherently connected to the nation of the United States. This connection is true organizationally and theologically. The Church of Jesus Christ of Latter-day Saints has developed in a manner that seems reversed from typical religious evolution. The Church began as a movement completely within the bounds of the American nation and within the context of American political structures, and has since expanded beyond American borders. As it has expanded, it has changed and adapted central tenets as the prophet has received inspiration to do so. These changes have, in part, served to accommodate a new global church. The American borders no longer contain Mormonism, and the global reach of the Church is impressive. As the Church expanded it actively sought ways to more successfully reach new parts of the world. In return, these new geographies and cultures affected the Church's place in the world and some of its organizational features.

Through proselytizing and conversion, missionaries attempt to harness free spaces in societies. The Mormon Church has been extremely effective in reaching out to new cultures and presenting a belief structure that appeals to a diverse network of believers. Conversion cuts across social categories of class, gender, age, level of education, and type of occupation. At times the growth of the Church takes place in parts of societies that have been without organized global religious traditions altogether. At other times, the most successful growth has occurred in the freshly made free spaces of war's aftermath. In the wake of violent struggles, the bonds of society are weakened. Relations to kin, company, and community are destroyed in war, and religion fills in to restore a sense of identity and order to a given community. This has been the case in many of the war-torn nations of Africa and South America.[1] The Mormon Church provides a rigorous organizational structure, with a strong sense of community and identity. Just as religions can repair society, so too can they instigate violence in the first place. Transnational religion provokes populations to armed struggle in dictatorships and democracies alike. The very future of the nation-state as the given unit of political power may rest on the development of contemporary transnational religions. The Mormon Church, however, has not had much experience with the kind of violence seen in other religious traditions. This is likely due, in part, to the relative youth of the tradition. Some of the lack of historical violence against political powers outside of the United States comes from the commitment to loyal citizenship taught by the Church.

Transnational religious movements, like Mormonism, are often considered an accommodation to modernity, or perhaps postmodernity. This particular phase of religious organizational history is a reflection of the increasing forces of globalization. Transnational cultural and religious networks provide a collective identity to peoples who are widely dispersed.[2] The Mormon Church is growing in size and importance as the communities of the Mormon diaspora grow throughout the world. Globalization, in terms of greater connectivity through faster communication and cultural exchange, has greatly contributed to the expanse of the Mormon Church. Missionaries present a belief structure that hinges on the importance of the United States to the future reign of God. This provides a connection to the attractive cultural identity of Americanism for people around the world. The more connectivity and globalization, the easier it is for a religious movement born in a specific nation to provide a sense of identity for new converts.

Transnational religions have political ambition insofar as they seek to expand beyond the limits of national borders. This ambition requires some attention to the larger global context of international politics. Many religious movements have yearned for a global state, but have been satisfied to settle for a nationalism specific to a particular country. In these cases the capacity of the religion to symbolize social identity is merged into national identity.[3] The Mormon Church balances its historical connection to the United States as a nation with its teachings of loyal citizenship for followers of other nations. The social identity of Mormonism is intrinsically linked to the nation of the United States, but over time this has been deemphasized in the work of missionaries and church materials in general. The cultural connection, though, to the power of the United States' appeal worldwide has meant rapid growth for the Church in the era of increasing globalization.

Forecasting the future for transnational religion overall, many scenarios exist that provide for the survival of the nation-state as an enduring structure of power. Many religions, such as Islam, have seen enough infighting among competing sects to maintain the salience of national borders and politics.[4] In other words, as religious traditions splinter they lose the organizational power to supersede the authority of the nation-state. This has not been the case for Mormonism. Little evidence of national or ethnic infighting exists so far in the Church's evolution. There is, of course, a natural competitive battle with the other religions of the world currently expanding in the same geographic locations of the world. As the Mormon Church competes for converts with Islam and Pentecostalism, for example, the opportunities for cultural and political struggle are more common. However, within the Mormon Church there exist a high degree of solidarity and few signs of division aside from those sects that have broken from the Church over various theological disagreements. These sects do not constitute a significant challenge in the context of global religion.[5] In fact, some of these divergent sects have come back to the mainstream organization after years of practicing in a manner that disobeys the contemporary edicts.

TRANSNATIONAL POLITICS

In much the same way religion provides a legitimating force for national governance, so too may it provide a similar legitimating force for transnational political structures and ideology. The future of political structures on the level of global governance may rely on transnational religion for a new sense of citizenship. For a time, a socialist movement attempted to strip people of their identity rooted in the state in favor of a larger ideological identity. Similar attempts may inevitably involve transnational religion as it provides a sense of identity needed to bind people together across national borders. The growth of transnational corporations and regional political alliances displays the political and economic consequences of globalization. Nevertheless, the nation-state continues to be critical in world politics as a unit of authority and power. The nation-state is still the essential unit of political order in the global economic system. Transnational religion challenges this unit as it fosters social identity that extends beyond the jurisdiction of the nation's political authority. These effects are not all negative for the nation-state. The larger social identity provided allows for easier political cooperation between nations that share religious traditions. Thus, it facilitates the globalization of political power by providing a larger base of legitimacy for governance.

At times Mormons have been described as a distinct subculture. The experience of Mormons has been seen as an isolated identity almost like that of the ethnic identity that sets Jews apart from other subcultures.[6] This subculture status does not change the global realities of the Church. A relatively small portion of the history and future history of the Church is used to make this characterization and can obscure just how global and diverse the Church has become and will likely be for the foreseeable future. Even the Church as it is contained within American borders has diversified considerably. The religious pluralism of the American culture has allowed Mormonism to spread, slowly, throughout racial and ethnic communities. In addition to this homegrown pluralism, immigration has also fueled diversity. From the mid-1800s, successive waves of immigrants from Catholic countries like Ireland, Italy, and Poland poured into the nation.[7] This wave of immigration was responsible for an enduring cultural divide in the United States. The Protestant traditions of the early United States clashed with Catholic traditions on political and cultural matters.

In this context, the Mormon faith represented a threat to both of these competing traditions. From the point of view of majority Protestantism, Catholics were seen as corrupt and tied too tightly to the pope, while Mormons were creating and innovating in the opposite theological direction. Thus, early immigration created a charged environment of religious identity and cultural division. More recent immigration has brought new citizens from parts of the world without the specific religious identity the earlier waves of immigrants had. This, in conjunction with the presence of the Mormon Church in immigrant home countries, has provided new opportunities for the Mormon Church to grow within the American context.

GLOBALIZATION

Globalization is not a new phenomenon. It is a force of interconnectivity that has existed from the earliest days of nations as a political unit. Contemporary globalization finds an increased pace of interconnectivity and more specific economic consequences. There is a growing connection of ideas, materials, goods, information, pollution, money, and people. The capacity of information technologies to shorten distance in time and space has increased geometrically.[8] Worldwide practices are more and more standardized, while new organizations have emerged to monitor or counteract these practices. Globalization means a shrinking world in which people of diverse religious backgrounds come into intense contact with one another. This contact requires theological traditions to negotiate exclusive beliefs with new cultures and competing faiths.[9] Religious identity requires inclusion and exclusion. Some are granted entry and can claim the social identity provided by religion. Some are excluded and these people define the boundaries of a religious tradition. These boundaries are more complicated to monitor as globalization challenges the standard notions of inclusion and exclusion.

While globalization creates challenges for religious identity, it also creates the conditions for a truly transnational religion, like the Mormon Church. The contact common between religious traditions is often less combustible on the global stage than when contained within nation-states. The ability to connect, as a minority religion, with the rest of the tradition worldwide is a secure reinforcement of identity and organizational strength. Thus, globalization helps connect minority religious traditions in a way that prevents the kind of isolation and limited options that lead to violent confrontations or forced assimilation. As a minority population is backed into a corner, as the Mormon tradition was for many years in the American context, the choices are limited. Fighting the majority population is not preferable, but has seemed the only option to many religious sects throughout history who are essentially viewed thereafter as terrorists. Assimilating, and so accommodating the majority, is a concession and not an ideal practice for any religious tradition that would like to remain distinct. A more global world means a more connected network of religious minorities, reducing the odds that such a group is isolated.

There are generally two responses to globalization from religious traditions. One is to view the increasing interconnectedness as a conspiracy to impose homogenous standards on all areas of life. Whether or not it is an active conspiracy or an indirect consequence, these traditions see the marketization and Americanization of the world as dangerous and detrimental to the health of distinctive religion. Such a response leads to an emphasis on the capacity for globalization to destroy those particular identities formed by religious bonds. This capacity undermines the principles of plurality and pushes toward uniformity.[10] This response is similar, in some ways, to the manner in which a religious tradition regards contemporary culture. For many it is a threat to the moral and spiritual health of its members, for others an ever-changing medium of opportunities for new theological applications and variations. As a threat, it must be limited and excluded when possible. As an evolving context for religious proselytizing, it can be harnessed for the powers of good. This second response to contemporary culture is reflected in the other major reaction of religious traditions to globalization. This reaction sees globalization as a positive force in the world that extends opportunities for the Church to have influence on the world. Traditions that view globalization through this lens emphasize global consciousness and the increased abilities to deal effectively with transnational problems.[11]

The Mormon Church certainly views contemporary culture as a threat to moral and spiritual health. Common church directives advise parents to shield their children from the moral degradation evident all around them. However, as it regards the globalization of world culture, the Church has embraced the opportunities that abound. This is made easier as the Church is grounded in the nation that is most associated with the standardization of culture. Religions whose heritage is decidedly non-American are more likely to view the perceived Americanization of world culture as a threat. The Mormon Church, however, has a decidedly American heritage. In fact, the belief that the Constitution is a spiritually inspired founding document likely leads to a reinforcement of American exceptionalism in Mormon populations abroad.[12] The reverence required of Mormon followers for the American experience is less a focus of international Mormon populations, but it remains a core piece of the faith. This creates a social identity that is linked through theology to the nation of the United States around the world. The biggest organizational challenge for the Church in the late twentieth century has been the immense international growth. For a church that is uniquely American, it is somewhat surprising to find it ranked atop the list of fastest-growing religions in the world.[13] Some of this success is due to the cultural and spiritual connection to the United States as a nation that spreads its culture successfully in this era of globalization.

The Mormon Church will soon achieve a worldwide following comparable to that of Islam, Buddhism, Christianity, and Hinduism.[14] Due to its relative youth as a religious tradition and its recent globalized success, the Church is in many ways a unique opportunity for scholars to study a religious movement across cultures. Among the many interesting avenues of study is the explanation for the Church's success in high and constant rates of membership growth. Some of the hypotheses for why the Church has been quite so successful focus on the level of exclusivity evident in the Church as a provider of strong cultural and religious identity. This explanation finds the barriers to entry significant enough to attract converts looking for a complete organization that provides meaning and structure in all aspects of life. This relatively high barrier of entry also aids in retention as the investment is significant on the part of the convert. Related to this explanation is the characterization of the Church as a demanding organization on individuals' time and resources. It requires the full attention and commitment of new members. Another contributing factor is the policy of splitting congregations in two when they reach a critical size.[15] This has allowed the Church to remain responsive to each member and fulfill the spiritual and material promises of conversion. The proven adaptability of the Church overall is an asset in the globalized world. The Church may represent a theology rooted in Americanism, but it has changed organizationally and theologically to be better equipped for proselytizing abroad.

Globalization presents a challenge for the Church in terms of its doctrine. As it grows in places where new converts are encouraged to build up their congregations in their homelands, it is remains to be seen how much these homeland cultures will eventually be a part of global Mormonism. It is unclear the extent to which international congregations should reflect the American culture through the workings of the Church. At the moment, these distant churches are closely supervised by the center of the Church in the United States.[16] As religiously based movements reach out to include wider and wider constituencies, they encounter a greater diversity of membership and become more tolerant.[17] The Mormon Church has certainly been affected in the specific category of racial diversity and tolerance. However, the Church remains a fairly tightly controlled worldwide organization with few deviations in practice and doctrine. The Church tends to feel the effects of globalization as a whole, rather than specific to certain regions. It has been successful in converting new members in different regions around the world, but with the same core theological and organizational principles at work.

Some of the most successful regions for Mormonism have been Central America, South America, and Africa. The Church represents one of the great success stories in modern Latin American religion. Close to one-third of Mormon membership lives in Central and South America. There will soon be 20 temples in Latin America overall. Mexico and the other nations of Central America constitute more than a million Mormon Church members.[18] Church membership in Brazil and the surrounding nations of South America grew enormously during the 1960s and 1970s and continues to grow today.[19] Most projections show that the portion of the Church that lives in Europe and the United States will likely shrink, while the proportion of the Church in Central America, South America, and Africa will continue to grow over the next few decades.[20] The shifting majority of the Church from European and American heritage to the southern hemisphere of the planet is likely to require further adaptations from the Church. Its experience with Latin America and Africa has already impacted church doctrine in one specific way. The experience with race in the Church has been a slow evolution from outright racism to gradual acceptance and embrace.

The success of the Church worldwide has some effect on the foreign policy preferences of Mormon Americans. In terms of national politics, the Church maintains a staff in Washington, DC, but does little actual congressional advocacy.[21] This is because the focus of the Church is on the accessibility of other nations for proselytizing. The Church does a lot of globalization advocacy that is specific to the missionary work that fuels the growth of membership. In this way it maintains relationships with embassies of foreign governments in an ongoing effort to secure access for its thousands of missionaries. While the practical international political efforts of the Church focus on missionary work, the broader political policy preferences are shaped by an overwhelming sense of the goodness of the United States. Latter-day Saints share a general agreement on American exceptionalism.[22] In other words, Mormons see the United States' place in the world as unique and of elevated importance. This colors each international political issue with shades of pro-Americanism. The pervasive belief that the United States is intrinsically good informs each Mormon citizen in regard to foreign policy actions the nation takes. Every deed committed by the United States in the global arena is seen with a special sense of goodness in the eyes of many

Mormons.[23] The global politics of the Church involve a special justification for American involvement in the world that extends beyond universal principles for the fair sharing of power worldwide. The United States is seen as a special case, with different moral justification that other nations.

RACE AND THE MORMON FAITH

Religion and politics are two large conceptual topics to tackle. Adding race into the mix often makes for overgeneralization. Race, religion, and politics cross over ethnic and regional backgrounds and can be difficult to parse.[24] The Mormon experience with black Americans, however, is an important chapter in the evolution of the Church. In many ways it is a history not unlike most American religious traditions. It is one rife with segregation and discrimination. Even today, the Mormon Church is rather segregated, but most congregations of all religion in the United States have little ethnic diversity.[25] The early years of Mormonism were shaped by the dominant Jacksonian culture of the United States in the nineteenth century. Reflecting this Jacksonian environment, Mormon society was structured by hierarchies of race and sex.[26] The Book of Mormon made the white race morally superior to the red and black races around it. The book of Abraham was read as a message to subordinate black people. The implementation of plural marriage further amplified the patriarchic order of the Mormon faith.[27] Mormons behaved much as the majority of religious Americans did in regard to sex and race. The pluralism that allowed for the religious innovation of Mormonism also led to many cases of racism. Pluralism may have an affinity with tolerance, but is likely to breed some amount of racism in the competitive struggle of the religious marketplace.[28]

As part of early Mormon racism, black members were excluded from the priesthood. The origins of this exclusionary doctrine are not completely clear. Some translations indicate a connection of black Americans to the Egyptian pharaohs.[29] The other doctrinal source of skin preference comes from an understanding of Native American history as a battle between good and evil tribes. The two tribes, the Lamanites and Nephrites, battled against each other. The Lamanites won and became so evil that they warred among themselves. By the time Columbus stumbled upon them, these so-called American Indians had become a filthy and loathsome people. They had no idea that their dark-skinned appearance was a curse traceable to a failure to correctly follow God.[30] From this particular history, the Mormon faith developed an aversion to darker skin tones and an affinity for lighter skin. Native Americans were evidence of evil turning a population's skin tone darker to reflect the sin of past decisions. Black Americans were burdened with the darkest skin and so indirectly labeled theologically as most evil. For this reason, black Americans were not allowed into the inner circles of the Mormon faith, nor were they actively recruited by the Church. Black Americans still joined the faith, but this only added to the Church's struggle to deal with race overall.

Prior to 1978, missionaries around the world were reluctant to teach blacks. It was typical of church instructions to guide missionaries to avoid areas where it was known black people lived.[31] Black church members often reported feeling prejudice and stigmatized. Eventually, the civil rights movement brought extensive pressure to bear on the Mormon Church. The pressures mounted from within as well. One young Mormon, Stephen Holbrook, was instructed by Church leaders not to work with blacks. He worked for Utah congressman Sherm Lloyd at the time of these instructions and found them disturbing. He went on to work with the NAACP in Utah to fight against the Church's position on race.[32] It was not an easy fight. Many rumors were spread about the radicalism of the NAACP and the potential dangers of Muslim black Americans. These rumors fueled a hysteria that forever prejudiced many Mormons against the NAACP and the cause of civil rights more broadly.[33] The bonds of racism were rather strong, especially considering scriptural guidance and constant church directives that reinforced the relative inferiority of black people.

The pressure to deal with the racism within Mormon practices came not just from the civil rights movement, from church members within the organization, but also from sources outside the United States. Church membership in Brazil and the rest of South America grew rapidly in the 1960s and 1970s. Determining who was black had always been a sensitive issue in Brazil, and the Mormon exclusionary doctrine made matters severely uncomfortable for the Church.[34] For a growing church with even greater potential, issues of race needed to be dealt with to secure that potential. Across the Atlantic Ocean, similar circumstances threatened to hurt the Church's prospects in Africa. Since 1946, Nigerian citizens had been requesting missionaries from the Mormon faith to visit their nation. They had organized churches based on the Book of Mormon and requested the Church's guidance through missionaries. In 1963 missionaries were sent, but the Nigerian government refused to admit them because of the faith's restrictions on priesthood.[35] Given its otherwise highly egalitarian heritage, including a lay clergy, the Church's racial policy was all the more noticeable.[36] By the time Spencer Kimball took over as president in 1973, the Church had been enduring non-stop pressure for many years to conform to a new understanding of race in the United States. Kimball understood that for Mormonism to continue its expansion, the Church would need to change its policy on blacks and the priesthood.[37]

In 1978, the president issued a new revelation. Every faithful man in the body of the Church could receive the holy priesthood. Most outside observers commented that foreign trends had more impact on the policy change than anything else.[38] The Church had found through active revelation a swift correction and adaptation to a new conception of racial equality, at least with males. National pressure mixed with a substantial amount of global pressure was eased with the new edict.[39] Following the policy change, Mormons were by and large pleased with the doctrinal adjustment.[40] The change was quickly adopted by the Mormon faithful if for no other reason than the facilitation of further missionary activity. The new doctrine created a whole new world of opportunities not only in South America but also in the formerly cursed geographies of Africa, the Caribbean, and Latin America. Not only was the social pressure and criticism eased, but also an entire population of millions were opened up for conversion.

The diversity of the Church lies in its global portfolio of nations and ethnicities. Within the United States, however, the religion is predominantly white. Over 94 percent of Mormons in the United States are white.[41] Overall, Mormon Americans are white, are Western, and exhibit strong conservative tendencies independent of their religion.[42] This means that the racial and cultural makeup is still skewed to a small slice of the racial and cultural landscape. While Mormon political thought and political preferences are not monolithic, they are rather well grouped ideologically and electorally. What divergence exists within Mormon political preferences can often be accounted for by race. There are not a lot of data to crunch for black American Mormons, because they are not a significant population. However, there is some indication that racial differences account in part for differences in Mormon political views.[43] White Mormon Americans are as reliable a conservative bloc of voters as any population in history. On the other hand, some surveys and interviews show that LDS black Americans are closer ideologically to LDS white Americans than they are to other black Americans. These data would suggest that little variation in ideology can be accounted for simply by racial differences. These more recent data likely reflect some kind of upward-mobility stream for black Mormons.[44]

Black Mormons in the United States have been in a unique position as the only group historically excluded from priesthood and temple worship. Since the policy change in 1978, missionary efforts have gradually increased among black Americans and the rate of conversion has been growing accordingly. The Church has seen noticeable growth in the inner cities of Charlotte and Greensboro, North Carolina. Birmingham, Alabama; Newark, New Jersey; New York City; Chicago; and Detroit have all been hot zones for Mormon conversion of black Americans. The educational backgrounds of these black converts range from sixth grade to graduate-level studies. There is seemingly no typical or easily defined black Mormon convert.[45] Most black Mormons find that they are accepted easily into the ranks of the Church, although they report a subtle undercurrent of discrimination.[46] The Church does not advertise its history with the exclusion doctrine, and many converts are never purposefully exposed to it. Those who report discrimination claim it dissipates with time spent in the Church. The Mormon Church within the United States is becoming less European. Native Americans, Hispanics, Asians,

Polynesians, and black Americans are joining the Church in increasing numbers. Much as the profile of the global Church is becoming less white, so too is the Church within the United States. As the Church diversifies, its connection to the past racism is lessened. The history of racial injustice is a mirrored story throughout American religious traditions. Not all of those other traditions, though, have the growing diversity the Mormon Church has. Most did not have as explicit a doctrine as the exclusion of blacks from church ceremony and authority, but their exclusion was no less effective. While the specificity of the doctrine appears initially more damning, the role of active prophecy more completely changed the attitude and practice of the Church than any other tradition in the American context. At its worst, Mormons were rarely hostile toward nonwhites. A more accurate characterization would be that Latter-day Saints have been ambivalent about racial issues and at times intimidated by racial differences.[47]

NATIVE AMERICANS

The Book of Mormon speaks of the ancestors of the Native Americans. Early Mormonism took an interest in these people and the American West. Missionaries traveled 1,500 miles, mostly on foot, preaching the Book of Mormon to natives. They taught the book as a religious history of the American Indian and a prophecy of their future role in God's plan. All in all, the missionary attempts met with little success.[48] And so began a strange relationship with a culture and race that figures prominently in the theological history of the Mormon tradition, but whose interactions have yielded mixed results from both perspectives. Overall the relationship is characterized by a set of tensions. Native Americans are linked to ancient Israel in Mormon teachings, but the history is somewhat checkered. Essentially descended from the tribe that fell into evil ways, the Native American lineage is still believed to be of vital importance in the history and future of God's plan. Aside from the cross-cutting theological impulses, the embrace of native populations early in the Church's history put the Church in a tough position in relation to the U.S. government.[49] Therefore it was somewhat costly politically to align with a minority population that was consistently ostracized and targeted by the national government. This cost added to the distance Mormonism kept from Native Americans. They were treated as a chosen people with a bright future, but somehow not quite ready. In some cases the place of Native Americans in the larger plan of God seems to be of a people not quite Mormon enough or spiritually intelligent enough to testify to the glory of God. Even today, stereotypes persist among the Mormon population as to the spirituality of Native Americans. Whether or not those who chose to join the Church should be fully assimilated into the predominantly white Church wards is an open debate. Both the Mormon Church and the Native American Mormon population seem somehow unable to resolve the proper place of these theologically important people.[50] Unlike the story of black Americans, there has been no significant external or global pressure for the Church to make any special adjustments for the Native American population. The isolated nature of Native American culture prevents globalization from playing the same role it did for the cause of civil rights. A lack of external pressure mixed with the dichotomy of a chosen and/or cursed people leads to an ambivalent and unresolved relationship. Despite a unique and very favorable theological outlook, the Church has a rather ambiguous policy for Native Americans.[51]

Native Americans and the Mormon Church share much of the same history. Part of this history is a shared subjugation of the eastern expansion of the United States under Manifest Destiny. The winning of the West caused both peoples to be driven into isolation and battled until deemed no longer threatening. A history of discrimination, persecution, and abridged civil rights is the story of both populations. It is not often that minority populations find enough common ground to join forces and repel the majority power. More often they turn on each other to gain whatever small advantage might be won in shifting the majority's attention elsewhere. Although a shared history exists, the Mormon Church chose to assimilate into American culture, while Native American populations clung to what culture, identity, and land they could. These divergent strategies also account for the strained history of relations. Many natives resisted the efforts of the Church to proselytize and viewed them as engaging in a typical Euro-American conquest. Nevertheless, many Native Americans have joined the Church and continue to struggle with their place in the theology and religious tradition.

This mixed history can also be attributed to an instrumental and political mobilization of rhetorical ammunition used to condemn American Indians during attacks. This strategic use of rhetoric in the nineteenth century further justified colonization and promoted evangelization. This is in contrast with the Church's success in the early twentieth century to attract people of color in Mexico and the rest of Central America. Despite central teachings that associated dark skin with a curse from God, the Church was able to explode in these nations with populations sharing much of the Native American heritage. This contrast illustrates that the meanings applied to racially charged symbols are not predetermined by church leaders or sacred texts. Instead they reflect the instrumental needs of the Mormon Church in particular times and places.[52] Mexican converts reinterpret the racial doctrines in ways that confirm a superior place in the plan of God. The focus for Mexican Mormons is on that part of the history that glorifies ancient Mexico. The Church of Jesus Christ of Latter-day Saints as it is controlled from Utah tolerates many subtle interpretations of the racial doctrine around the world to the extent that the Church's organizational power is not undermined.[53] Thus the racial doctrines have different interpretations and results in the context of the United States in the nineteenth century when compared to twentieth-century Mexico.

GLOBAL MORMONISM AND WORLD POLITICS

New religious growth is fueling the essential elements of democracy in some parts of the world. As secular nation-states look to religious ideologies to legitimize the morality and authority of modern governments, religious values reinforce the foundational ideals of the modern state.[54] Tolerant forms of religion serve to push an agenda of democratic values as they seek to coexist within developing societies. While some of these religious movements turn to violence, moderate churches expanding their reach, like the Mormon Church, secure the nation against intolerant extremists. Mormonism can be seen as part of the spread of democracy worldwide. The theology and cosmology of the religion is not especially democratic, but its connection to American identity and culture certainly engender new populations with receptivity to American-style democracy. Furthermore, Mormonism's rigorous organizational obligations require much of its members. This organizational burden yields all the potential benefits of a civil society with a fair amount of social capital.

The impact of Mormon religion on a society's economy is another effect conducive to the development of market economics. Mormons cultivate a sense of communal bonds through the support of fellow Mormons in the marketplace. Mormons patronize Mormon establishments and foster a system of in-buying that supports entrepreneurial endeavors among members. Indirectly, the contemporary Mormon faith breeds classic individualism, which can be an interesting cultural transition in more communal societies. This cultural transition facilitates the development of liberalized markets and economies. Sacrifice and discipline are core Mormon values and they support church members' efforts to compete in the marketplace. Along with supporting fellow member businesses, successful church members reinvest heavily in their community, church, and businesses. In this way the Mormon effect on a foreign economy can be rather Weberian[55] in developing practices of reinvestment and growth. In many of the places where the Church is growing fastest, it is adapting to native communal systems and injecting some commercial and capitalist energy. Conversion to the Mormon Church also connects new members to an American economic culture that is the dominant system of world economics. Whether this is good for the preservation of local traditions or not, it has specific positive effects on the development of regional economies. They become more connected with the global economic system and more likely to diversify in terms of income and wealth distribution. Mormon members around the world are significantly wealthier than surrounding populations and more likely to support middle-class notions of economic and political power. Thus, insofar as the development of democracy depends on the effects of a healthy middle class,[56] Mormon expansion has an indirect positive impact on the prospects for democratization in the developing world.

The structure of the Church, however, raises some doubts about the impact of Mormonism on the political development of any converted region. The Church of Jesus Christ of Latter-day Saints is strict in its hierarchy and authoritarian in its adherence to the president of the Church. A similar case is the Catholic Church. In the study of political development, Catholicism has received some criticism for the indirect cultural effect it has on the prospects of democratization due to its hierarchical structure of power. Some regions of the globe have seemingly had an easier time transitioning to democratic forms of power than regions rich in Catholic heritage (like Latin America).[57] Cultures that are used to hierarchical structures in their religious experiences are more likely to produce, or at least tolerate, political structures with similar authoritarian hierarchy. The pope is the figurehead for the Catholic Church and an intermediary between God and His flock, but the similarities with the president of the Mormon Church do not extend much further. The structure of the Mormon faith is rather different as well. There are theological tenets that foster democratic organizing within the Church and the formal roles of church leadership are less related to functional positions of power than positions of guidance. Despite a strict doctrine and adherence to one president, the Mormon Church is less like the Catholic Church in its cultural footprint and more akin to Protestant traditions in the Weberian sense.

Meanwhile, the institutional norms of the Church contribute to a more governable population. Patriotism and obedience to authority are core values. At one time, the patriotism encouraged was specific to the United States, but recent global outreach has become more flexible, encouraging citizens to identify openly with their given nations. Aside from obedience to national authority, the Mormon Church teaches members to be good and active citizens. Mormon citizens are well practiced in participating in meetings and fulfilling necessary duties. This active citizenship is conducive to the kind of civil society that fosters democracy.[58] Generally high expectations for church participation throughout Mormon culture help to increase civic skills and political activity.[59] The Mormon Church has shown a surprising resilience in the face of educational attainment, which usually has a secularizing influence on most religious groups. Latter-day Saints become better educated and more active citizens than neighbors, but remain devout and theologically attached to Mormon traditions.[60] This is important for the Church since it encourages members to be active in the governance of secular society and obedient to secular authority. Many religious traditions shelter members from these secular forces, and from the value of education, in fear that such dabbling will diminish religious zeal. These fears lead many traditions to pull back from the sordid world of politics and corporeal power.

Table 8.1
Religious Political Activity

	Mormons	Southern Baptist	Catholics	No Religion
Political activity	2.16	1.9	1.78	1.81
Electoral politics	2.98	3.14	2.89	2.67
Protest scale	1.10	.91	.97	1.13
Social trust	.29	−.03	−.01	−.14
Civic participation	1.87	1.68	1.54	1.51
Volunteering	7.6	5.3	4.9	3.1
Volunteer events	13.1	7.3	7.7	5.9

Political engagement is seen as necessary to secure the rights a tradition requires to be able to withdraw from secular society. Often, it is as if religious movements fight for the rights and freedoms associated with modern society explicitly for the purpose of living separately from it.[61] One might expect to find this same impulse within the Mormon faith, but on the contrary, it is more engaged than most other traditions. It is possible that the history of persecution and eventual assimilation presents a trajectory for the Church to increased civic involvement.

Table 8.1 shows the relatively high levels of engagement the Mormon Church produces compared to other religious traditions and nonreligious citizens.[62] Significantly higher levels of citizenship overall reflect a church culture that is sincerely engaged in and integrated with its surroundings. Mormon connection to politics and volunteerism is greater than other religious traditions.

These higher rates of political activity come from being engaged in church activities. They do not come as a result of explicit mobilization from LDS leadership as this direction is relatively infrequent.[63] In other words, the daily practice of being a Mormon leads to an increased likelihood of civic and political engagement. Members are provided civic skills and social networks that facilitate connections with public affairs.[64] On the other hand, the demands of the Church are such that volunteerism tends to serve the Church as much as the community. The involvement in politics may be strong and persistent, but the number of hours available to members to actively participate is limited. It is worth considering the limited time and resources left to members after the demands of the Church are taken into account. Nevertheless, the commitment and civic skills of Mormon citizens contribute positively to healthy secular governance.

GLOBAL MORMONS IN AMERICAN POLITICS

Many religious movements around the world have authoritarian tendencies, especially when in positions of minority power. Nevertheless, the rhetoric of most religious movements suggests a high regard for democracy and human rights.[65] As religious traditions struggle for rights, they seek the protections of liberalism. This pursuit of rights leads religious traditions to covet the natural rights that make up classic liberalism. Religion then serves to reinforce the legitimate power of liberalism and so supports the possibility of liberal democracy taking root. Religious traditions are often sources of democratic strength. This can be seen even in the less likely national settings of the Islamic world. The Republic of Iran, for example, is an Islamic nation. The Constitution of Iran, though, resembles those of secular Western nations. Passages deal with civil rights, minority rights, and a separation of powers in three distinct branches of government.[66] As a religion relates to rights and democratic governance, so too does it relate to the secular political context of the nation.

The Mormon Church survived early persecution by retreating from majority powers, and by exercising the basic rights afforded to any minority population in the American context. The Mormon Church throughout the world continues to depend on the formation of these basic rights for its survival in new cultures and governments. As it grows in membership on the global stage, it grows in significance within the American political setting as well. The relatively secure position the Church now holds in the United States allows for less focus on the politics of minority rights and more focus on the democratic possibilities of cultural identification with traditional American values. Although the formation and health of basic human rights worldwide is fundamental to the Church's ability to spread and grow, its role in American politics is not focused on issues of minority rights. The fact that the Church is now a global institution has indeed led to significant changes, such as in its position on race discussed earlier. The contemporary activism of Mormonism, however, is not focused on securing rights for minority populations. The Church of Jesus Christ of Latter-day Saints occupies a position in American cultural politics that is more likely to pursue democratic majority initiatives than it is to seek judicial protections from majority power. The Church is not often openly political, but when it is, the politics in question are mostly cultural issues in which the Church takes a traditional American majority stake. Thus, the Church mobilizes to fight the politics of homosexuality on the side of majority morality and not the rights of the minority.

Mormons in the United States are citizens with a significant political capacity. This capacity is activated only when church leaders give clear instructions on political matters, which they are reluctant to do.[67] The Church prefers to work behind the scenes to mobilize support through congregations. When exceptions are made and mobilization occurs openly, the matters involve political questions of cultural morality like gambling and gay marriage. In these struggles the Church seeks majoritarian power to resist the degradations of modern society. The global reach of the Church adds to its political presence in American politics. In terms of practical electoral politics, this is not an important change. Only those Mormons who live in the United States constitute any kind of electoral threat. The Church is growing much faster outside of American borders than within, but the place of the Church in the world has changed and it can no longer be considered a parochial or regionally contained religion. This may not translate into much increased domestic electoral power, but it does mean increased economic and international power. The Church is a financially powerful institution and its use of these resources will have a significant impact on elections and political mobilization for years to come. The more diverse makeup of the Church has not changed the focus of its international politics. The Church still primarily cares about those policies that best facilitate proselytizing around the world.

Religious traditions throughout the world personalize large forces and conflicts. Antimodernism is common where cultures feel threatened. Antiglobalization ebbs and flows with the incursion of global economics in the lives of different people. Anti-Americanism surges as cultures feel the pressures of assimilation that portend change. These responses to a globalizing world are filtered through a given religious tradition. Religion provides a personal context for that which is beyond a member's control.[68] From the point of view of American strategic interests, the particular ways in which these forces are personalized by religion matter. If a religious tradition provides a context that pits members against the cultural superpower of the United States, an enduring threat will exist. The Mormon Church is a positive force in the world for American interests because of how it personalizes the larger struggles of the world. The Church is not anti-American. The Church teaches of the special place for the United States in the Second Coming and as the future site of Zion. Globalization may present some immoral cultural effects, but it is hard to argue that the fastest-growing church in the world would come down too hard on the very force that provides for that growth. A more globalized world has meant a stronger and larger Mormon Church. The Church personalizes these larger forces with its vision of a future kingdom of heaven on earth and the special role of the Mormon Church in that future. Antimodernist impulses have given way in some cases and held strong in others. The following chapter takes a look at how the Church accepts economic modernity while maintaining hostility toward cultural modernity.

9

Mainstreaming Mormonism

SECULARIZING FORCES

Religious traditions face many challenges in maintaining membership and theological purity. As material goods and technology allow for higher standards of living, the secular world of progress can threaten the spiritual constants of religion. As education levels increase, the mythologies of religious belief are tested. When the sacred is either taken for granted or no longer taken at all, secularization has occurred.[1] Secularized religion is demystified by science and education. Its message is disenchanted and its place in society is diminished or replaced. For many years the European continent provided evidence of an inverse relationship between education and economic development, and belief in God. Political and sociological observers saw the rate of belief and church attendance decline dramatically over many centuries. This process became known commonly as secularization and, for some, became an inevitable result of a changing world. Religious belief and church membership, however, did not continue to disappear elsewhere and are still vital to humanity. There are certainly secularizing forces in contemporary civilization, but the role religion plays in the lives of people around the world remains integral to human existence. Religions push back against the secular world as the forces of spiritual belief contend with the secularizing forces of the nonreligious world.

Secular institutions regard religions as subpopulations that can be tolerated, but are separate from the structures of political power. The separation of church and state is an obvious necessity for peaceful existence from the point of view of secular logic. Religious leaders, though, tend to reject the idea that spiritual and political matters are separate.[2] From a religious point of view the separation is artificial and to accept it would be to capitulate to secularism itself. Secular logic provides for the existence of political power separate from spiritual belief. Minority religious traditions have no problem playing along with this separation since it helps preserve their survival, but in terms of theology, the separation is temporary. To accept a separation of church and state is to accept secularism and thus secular power as righteous, which no religious theology can accept. The Mormon tradition has faithfully upheld the American commitment to a separation of church and state. This commitment is possible, though, because of the eventual Second Coming that will sweep aside the temporary secular authority and replace it with a theocratic kingdom. The separation of church and state is a secularizing force in the practice of religions, but one that is tolerated for practical purposes and because of a theological belief in its eventual collapse.

Understanding how the pressures of secularization change the religious landscape is a challenging endeavor. The entire concept of secularization is largely contested and inherently problematic.[3] It can be an exercise in circular logic to identify ways secular society replaces sacred values as sacred values endure within secular society. One way to make sense of how secularizing forces might impact the Mormon Church is to look at religion as a changing institution in the context of society's complexity. As a civilization evolves from simplicity to complexity, religion becomes more about legitimating the prevalent form of society.[4] Rather than challenge the existing norms of marriage as the early Mormon Church did, contemporary Mormonism seeks to uphold all that is traditional about American marriage and culture in general. Another way to see secular forces at work is to assume that the spread of scientific thought somehow demonstrates the implausibility of religious belief. The Mormon Church as a body of believers does not embrace many of the mainstream understandings of history and science. Overall levels of education among Mormon faithful are rather high, though. The Church may be reluctant to accept certain scientific knowledge, but does not shy away from the accumulation of knowledge. The focus that liberalism puts on individualism can be challenging to religious traditions that draw spiritual strength and clarity from social understandings of existence.[5] Individual rights, and the political order based on individuals, pose a challenge to the theocratic shape of authority followed by most religious traditions. Mormonism has not had a difficult time reconciling individual rights with the Church as a body of worship since those individual rights helped secure the early survival of the Church. Nevertheless, secularizing forces put pressure on the Church, and the Church pushes back against these pressures.

One of the only things religious activists around the world have in common, aside from fervent belief, is a rejection of modern secularism.[6] The perceived threats secularism poses for religion as a function of society are genuine, but so are the strengths religious traditions can draw from in the belief of members. The Church of Jesus Christ of Latter-day Saints does not overtly condemn or battle with the secular world. It does take issue with many of the effects of contemporary secular culture, but rarely directly acknowledges secularism as the culprit. The Church resists secularism through constant growth in membership and through regular prophetic denunciations of certain secular beliefs. The success in membership growth has made the Mormon Church one of the least sensitive religious traditions to secularism in recent years. Furthermore, just as the sacred may dissipate in the face of secular pressures, so too may the secular become sacred.[7] Forces of secularization and sacralization are two sides of a metaphoric coin. Secular American politics requires some extra glue to hold its citizenry together. This social glue is often provided by religion. In the case of Mormon doctrine, the secular creations of the American founders are imbued with some sacred value. The belief that the founding documents are heavenly and touched by God is a clear example of the secular being made sacred. In fact, the Mormon Church is as effective at this sacralization as any other. The American political system is secular and pressures religion in the way secular powers do, but the Church is able to push back through the sacralization of that system's foundational documents.

Were secularization an inevitable process of the modern world, religion would cease to exist. Secularizing forces, however, are met with sacralizing forces and this mirrored pressure wards off the extremes of either.[8] What is considered sacred may shift and adapt over time. With the continual revelation at the Mormon Church's disposal, such shifts are not impossible to accommodate. Secularization is a historical process by which religion loses its sacred claims and urgency.[9] But this process is not inevitable and is met by the countervailing force of an institution like the Mormon Church creating new sacred space. The American experience with secularism has tended toward a neutrality concerning religion. This kind of secularism poses no threat to the Mormon faith. The kind of secularism the Church finds reason to battle with politically is that which seeks nonreligion as an explicit ideology. It is this form of secularism that the Church spends considerable time and energy combating and framing as evil. The Mormon Church turns to politics in an attempt to stem the tide of this explicit nonreligious impulse. Other religious traditions, often with different agendas, have launched into American political life, trying to halt the perceived decline that threatens traditional American religion, values, and culture.[10] Traditional American values are a big part of the Mormon way of life. Protecting those values means fighting against antireligious secularism, but not necessarily pushing much past it. The kind of neutral secularism that does not punish, favor, or establish any particular religion is not dangerous enough to prompt Mormon political action.

MODERNITY AND POSTMODERNITY

For many religious traditions, the forces of secularization have overmatched the sacred to the point that the world has lost its cultural and sacred bearings. Modernity and postmodernity account for this perceived loss, and religions fight against those features of modern and postmodern life that contribute to a continuing trend.[11] Of course, many features of the modern world facilitate religious and spiritual growth. Naturally these features are not highlighted by religious teachings against the modern world. It is the specific cultural developments that challenge an institutionalized norm of behavior that are evidence of modernity's corruption. Religious traditions as a whole are criticized at times for being out of step with modernity, but this is usually when they fail to place enough value on the role of individualism in the world. Modern secular culture revolves around the individual as the ultimate value, and when religions behave differently they are cited as somehow opposed to contemporary culture.[12] Modernism has more than one meaning, though. One form of modernism within religious traditions accepts the bureaucratic order and technological innovation of the modern world. Another more ideological modernism requires the acceptance of individualism and a relativist view of moral values.[13] Mormons are decidedly modern in the sense that they embrace the authority of the U.S. government and are not theologically opposed to technological advancement. But the Church is not modernist in the sense of accepting ultimate individuality and relativity.

Although the early Church experimented with communal systems of social and economic life, the contemporary Church of Jesus Christ of Latter-day Saints embraces capitalism and the economic features of modernity. On the macro level of capitalism, Mormons find value in its rewards for discipline and hard work. As an economic system it reinforces an ethic that is in keeping with the larger Mormon system of ethics. Plenty of theological reasoning exists to support other more communal economic systems, but the Church has become integrated in a globalized capitalist economic system and has thrived financially because of it. This translates to a political ideology that is in favor of free markets and less government intrusion in the economy. Culturally, however, Mormons fight against the effects of modernism. The materialism of modernity is fine with Mormons when it is part of the reward system for hard work and discipline. The kind of excess likely in a materially productive economic system is not necessarily morally acceptable to the Church, especially when that excess breeds idleness or substance abuse. The interpersonal norms of modernity also challenge Mormon sensibilities. Sexual behavior in the modern context is seen as promiscuous and sinful. On the whole, Mormons feel they are engaged in a culture war. They reject modern images of sexual immorality and condemn the content of television.[14]

The Mormon subculture has traveled a long way toward modernization, especially as it relates to economic matters and the acknowledgment of civil authority. Most religious traditions disdain features of the modern society, but some go further and reject the secular ideologies that undergird modern cultures.[15] The Church Jesus Christ of Latter-day Saints makes use of the features of modernity that aid in proselytizing and in the material rewards for diligent behavior. The Church has accommodated features of modernity in the same way it has accommodated and assimilated to traditional American society.[16] The Church now rejects and fights with political tools against those features of modernity for which it can harness the political power of traditional American values to fight.

WOMEN IN THE MORMON CHURCH

The understanding of gender in the Mormon faith has changed rather drastically since the early days of the Church, while gender roles have not. As was true for many other religious traditions, women were once viewed as objects to be owned. At times a man thought no more of taking a wife than of buying a cow.[17] These views may not have been as widespread as some reports contend, but the place of women in the world was not one of considerable political strength. Nevertheless, Mormons were at the forefront of attempting to change that political position. The territorial legislature of Utah gave women the right to vote in 1870. The right was revoked by the U.S. Congress.[18] Rather than disappear into meek obscurity, Mormon women asserted themselves in politics and enthusiastically joined the campaign for national woman suffrage.[19]

The fact that Mormons were willing to establish women's right to vote 50 years before the rest of the nation got around to the same task speaks to a more egalitarian church than an outsider might suspect. The voice of women within the Church and in the political sphere is important to the Mormon faith. That importance, though, does not always translate into political or church power. The Church's leadership is male at almost every level.[20] There is a particular balance between the equal rights and egalitarianism evident in the 1870 right to vote and the male-dominated organizational authority of the Church.

These Mormon male leaders have generally encouraged women to speak up and seek education, but the organization remains male dominated.[21] Again, this is not unlike the path of other religious traditions in the United States, but it is somewhat unique in its progressivism on political power as matched with the conservatism of church power. A majority of Mormon women are devoted, obedient, and uncritical of the Church.[22] A minority of Mormon women express frustration with the male-dominated structure of the Church. This frustration reached its high point in a feminist push during the 1980s. Although Mormon feminism still exists, it has receded significantly since its high point and speaks mostly from the fringes of the membership.[23] This is partially due to the mixed history of the Church with the feminist struggle. During the 1970s, many Mormon women openly fought against women's rights. This revealed an internal acceptance of the Church's teachings about proper gender roles, male-female relations, and the submission of women.[24] These teachings take a traditional view of family values and female roles in the family. As to the role of women in society at large, the Church of Jesus Christ of Latter-day Saints takes a traditionalist view of women as primarily bound to the household and family.[25] "Mothers are primarily responsible for the nurture of their children."[26] This is no small role as children are of the utmost importance to Mormon theology and cosmology. Nevertheless, it is a rather succinct description of a limited societal role for women to play.

Despite the limitations, the revival of feminism in the United States did leave its impact on the Mormon subculture. Contemporary Mormon women are vocal, articulate, and well educated.[27] The actual gender roles of contemporary Mormon families are not so different from non-Mormon gender roles. The official ecclesiastical position proclaimed by the Church does not regulate all gender behavior. The official patriarchal rhetoric, in fact, is countered by a high degree of egalitarianism between spouses.[28] Like many American religious traditions, gender roles are vaguely patriarchal, with much variance from household to household. Even the Church's official doctrine expresses the need for equality between spouses. "In these sacred responsibilities, fathers and mothers are obligated to help one another as equal partners."[29] For a traditional and conservative religious tradition, that is a clear position of egalitarianism within the household for women. Mormon women have used this doctrine to assert themselves in politics and, to some extent, in the Church.

The role of women in the Church of Jesus Christ of Latter-day Saints continues to evolve. In 1990 changes were made in the temple endowment ritual. Language was rewritten to reduce the rhetoric reinforcing female inferiority. Women are no longer required to promise to obey their husbands. In a more symbolic change, women are no longer required to wear face veils during certain parts of the ritual.[30] Such changes are indications of the flexibility of the Church on the interactions between male and females. The primary place for a woman in society is still seen as the role of motherhood. This part of the traditional theology has not changed. But as to the second clause of the Proclamation, much effort is put forth to secure egalitarian relations between fathers and mothers, which is another way of saying males and females in the context of Mormon rhetoric. The place of feminism within American religion is ever changing. The equality of women within religious traditions is shrouded in patriarchal legacies of church leadership, and efforts to increase the voice of women usually cause some backlash. The Mormon doctrine on equal relations is balanced by the Church's broader position in a culture war ideology. Feminism is often linked with the kind of misdirection that modern values bring to a traditional understanding of right and wrong. How culturally traditional churches deal with the presence of feminist influences is something to watch closely in the coming years.[31]

ASSIMILATION

Part of the changing gender roles of the Mormon faith is due to the slow and steady assimilation of the Mormon subculture to American cultural norms. Latter-day Saint history and doctrine is full of communitarian principles that are less prevalent today because church members have had to assimilate.[32] This process of assimilation continues today as members are taught to be upstanding citizens and identify with traditional American culture. The overarching story of Mormon assimilation is illustrated in the Church's adaptation to marriage norms by getting rid of polygamy and in several other doctrinal changes that have eased a merge with dominant American custom. This assimilation has been guided by church leaders as Mormonism has become more mainstream and more easily blends into the American mosaic. Mormon self-identity has changed dramatically from a separate subculture to a traditional American citizen. Mormonism has undergone a rapid transformation from a remote, disreputable sect to an easily recognized regional religion.[33] At early points in the Church's history, what it meant to be Mormon was distinctly outside of American norms. To be Mormon was to be un-American in a sense, and certainly excluded from the mainstream. Contemporary Mormon identity is intertwined with American identity. In the first half of the twentieth century, young Mormon scholars sought graduate study in prestigious universities outside of Utah.[34] These scholars are responsible for much of the early literature on Mormon communities and families, and are an example of a changing identity. A new and larger generation of Mormon scholars is a remarkable development and shows a religion that was once excluded and now identifies enough with the mainstream to measure society against the traditional majoritarian norms it represents.

The options for minority populations are limited. If assimilation does not occur, that population may face extermination or expulsion. Less drastic responses from the majority population include segregation, assimilation, and cultural pluralism.[35] Early Mormon history is full of the segregation necessary to provide space for unpopular doctrines like polygamy. This segregation provided only a short window of freedom before the majority population pushed in with military force. It is possible that the American culture could have responded with cultural pluralism. In other words, the nation could have simply accepted that Mormons had nontraditional marriages and did things their own way in Utah. This is rarely the route majority cultures take because assimilation is preferable. Dominant cultures nearly always choose assimilation above segregation or pluralism because it requires the minority population to adapt and requires very few adjustments from the majority. This was not completely involuntary on the part of the Mormon Church. It made decisions throughout the twentieth century that allowed the Church to move past basic assimilation and into mainstream traditional culture.

There remains a tension between the history of strife members suffered at the hands of the larger culture and the contemporary embrace of that majority culture. Persecution was stark and persistent enough to drive Mormons together into a very cohesive social group with a remarkably cohesive outlook on the world.[36] As Mormons retell and relive that history, they are reminded of their uniqueness and otherness. The institutional memory of being an unpopular minority is strong and leads to an urge to distrust government. If the Church cannot trust government, then it needs local political control. The assimilation required to become a state, though, pushed the Church into the world of national political institutions. In the long run, this step had greater assimilating effects than the legacy of isolation had in stimulating the impulse to withdraw from the mainstream. The Church was forced to assimilate to some extent, but continued to purposefully support a process of assimilation to transform the Church from ultimate outsider to defender of American propriety.

In an open letter in 1903, the Mormon Church told all foreign-born members to learn to speak English as soon as possible and to adapt to the American way of life.[37] From the earliest moments of the twentieth century, Mormon immigrants were taught to consider it a virtue to accept the dominant culture. They were to become loyal citizens and do good work. In stark contrast to immigrants from other cultures and traditions, Latter-ay Saint immigrants worked actively to adopt the English language and way of life. In other parts of the United States where Scandinavian and German Lutheran immigrants were common, the native language was maintained and held those communities together, but separate from American culture for generations.[38] Immigrant converts accepted American culture as a part of becoming Mormon. Conversion was more than religious; it was a cultural transition to a new societal and political tradition of Americanism. From an outsider's perspective, to be Mormon required assimilation to the American culture, and the Church fostered a strong sense of nationalism through this conversion.

An understanding of what American culture and the American way of life meant was guided by the Church, and so a particular version of Americanism was promulgated. The simplest and most clear-cut of American ways Mormon converts needed to accept was the American capitalist economy. Latter-day Saints adopted some of the ideas of early American Puritans in regard to wealth. Prosperity is seen as somehow an indication of successful spirituality and God's favor. For the Puritans of the early United States, this led to many new endeavors to test and prove one's success, and there is a similar spiritual-economic connection in Mormon daily life.[39] Latter-day Saint doctrine is flexible enough on economic life to support a variety of viewpoints. The early emphasis on the redistribution of wealth and economic communitarianism is gone. Where the Church once emphasized the good of the community and the need for communal property, it now emphasizes free-market capitalism and individual hard work leading to success. Based on survey research, most Mormons are broadly opposed to the redistribution of wealth.[40] For many American religious traditions, the early twentieth century was a time to reevaluate the effects of the capitalist economic system. The stratification of society as a result of the Industrial Revolution led to extreme concentrations of wealth and poverty. In many mainstream Protestant faiths, a new surge of social consciousness spurned a movement called the Social Gospel movement. This movement sought to bring a more equitable distribution of resources to bear on the United States through the teachings of Christ. It is interesting that at this moment, the Mormon Church was transitioning in the opposite direction and adopting economic individualism and requiring new immigrants to do the same. Of course, most of the Mormon faith was not located in the urban areas where the Social Gospel movement would be found. Industrialization was not as extreme in its distributive inequalities in Utah as in New York for instance.

The Mormon Church adapted its family structures and economic relations to better fit American culture. The contemporary Mormon faith is a relatively wealthy church membership. Its members easily fuse doctrine with the market-based economics of the twenty-first century. This is quite a contrast from the 1830s when Joseph Smith announced a system of property holding for the faithful. The system was officially designated the "United Order," but is more commonly referred retrospectively as "The Order of Enoch."[41] Members transferred their property to the Church in an act called "Consecration," and the subsequent distribution and holding of property was known as "Stewardship."[42] The Order of Enoch bound the community together and helped early Mormon communities weather the storm of economic uncertainty and persecution. There are many examples of similar impulses within religious movements where material security is at risk on a communal level. The property sharing was a practical solution to a tenuous existence, but also reflected Mormon theology. There are ample selections from Mormon sacred texts that discuss the communal spiritual foundation for such property restrictions.[43] This communal system represents a very different kind of politics from those found in the 1960s Mormon Church. President Ezra Taft Benson condemned the 1965 civil rights demonstrations in Utah as proof positive that the Communists were using the movement to promote Communist revolution. The era of the Benson presidency was marked by a great deal of conservatism and anti-communism. This era represents the complete transformation of the Church from the kind of fledgling religious movement that might dabble in communal property sharing to an established, mainstream part of the American religious tradition invested in the given historical majoritarian panic. Like other traditional Americans, the Church of Jesus Christ of Latter-day Saints was focused on rooting out the communists and their minority viewpoints.

CULTURAL EFFECTS ON THEOLOGY

The Mormon Church of the mid-1800s was an autonomous and isolated organization. Its journey is a long and slow retreat from this autonomy to an accommodation and acceptance of American culture.[44] On this journey the theology of Mormon belief changed along with the changing social realities. The Church focused much less on its hermetic aspects and much more on those parts of theology that align with mainstream Protestantism. In order to blend into the American culture, the Church partially abandoned those parts of the faith that highlighted a sense of magic and the spiritual evolution of the cosmos to the point that some observers comment that the Mormon trajectory might well lead to the tradition becoming indistinguishable from contemporary conservative Christianity[45]—indistinguishable, that is, from an outsider's perspective. From such a vantage point, it is difficult to assess the extent to which the Church's theology fundamentally changed and the extent to which the Church simply began to filter what others knew and saw about that theology. Substantial adaptations of doctrine have occurred and are most visible as proclamations from the president of the Church. A greater awareness of the image of the Church has grown alongside these doctrinal changes, allowing the Church to better control the impression Americans have of the Church overall.

Much of the early church's conflicts with American society stemmed from those theological innovations that distinguished the faith as a fringe movement. Theological tenets like polygamy, communalism, and political unity set the faith apart from mainstream Protestantism. Other religious movements, with their own theological innovations, existed alongside Mormonism. Utopian religious groups like the Oneida community and the Shakers formed in the same era as the Mormon faith.[46] All three traditions faced persecution and isolation as minority religions. One of these three had a rather short-lived experiment with utopian or idealized communal life. The other two maintained their commitment to such an existence. The results are evident in the state of these three churches today. The Church of Jesus Christ of Latter-day Saints adapted to the mainstream United States, abandoned those tenets that conflicted with broader society, and became a global religion while the other two movements receded into obscurity.[47] The theological adaptation did not take place over centuries or many decades. Rather, by the early twentieth century, the Mormon faith had shed the most controversial of its theological innovations.

One of the theological and structural changes the Church has made while becoming more mainstream is the practice of referring to its president as a prophet. Before 1955 just about every mention of the Church's leader used the term "president." The term "prophet" was reserved for Joseph Smith as the founding prophet of the faith and certain figures found in the Bible and the Book of Mormon.[48] Beginning with David O. McKay's presidency, church publications began referring to the president as the prophet. By the 1960s, the two words had become interchangeable. This is more than a rhetorical alteration. There is a strengthening, theologically speaking, of church leadership in the lives of its members. The Church's ability to adapt and alter doctrine is enhanced to the extent that the president of the Church has the spiritual authority granted to the title of prophet. This change also allows for faster and more organized mobilization on political issues. The practical organizational effects are that the Church remains unified and tightly managed from the top. The Church is authoritarian in its adherence to orders from the president. There are practical organizational benefits from a transition from terminology, but also theological benefits.

Beginning in the mid-1900s, the Mormon Church began to face something of a paradox in that it was moving into mainstream American culture while many aspects of that culture were morally reprehensible to the faith. Mainstreaming meant becoming a part of the traditional conservative values of American culture, but it also meant exposure to those aspects of modern American culture that were most unsavory to the Church. The active prophecy of the president from this point on would be of great value to a church that views itself in the midst of a culture war. Entering mainstream American culture meant entering into this ongoing battle between modern forces of moral decay and the traditional American way of life. The spiritual guidance needed in a time of cultural and spiritual struggle was found in the president through active revelation. With the Church able to clarify theological implications of individual aspects of modern society, the faith could more easily move into the mainstream without risking the theological drift that might occur without specific prophetic guidance. The authoritarian leadership provided by the president, however, illustrates another paradox in the Mormon Church. The fusion of structures of authoritarian control is in contrast with the need for active popular participation in the Church.[49] Religious traditions with a tight organizational control from the top usually have a more difficult time accommodating large numbers of diverse converts. The Mormon Church has been able to maintain tight organizational order, while vastly increasing membership. This is partially due to the fact that the larger structure of Mormon power is more flexible than active prophecy might indicate. The head of the Church is clearly defined and actively issues theological proclamations. The rest of the leadership structure, though, has been flexible enough to allow for some local variance on rituals. Alterations over time in the temple ritual highlight this central tension between authoritarian structure and an ever-growing membership base.[50]

STRATEGIC MAINSTREAMING

The practice of polygamy is gone. Communal property sharing is gone. The Church has redefined itself as a protector of the traditional family and traditional values, reversing the role it played as persecuted minority in the nineteenth century.[51] This redefinition has happened both from without and from within. External pressures forced the Church to adapt in order to survive. Many of the changes, though, were initiated from within the Mormon leadership with a conscious understanding of the benefits of mainstreaming. One symptom of the process of assimilation is the persistent Mormon concern with the Church's public image. Church leadership has established a powerful and competent public relations office.[52] Significant efforts on the part of the Church to have some impact on the perception of the faith overall have had mixed results. The stain of polygamy is a constant struggle for the public relations office. Nevertheless, the existence of a powerful public relations office is an indication of the awareness by church leaders of the importance of perception.

Part of the strategic considerations for the Church is where to fit in to the larger American religious context. The Church is constantly adjusting its position on the spectrum from fundamentalist to progressive. It is a church with specific sacred texts and established doctrines that allow for some legalistic attributes. In other words, there are parts of the faith that behave in the same way other conservative and fundamentalists sects behave. However, the Church of Jesus Christ of Latter-day Saints has an active prophet that adjusts church doctrine as needed, and this would indicate some level of progressivism at least in the sense that the Church can adapt and change to changing social conditions. In American history, legalistic Protestant traditions often opposed social policies on religious grounds until that opposition became socially and politically untenable.[53] Racial integration and interracial marriage were denounced regularly based on biblical scripture. Many of those same sects have since repudiated the biblical passages associated with the doctrinal reasons for opposition. The Mormon Church's ability to change its positions does not exclude it from consideration as a legalistic or fundamentalist tradition. In the context of American religion, the Mormon faith occupies a space that is alongside the more legalistic strains of other traditions. At least in the contemporary United States, Mormons have much more in common socially and politically with conservative evangelical Protestants than with Catholics or progressive Protestants. Two distinguishing characteristics allow the Church to occupy a somewhat less legalistic space, though. One is the active revelation of the prophet. This theological guidance adds an element of heavenly purpose to the changes the Church undergoes. The second characteristic is the tight organizational structure in comparison to Protestantism's tradition of dispersed authority. This organizational clarity provides an element of progressive capacity that decentralized Protestant authority cannot.

The most important strategic consideration for the public relations of the Church in recent years has been to secure the religious tradition as one of the United States' Christian traditions. There is quite a bit of debate among other religious sects as to the extent of Christianity evident in Mormon belief. Latter-day Saints are quite certain of the fact that they are Christian. Yet conservative and evangelical Christians reject these claims.[54] Mormon belief includes the Christian Bible, but Mormons also use additional scriptures that extend beyond that text. There are also some significant differences in the interpretation of doctrine and of Jesus Christ as a man and God. The Mormon faith is not alone in its precarious claims to Christianness. Many African and Asian independent churches that claim the label of Christian are problematic for similar reasons.[55] Some mixture of local myth or difference in the understanding of Jesus as part of the trinity puts these traditions on shaky ground for mainstream Christians. The Mormon cosmology is filled with theological understandings of heaven that run counter to the cosmology of mainstream American Christianity. Jesus plays a central role as a prophet in both Mormonism and mainstream Christianity, but his unity with God and the Holy Spirit is not a central tenet of the Mormon faith. The nuances of Mormon belief (like the potential for all men to become gods) are generally exposed as the most controversial pieces of evidence that it is not a Christian faith. Critics of Mormon claims to Christian status point out that Judaism and Islam both share Christian heritage and some belief in Jesus, but in their differences of belief about Jesus lie the most important differences of religious tradition.

Mormons believe their proper status is as traditional American Christians. To be characterized as anything else is not conducive to a greater inclusion in the mainstream United States. The Church is actively engaged in shaping public perception of Mormonism as a Christian tradition. To this end, the Church continuously makes stylistic changes to appear more Christian. The Church added and put more emphasis on the name "Jesus" in most of its public documents. In the discussion of contemporary cultural subjects, the Church has adopted the terminology of other Christian sects. In an effort to play down the cosmology that teaches that godhead status is possible for men, the Church changed the phrase "We can become Gods like our Heavenly Father," to "We can become like our Heavenly Father."[56] The concept of becoming godheads not only would be foreign to most Christian sects, but would be evidence of substantial theological separation. In 1982, the phrase "Another testament of Jesus Christ," was added as a subtitle to the Book of Mormon.[57] As an additional text that other Christians point to as evidence of separate tradition, the new title sought to connect more concretely with that part of the religion that shares Jesus as a central figure. Since 1995 when Gordon B. Hinckley took over as president, the Mormon Church has distanced itself from each aspect that causes other Christians to doubt its status as a Christian tradition.[58]

The motivation to appear Christian is connected to an overall desire to align with traditional American culture. The Mormon Church does not need to be considered Christian to survive as a religion in the world. It is the fastest-growing religion on the planet. As its history of persecution would suggest, the faith is substantially different from other Christian traditions. These differences have contributed to the overwhelming success of the Church in the world. The fact that such a successful faith would go to great lengths to be counted among the mainstream traditions of American culture is evidence of the conscious strategic efforts of the Church. A history of isolation, a contemporary disdain from other traditions, and a thriving membership on its own accord have not deterred the Church from pursuing this particular aspect of mainstreaming. In other words, efforts to appear Christian are not likely responses to exterior pressure to do so. There is no organizational need to adapt in this manner. It is a conscious and strategic decision on the part of the Church that it would best be represented culturally and theologically by aligning under the larger banner of American Christian traditions.

COSTS AND BENEFITS OF MAINSTREAMING

Assimilation leaves a minority culture with some positive and some negative experiences. There are the benefits of joining majority society and the security from persecution. There is also a loss of cultural distinction and uniqueness. Private and public spheres overlap and display the tension that results from giving up a cultural history to more effectively assimilate. Of course that assimilation leads to the growing success and ability to thrive for that newly assimilated culture. This new success, in turn, brings a different kind of pressure. The Mormon Church experienced the costs and benefits of assimilating into American culture. It subsequently has also experienced the effects of overwhelming success. International growth has dramatically affected the Church's programs throughout the world. The effects are simplification, standardization, correlation, and an extension of Church authority to all the people of the world.[59] Some of these effects work well with the Church's existing organizational structure. Standardized practices lead to more unified and effective control. Simplification resulting from widespread success is a potential hazard as it reduces theological nuance and clarity. Success also has costs in terms of what imperfections the spotlight of international attention can reveal. As the Mormon faith has grown, the knowledge of its history as a faith with quirks has grown. Interest in the practice of polygamy has been consistently greater than the knowledge of its discontinuation. Despite the Church's renunciation of the practice more than a hundred years ago, for many it is the first thing that comes to mind when thinking of Mormonism.

It is worth noting that the strategic costs or benefits that come from mainstreaming would not be viewed so instrumentally from within the Church. To suggest that the president makes active changes to theology to suit organizational goals of membership or acceptance is to ignore the theological role of a prophet. Members would be quick to point out that such leadership is guided by God and not by the external realities of human existence.

Nevertheless, religions do not exist in a void, and whether the Mormon religion has mainstreamed due to shrewd human leadership, heavenly guidance, or both, the effects in a contemporary setting are the same. From an outsider's perspective, the Mormon path seems less set by theologians than by businessmen and publicists.[60] The irony of mainstreaming for any religion is in how distinct the center theological tenets remains while softening the details enough for expansion. The more the Mormon Church mainstreams, the more it pulls away from the more rarified tenets of its original disposition. The more distance the Church puts between itself and these distinct tenets, the more likely it is that radical groups at the fringes of the religion grow. This creates a public relations problem for the Church because it is precisely these fringe groups that receive the kind of attention that detracts from the efforts of the Church to distance itself from the more controversial pieces of theology. These are the sects that receive television coverage and widespread media attention because of their novelty. This attention perpetuates the image of the Mormon Church as polygamist or radical in some other cultural way.

Defining the borders of Mormon tradition is no easy task. To some extent a faith's level of fundamentalism or progressivism can be determined by how inclusive or exclusive the faith intends to be. The Mormon tradition is steeped in a history of exclusion. Its membership was exclusive in the sense that it was a rare faith. Its overall position in American society was one of exclusion from the mainstream. The early years of the Church are all about exclusion. As the Church has entered the mainstream and continues to adapt to an image of mainstream Christianity, inclusivity has been the norm. An inclusive church has adapted to a global setting and new cultural surrounding. For other more fundamentalist Christians, any approach to salvation is suspect to the degree that it is inclusive. "The door to heaven is precious in exact proportion to its narrowness."[61] It is difficult to sum up the contemporary state of Mormon exclusion and inclusion. It remains a faith with a relatively high barrier to entry due to the financial and temporal demands it puts on members. The theological tradition is distinct enough to cause controversy from conservative Christian traditions. And yet the expansion worldwide and the efforts to appear more mainstream point to a rather high level of inclusion. The Church's current dilemma is in deciding how inclusive to be with such a successful organizational trend in motion. With 13 million members worldwide, the Church of Jesus Christ of Latter-day Saints is the fourth-largest church in the United States. It is the richest per capita and fastest-growing faith worldwide.[62] Cultural integration is evidenced in the many Mormon public figures. Mitt Romney, Harry Reid, Glenn Beck, and Stephanie Meyer[63] are all prominent political and cultural figures in the United States. A mainstreamed church provides for more and more inclusion in the majority culture, but also presents some challenges to a faith long defined by exclusivity.

MAINSTREAM MORMONS IN AMERICAN POLITICS

When religious traditions assimilate into the political process in a nonrevolutionary way they often use political parties or harness political support to back particular candidates.[64] The Mormon Church has used both of these processes early in the life of the tradition, but receded from politics for a few decades. Much like the fundamentalist and conservative sects of Protestantism withdrew from the political process from about 1920 to the 1980s, so too did the Mormon Church steer clear of concerted political endeavors. Instead, the Church slowly adapted from minority to majority cultural identity and now has the political power of traditional American values to back up its policy interests. Compromise with secular political order tends to lead to the formation of extremist splinter groups.[65] While there are splinter Mormon sects that receive a fair amount of attention, these groups are rather inconsequential on the stage of American politics.

Religion plays a significant political role in the United States by sustaining an individualistic political culture and the government institutions that rest on that culture.[66] This is not usually accomplished through active engagement in politics but by offering a source of morality and community. For most of the twentieth century, the Mormon Church stayed out of the daily politics of the nation but became one of the cultural forces that strengthen the government and political system overall. The Church reconstructed its society on the basis of American patriotism and conventional morals. Mormons became respectable, while remaining removed from society.[67] The position held in society and politics by the Church is a powerful position. There is a strong antimodern cultural sentiment to tap into and from which the Church can use classic restoration rhetoric. This is the kind of rhetoric that harnesses a sentimental urge in Americans to restore honor, glory, and moral fiber to a deteriorating society. The Mormon Church presents an image of a population that is clean, industrious, and wealthy. This image gives the Church the credibility to back up visions of restoration. Throughout American political history the rhetoric of restoration has been a powerful political tool. Often, the rhetoric masks some new political need by wrapping it in the language of restoration and returning to something already proven and accepted.

This powerful position gives rise to many predictions of the future power of the Mormon Church in American politics. Author Harold Bloom made the provocative observation that Mormon political and financial power will soon be strong enough to disregard the American mainstream and secure perpetual Republican occupation of the White House.[68] The effect on presidential politics is certain to be a boon for the Republican Party in the near future, but the rest of this comment misses the evolutionary truths of contemporary Mormonism. The idea that the Church could one day be powerful enough to ignore the mainstream is misleading since a primary reason for its rise in political and cultural power is the fact that the Church has become part of the mainstream United States. The place of Mormonism in American politics is at a bit of a crossroads, however, as the power of the Church becomes more evident to the citizens of the nation. Like Catholics and black Americans, Mormons have in the past been judged a threat to society.[69] This led to exclusion and violence. The Mormon Church receded from active political action and mainstreamed. As it reenters the political world in a new, more powerful way in the twenty-first century, it remains to be seen how the average citizen will judge the contemporary Mormon faith: as friend or foe.

As for Mormon citizens themselves, they express relatively high levels of political efficacy.[70] This indicator, common in political science, measures how much a citizen thinks his or her voice matters in the scheme of political power. Mormons are relatively convinced that they can make a difference in the political world. The Church of Jesus Christ of Latter-day Saints is highly organized and thriving. Its members are engaged in local, state, and national politics all across the country.[71] This is no accident or indirect result of some cultural phenomenon. Church leaders encourage involvement in politics and foster a setting where conservative values and politics are a way of life.[72] This surge into political action mirrors that of the Christian Right and is evidence of a larger trend in American politics. In much of the twentieth century, secular institutional politics was the center of ambitious drive and focus while religion was passive and withdrawn. Since the 1980s this equation has changed. Political institutions seem to breed apathy while religion provides the dynamism to shake people from apathy and help them see the political problems of the world in new ways.[73]

Religious traditions that were once on the edges of society and persecuted often find reason to resent the majority political structures of their nation. The leaders of these religions are able to exploit this resentment and translate it into political empowerment. Once this translation is complete, the leaders and constituents sense their capacity for impacting the political system.[74] The Mormon religion did not exactly follow this typical route. Rather than focus on the politics of resentment, the Church assimilated and draws strength from the American culture. Some of this has to do with the theological connection to the nation and to the founding documents. The prophetic future of the Church is to save the nation from destruction and pave the way for the kingdom of heaven on earth. This vision is more politically powerful than that of resentment. Religious Americans will probably continue to focus their political energies on policy-specific efforts.[75] Mormons have picked their political battles carefully and on an issue-by-issue basis. This suits the theological needs of the Church, but is also typical of religious sects that do not have a conclusive enough national political connection to work from an ideological perspective. The influence of the Church is somewhat constrained because it is not able to form the kind of political coalitions that would facilitate actions larger than the occasional policy rebuttal.[76] The most natural political coalitions would appear to be their natural allies in the Christian right, but there is a division between the Mormon Church and the evangelicals in the United States.

This division that prevents the Church from forming larger political alliances stems from the argument of whether or not Mormons are Christians. Although the two traditions now occupy the same space on the ideological spectrum of American politics, there are some fairly big cultural differences aside from the Christian status debate. One essential difference is the nature of human existence. The Mormon tradition teaches that human nature is good and has a spark of eternal goodness buried within. Evangelical and conservative Christians tend to focus on the inherent sinfulness of humans and are less optimistic that humanity has any intrinsic worth aside from being God's creation. Both traditions use the language of nostalgia and restoration. In this regard, the Mormon Church co-opted most of this rhetoric from the long tradition of Protestantism. The future prophetic understanding of Zion's restoration in the United States, though, is a fairly substantial difference from the evangelical theology of humanity's descent into Armageddon. Thus while both traditions fit in with contemporary conservative ideology, the implications for the future political order are different.

Mormon political ideology is not especially explicit or established. As with many other traditions, the political implications of religious philosophy are not always consistent. The Church has a serious commitment to some level of theocratic governance in contemporary society, and a great deal to the future kingdom of heaven. It has a history of withdrawing from mainstream culture and existing in a separate sphere of authority. These theocratic and separatist urges are counterbalanced by democratic and patriotic motives. There is a great deal of egalitarianism evident in Mormon households and in local congregations. Mormons feel a strong sense of efficacy and are taught to be patriotic and loyal citizens. These countervailing forces are both equally grounded in Mormon doctrine.[77] Theocracy is almost the perfect opposite to democracy. Separatism is nearly the mirror concept for active citizenship. Somewhere in this paradox, Mormonism offers an alternative to the pragmatic idea of popular sovereignty as balanced against constant moral authority. Revelations that come through the president locate power in the hands of individuals, but leave the authority with God. Average citizens are active in their agency, but are inevitably accountable.[78] Actors are accountable not just on the individual level in their soul's reflection to God, but in the eventual theocratic kingdom. The sovereignty rests with the people, but the actions of the political system overall will be judged and potentially fall short. When this happens the Church will be there to rescue the nation.

These tensions are joined by the place of Mormon theology in the American political spectrum. Parts of the mainstream church rest easily in the political conservatism of most Mormons. There is, however, a social idealism that rests at the core of Mormon prophecy that Zion will rest in the United States and that somehow the nation is a part of that prophecy with its heavenly inspired founding documents. This tension between conservatism and idealism is heightened when considering what culture the Church seeks to conserve. It is certainly not the political order of the nineteenth century that persecuted members. It is some particular elements of American society that the Church supports in terms of how those values mesh with theological truths. As the Church aligns itself with the conservative mainstream United States, it is pulled in the other direction by a sense of group particularism.[79] The Church is special and its members are special. The special status means some level of superiority. Democratic values do not have much room for superiority. Mormons are superior in the prophetic sense. They are loyal citizens who will rise up to meet the challenges the nation will one day face.

When looking at Mormon voters from an electoral point of view, the social group identity has much to do with candidate choice. What it means to be a Mormon American is informed by a mix of historical development and contemporary Church guidance. As this identity has been threatened from different directions, the social identity has responded and this has translated into more or less political action. The contemporary threats to Mormon social identity are the perceived threats of moral degradation evident in modern culture, and more practically, those Christian churches that make it their missions to expose certain aspects of the Mormon faith. The moral threat pushes Mormon social identity into the realm of social conservatism. What it means to be a Mormon American is largely informed by the social issues of the day: gay marriage, drugs, and abortion. The threat from conservative Christianity informs the social identity of Mormons in their efforts to appear more Christian and validate their status as a Christian tradition. This is a rather defensive response to a divisive issue that prevents larger political coalitions.

The mainstreaming trend of the Mormon Church may be an indication that eventually the Mormon faith could be coalition partners with the Religious Right. This seems unlikely in the present cultural context as the exclusionary politics of conservative Protestantism are not likely to withdraw severe claims of distinct otherness from the Mormon Church. Some of this political possibility lies in how much further the Mormon Church is willing to accommodate and adapt the controversial pieces of theology. The rest lies in the larger electoral successes of the Mormon electorate. Continued increases in this electoral power may convince conservative Protestants that the theological differences are not as important as the shared cultural and political values. This confluence of events is unlikely in the near future. Mormonism was seen by Protestantism as a threat from day one. It is unlikely that conservative Protestant sects, who are in direct competition for church membership with the Mormon Church, are soon to warm to the idea of co-operation. Residual hostility remains. Evangelical bookstores continue to feature exposés of the "Mormon Cult."[80] Internal cleavages, such as the one between Mormonism and conservative Protestantism, have made a Protestant political majority no longer possible in American politics. A transdenominational Judeo-Christian coalition that includes Catholics, Jews, Protestants, and Mormons seems unlikely in the next few decades of American politics.[81] A grand coalition may be out of reach, but certain marriages of convenience might work for particular issues. Temporary coalitions are likely in this sense as religions continue to pour support into interest groups that tackle individual social concerns.

A modern, global, mainstreamed Mormon Church is a part of the American political system that is likely to increase in power. How it will use this power is broadly guided by the prophetic future the Church's theology portends. Mormons believe one day the Constitution will hang by a thread and the Church of Jesus Christ of Latter-day Saints will step forth and save it from destruction.[82] This is not a new revelation. This future was predicted by Joseph Smith and later by Brigham Young. In 1988, President Benson reminded the Church of this prediction. This is an important piece of Mormon theology as it has continued through all phases of the Church's history. Many of the proclamations of Joseph Smith and Brigham Young are dismissed by contemporary Mormons as relics of the early faith. In other words, the active revelation of prophecy means observers should not put too much stock in or overemphasize things Smith or Young said. This doctrine of the Church saving the nation, though, is constant. The place of Mormons in American politics is justified succinctly with this document. While some religious traditions see political maneuvering as somehow dabbling in the sordid world of humanity's machinations, the Mormon Church sees eminent value in placing fellow Mormons near the center of power. This is how to best be in position to one day save the Constitution from destruction.

MAINSTREAM MORMON CANDIDATES

The Mormon faith has many strengths for Mormon candidates to draw on and many weaknesses that can be exposed. Contemporary candidates, like Mitt Romney, are not taking advantage of the potential strengths because the Mormon faith in general has a memory of persecution. The Church believes in theocracy. This exposes a candidate to the same kind of challenges faced by Catholic candidates in the mid-twentieth century. The role of the president is more active in the Mormon Church than that of the pope in the Catholic Church. This further disadvantages a candidate in connection to competing moral authority. However, this weakness is easily turned around as strength. Unlike the Catholic tradition, Mormonism sees a connection between God and the Constitution. This connection is rarely discussed by Mormon politicians who, at least at this point in American politics, would rather avoid discussing their religion so as to sidestep the more controversial theological pieces. Every religion has some passages from sacred texts that can appear controversial. The Mormon tradition is no more vulnerable in this sense than any other. The potential dangers of having a prophet with influence over a U.S. president can be ameliorated by the theological connection to the Constitution the U.S. president swears to protect. That oath takes on a new meaning in this light, and the threat of competing authority is lessened due to the shared goals of preserving the Constitution. Not only does the tradition have the rescue of the Constitution in its prophecy, the active teaching of the Church is that members should be good, loyal, patriotic citizens. This is a much more overt religious teaching as it relates to existing structures of government than almost any other in the world. Conservative Protestantism is rife with patriotism, but falls short of endorsing anything specific about the constitutional institutions of government.

The Mormon Church is a highly social organization where new members are warmly welcomed. The veneer of the religion is rather American in the classic majority vision of what it means to be American. The Church advocates traditional values, family togetherness, and healthy lifestyles. The Church openly discourages alcohol consumption, smoking, and illicit sex. It is one of society's most appealing bastions of conservativism.[83] These positions are not merely suggested norms for local congregations to interpret as they choose. The Church is tightly organized and these norms are widespread and consistent among the Mormon population. This is a position of strength for a candidate wishing to exhibit some strength of character and a connection to moral religious tradition. The Church is part of the mainstream conservative United States. However, it also has the benefits of a history full of minority status and persecution. It is rare for a candidate to be able to draw on majoritarian traditional values in a religion with high per capita income and still draw from a history of persecution. This is a powerful combination of cultural knowledge to harness in modern political rhetoric. A Mormon candidate should be able to convey the sense of moral outrage common to majority sensibilities, and add to that the sense of moral outrage common to minority populations that have been persecuted by majority values. Keeping these rhetorical tools separate poses some challenge, but it is certainly better as a candidate to have both available.

10

The Saints Go Marching On: A Conclusion

Scholarship on Mormons in politics is limited. There are several potential areas for additional scholarship. Chapter 2 examined the development of Mormonism through the leadership of a living prophet. The living prophet aspect of Mormon doctrine is one of the most thought-provoking aspects of Mormons in American politics. There is the omnipresent possibility that an LDS president can receive revelations that pertain to political behavior and make theologically premised requests of Mormons in positions of political power. The theoretical questions of the prophet's influence over the chief executive have become a matter of practical and prudent inquiry with Mitt Romney becoming the first Mormon to successfully earn a presidential nomination from a major party. Strategically, empirically, and rhetorically, there is little evidence to support the notion that a Mormon prophet would meddle in national political affairs. Still, little is known about the nature of relations between LDS leaders and Mormon members of government. Related scholarship would benefit from systematic research on political interaction between prominent members of government who are Mormon and the Mormon religious leadership. This will be difficult given the relatively closed nature of Mormon life and the reluctance of Mormon elites to publicly share details of private meetings and deliberations. Previous literature has focused on voting patterns of Mormon members of Congress to test whether Mormon political behavior was unique compared to other members of Congress. Examination of both inputs and outputs in regard to the relationship of Mormonism and political behavior would add important empirical data to the largely theoretical debate over the influence of the Mormon hierarchy in American politics.

Chapter 3 examined the legacy of Mormon persecution and the gradual development of a unique Mormon subculture centered in Salt Lake City. Mormons can be understood as a challenge to a predominantly Christian nation who claims to protect religious freedom because of their atypical Christian views and unique religious practices. The limited application of the First Amendment to Mormons throughout American history serves as a vivid reminder that the United States' tradition of religious freedom is an imperfect work in progress. Intolerance toward religious minority groups in the United States, such as Mormons, suggests that greater tolerance, politically and socially, would best serve the United States' democratic tradition moving forward. This would be most applicable to contemporary Muslims and atheists, who are the two religious groups in the twenty-first century who create more discomfort in the American electorate than Mormons. Related scholarship would benefit from comparative analysis of Mormon persecution in the nineteenth century to American attitudes and treatment of Muslims in the twenty-first century. Religious studies scholarship has drawn parallels between the beliefs and practices of these two religions. Explicit focus on cultural understandings of each religion and related political responses would help measure continuity and change in regard the United States' interaction with minority faiths viewed by society as a whole as nationally threatening.

Chapter 4 examined the rise of Mormons in federal politics. The most prolific Mormon in politics is Mitt Romney. Romney faced a political environment toward Mormons that resembles what his father faced as a presidential candidate in 1967. Nearly 20 percent of Americans would not vote for a well-qualified presidential candidate who was Mormon. Identifying what exactly about Mormons causes one in five Americans to withhold their support would be a highly valuable area for further research. Previous studies have found that lack of education is one variable that helps to explain opposition to Mormons in politics. Explicit focus on identifying other relevant explanatory variables would be helpful in understanding this phenomenon.

Chapter 5 examined the political thought of Mormons. Mormon theological and political attitudes are not monolithic, but do provide extensive coherence in several policy areas. The deeper theological underpinnings of the American Mormon worldview is likely to have political repercussions. Relevant scholarship would benefit from greater examination of Mormon political rhetoric and the use of general political appeals that hold specific theological significance for Mormons. For example, when Orrin Hatch, the longtime Utah senator, speaks of the Constitution hanging by a thread, this is an important reference to Mormon prophecies, not a secular statement of overreaching government. Explicit focus on the degree and nature of blending spiritual and political appeals in the Mormon political tradition would be beneficial. Furthermore, Democratic Mormons have been largely ignored in scholarly and popular accounts of contemporary Mormons in politics. Reconciling this oversight would help to provide a richer and more accurate understanding of Mormons in politics, while exploring the uneasy relationship Mormon liberals have had with the Mormon religion since the strong conservative shift within Mormonism since the 1950s.

Chapter 6 examined Mormon opposition to the legal recognition of same-sex marriage at the state and federal levels of government. The issue of same-sex marriage helps to illuminate the belief among Mormons that they are engaged in a cultural war against the degradation of traditional values. The threats of vigilante justice and state-sponsored persecutions have been replaced by a deteriorating moral fabric of American culture. Although the Mormon Church claims to be relatively apolitical, they have not been when it comes to key battles in this culture war, such as Proposition 8 in California. Relevant scholarship would benefit from greater examination of the perceived risks and rewards for the Mormon Church in becoming a major political player in opposing same-sex marriage. Rights for gay, lesbian, bisexual, and transgender Americans are quickly becoming a prominent civil rights issue in the United States. The Mormon Church is well aware of this and currently believes that the marriage battle is one worth fighting. Explicit focus on the extent to which the Mormon Church is willing to sacrifice potential support, religious, social, or political, would be beneficial. The situation in Utah and other Mormon communities would become very interesting if the federal status of marriage changes and marriage becomes a matter of federal protection. The Mormon Church has recently begun to distinguish their opposition to same-sex marriage from other rights gays and lesbians are pursuing, such as equality in housing and the workplace. An important question is whether the LDS Church will continue to maintain a hard line on marriage or continue to reshape their position as they have in shifting from blanket opposition to homosexuality to targeted opposition of same-sex marriage.

Chapter 7 examined Mormon patriotism. Mormons have engaged in party politics in a highly pragmatic and utilitarian fashion. There is little scholarship explicitly examining the causes and consequences related to the widespread support of the Republican Party among Mormons. Mormons gradually shifted from a valuable swing vote in the nineteenth century to a cornerstone of the Republican base. Greater examination of the political benefits and drawbacks for Mormons, given their current electoral position, would be a valuable area of study. Early LDS leaders were very conscious of the political positioning of the Mormon community. Little is known about the thoughts of modern LDS leaders in regard to this issue. Furthermore, liberal Mormons are becoming an increasingly isolated minority. Greater examination of the religious implications for liberal Mormons holding liberal political beliefs would be highly valuable in understanding ways in which political attitudes can create religious tensions within a homogenous American Mormon community.

Chapter 8 examined the global expansion of Mormonism and Mormon religious identity. Over 90 percent of Mormons in the United States are Anglo-Saxon. Black Mormons in the United States are in a unique position as the only group historically excluded from priesthood and temple worship. Missionary efforts have gradually increased among black Americans, and conversion rates have grown accordingly since the priesthood was desegregated in 1978. There has been little research on African American Mormons. Previous studies have found that black Mormon Americans are ideologically closer to white Mormons than to black Americans at large. Explicit focus on the relationship of black Mormons within the larger community of Mormonism would be beneficial as would research on the social and theological impact of immigration from Central and South America on Mormon communities in the Mountain West.

Chapter 9 examined the relationship between Mormonism and the mainstream United States. Mormons established the right for women to vote decades before political equality was established nationally. The Mormon Church is more egalitarian than most outsiders suspect, but this has not translated into theological or political power. The majority of Mormon women are devoted, obedient, and uncritical of the Mormon Church. A minority of Mormon women express frustration with the male-dominated structure of the Church. This frustration reached its high point during the feminist movement of the 1970s and 1980s. Relevant scholarship would benefit from greater examination of the lack of female Mormon politicians at the national level and at the state level in Utah. Mormon gender roles appear to be significantly limiting opportunities for Mormon women to embark in public service. Explicit focus on the connection of the patriarchal tradition of Mormonism to economic, social, and political life would be particularly valuable.

The study of Mormons in American politics is a fascinating and timely subject, but there is little comprehensive scholarship on Mormons in American politics generally, and undertaken by non-Mormon political scientists, in particular. This book was an effort to help change this. The 2012 presidential election attests to the tremendous progress Mormonism has made from its origins as a persecuted religious minority group to having one of its own representing a national party and competing for the most powerful political office in the world. Mormons will continue to be an increasingly prominent political, economic, and social force in the United States into the foreseeable future. Non-Mormons would be well served by learning more about this unique and powerful element of American Society.

Notes

CHAPTER 2

1. Ostling and Ostling 1999, xvii.
2. Bushman 2008, 9.
3. Givens 2007, 202.
4. Bushman 2008, 17.
5. Bushman 2005, 41.
6. Exodus 28:30.
7. Bushman 2005, 61.
8. Ibid., 70–71.
9. Ibid., 78.
10. Ibid., 82.
11. Ibid., 84.
12. Ibid., 107.
13. Ibid., 101–2.
14. Ibid., 102.
15. Ibid., 104.
16. Doctrine and Covenants, 1:30.
17. Bushman 2008, 25.
18. Interview with Michael Coe (May 2006).
19. Bushman 2005, 98.
20. Interview with Terryl Givens (June 2006).
21. Olson 2007, 28.
22. Doctrine and Covenants, 21:1.
23. Ibid., 21:2.
24. Bushman 2008, 29.
25. Interview with Gordon Hinckley (January 2007).
26. Interview with Terryl Givens (June 2006).
27. Interview with Marlin Jensen (March 2006).
28. Interview with Michael Coe (May 2006).
29. Ibid.

30. Interview with Terryl Givens (June 2006).
31. Interview with Michael Coe (May 2006).
32. Interview with Daniel Peterson (February 2006).
33. Ibid.
34. Interview with Kathleen Flake (April 2006).
35. Interview with Jon Butler (May 2006).
36. Interview with Sarah Gordon (April 2006).
37. Interview with Jon Butler (May 2006).
38. Interview with Jeffrey Holland (March 2006).
39. Bushman 2005, 143.
40. Bushman 2008, 4.
41. Ibid., 5.
42. Interview with Terryl Givens (June 2006).
43. Ostling and Ostling 1999, xix.
44. Interview with Terryl Givens (June 2006).
45. Bushman 2008, 27.
46. Interview with Kathleen Flake (April 2006).
47. Interview with Gordon Hinckley (January 2007).
48. Interview with Terryl Givens (June 2006).
49. Interview with Kathleen Flake (April 2006).
50. Interview with Terryl Givens (June 2006).
51. Nephi 2:14–27.
52. Bushman 2008, 6.
53. Doctrine and Covenants, 130:22.
54. Bushman 2008, 7.
55. Jensen 2000, 8.
56. Ephesians 5:22–23.
57. Bushman 2008, 61.
58. Interview with Gordon Hinckley (January 2007).
59. Interview with Marlin Jensen (March 2006).
60. Interview with Jon Butler (May 2006).
61. Bushman 2008, 30.
62. Interview with Greg Prince (June 2006).
63. Interview with Greg Prince (June 2006).
64. Cowan 2000, 20–22.
65. Top 2000, 44.
66. Jensen 2000, 4.
67. Black, Bott, Darling, and Woods 2000, vii.
68. Jensen 2000, 4.
69. Ostling and Ostling 1999, xix.
70. Interview with Greg Prince (June 2006).
71. Ostling and Ostling 1999, 118.
72. Hinkle 2008, 6–7.
73. Ibid., 258.
74. Ibid., 50.
75. Doctrine and Covenants, 107:14.
76. Ibid., 268.

77. Ibid., 54.
78. Ibid., 269.

CHAPTER 3

1. Interview with Terryl Givens (June 2006).
2. Interview with Sarah Gordon (April 2006).
3. Bushman 2008, 42.
4. Givens 2007, 205.
5. Interview with Terryl Givens (June 2006).
6. Ibid.
7. Interview with Jon Butler (May 2006).
8. Bushman 2005, 122–26.
9. Ibid., 144.
10. Ibid., 191.
11. Ibid., 163–65.
12. Ibid., 217.
13. Ibid., 116.
14. Ibid., 178–79.
15. Ibid., 222.
16. Ibid., 223.
17. Ibid., 235.
18. Ibid., 226.
19. Ibid., 226.
20. Ibid., 235.
21. Ibid., 236–37.
22. Ibid., 244–47.
23. Ibid., 324–25.
24. Ibid., 331.
25. Ibid., 332.
26. Ibid., 170.
27. Ibid., 327.
28. Interview with Terryl Givens (June 2006).
29. Bushman 2008, 342.
30. Ibid., 358.
31. Ibid., 349.
32. Ibid., 352.
33. Ibid., 364.
34. Hartley 2001, 7.
35. Bushman 2008, 365.
36. Ibid., 369.
37. Ibid., 391–93.
38. Ibid., 415.
39. Flanders 1970, 27.
40. Bushman 2008, 501.
41. Ibid., 449–50.

42. Ibid., 511.
43. Ibid., 437.
44. Ibid., 491.
45. Ibid., 493.
46. Ibid., 473.
47. Ibid., 534–35.
48. Ibid., 528.
49. Ibid., 544.
50. Ibid., 549–50.
51. Ibid., 560.
52. Ibid., 552.
53. Bushman 1999, 37–41.
54. Ibid., 44.
55. Ibid., 46.
56. Ibid., 47–50.
57. Ibid., 51–52.
58. Phillips 1999, 53.
59. Bushman 1999, 53.
60. Phillips 1999, 73.
61. Bushman 1999, 54.
62. Ibid., 55.
63. Ibid., 55.
64. Ibid., 56–57.
65. Interview with Sarah Gordon (April 2006).
66. Bushman 2008, 442.
67. Ibid., 443.
68. Ibid., 439.
69. Ibid., 440.
70. Interview with Sarah Gordon (April 2006).
71. Elisha 2002, 45.
72. Ibid., 46.
73. Interview with Sarah Gordon (April 2006).
74. Elisha 2002, 47.
75. Interview with Jon Butler (May 2006).
76. Interview with Sarah Gordon (April 2006).
77. Ibid.
78. Interview with Kathleen Flake (April 2006).
79. Interview with Sarah Gordon (April 2006).
80. Jensen 2000, 3.
81. Hauss 1984, 440.
82. Bushman 2008, 48.
83. Interview with Kathleen Flake (April 2006).
84. Bushman 1999, 100.
85. Ibid., 96.
86. Givens 2007, 203.
87. Bushman 2008, 36.
88. Interview with Greg Prince (June 2006).

89. See the cover and title story of *Newsweek*, June 6–13, 2011.
90. Bushman 2008, 2.
91. Pew Research Center Forum 2011b, 10.
92. Bushman 2008, 3.
93. Interview with Gordon Hinckley (January 2007).
94. Pew Research Center Forum 2011b, 9.
95. Ibid., 12.
96. Ibid., 12.
97. Interview with Kathleen Flake (April 2006).
98. Pew Research Center Forum 2011b, 16.
99. Bushman 1999, 92.
100. Pew Research Center Forum 2011b, 12.
101. Ferrin, 2012.
102. Pew Research Center Forum 2011b, 17

CHAPTER 4

1. Garr 2009, 49.
2. Ibid.
3. Poll 1968, 17.
4. Garr 2009, 51.
5. Hickman 1968, 27.
6. Ibid., 25.
7. Ibid., 23.
8. Ibid., 25–26.
9. Garr 2009, 51.
10. Poll 1968, 20.
11. Ibid., 19.
12. Ibid., 21.
13. Ibid., 21.
14. Ibid., 18.
15. Mikkelsen 1974, 26–27.
16. Cann 2009, 112–13.
17. Ibid., 113.
18. Flake 2004, 4.
19. Ibid., 36.
20. Flake 2004, 40.
21. Ibid., 41.
22. Ibid., 22.
23. Ibid., 24.
24. Ibid., 44.
25. Ibid., 26.
26. Ibid., 35.
27. Ibid., 5.
28. Ibid., 46.
29. Event Transcript of Richard Bushman (May 2007).

30. Flake 2004, 46.

31. Ibid., 90.

32. Ibid., 8–10.

33. Interview with Kathleen Flake (April 2006).

34. Ibid.

35. King and King 2000, 21.

36. Ibid.

37. Ibid., 22.

38. Ibid., 3–4.

39. Ibid., 7.

40. Ibid., 11.

41. Ibid., 13.

42. Ibid., 13–14.

43. Ibid., 15.

44. Ibid., 18–19.

45. Ibid., 7.

46. Ibid., 3.

47. Ibid., 20.

48. Pew Research Center Forum 2011a.

49. Walsh, 2005, 3.

50. Ibid., 5.

51. Ibid., 3–4.

52. Cann 2009, 115.

53. Ibid., 115.

54. Ibid., 117.

55. Kranish and Paulson 2007, 1.

56. For example, Apostle Delbert Stapley wrote Romney a letter at the Governor's Mansion expressing personal concern for Romney's civil rights views. Stapley referred Romney to "The Status of the Negro" in the Teachings of the Prophet of Joseph Smith and "The Prophet's Views on Abolition" in History of the Church. Stapley cited the demise of three presidents "who were very active in the Negro cause" and acted "contrary to the teachings of the Prophet Joseph Smith." God "placed the curse upon the Negro, which denied him the Priesthood; therefore, it was the Lord's responsibility—not man's—to change His decision." See Stapley (1964).

57. Swidley and Paulson 2007, 2.

58. Ibid., 8.

59. LeBlanc 2007, 4.

60. Swidley and Ebbert 2007, 6.

61. Ibid., 9.

62. Medhurst 2009, 196.

63. Ibid., 196.

64. Saslow 2007, 2.

65. Cohen and Agiesta 2007, 1.

66. Saad 2007.

67. Medhurst 2009, 198.

68. Ibid., 197.

69. Romney 2007.

70. Ibid.
71. Kaylor 2011, 499.
72. Romney 2007.
73. Ibid.
74. Ibid.
75. Ibid.
76. Ibid.
77. Medhurst 2009, 210.
78. Saad 2007.
79. Medhurst 2009, 28.
80. Kaylor 2011, 504.
81. King and King 2000, 20.
82. Saad 2011.
83. Doherty 2011.
84. Event Transcript of Richard Bushman (May 2007).
85. King and King 2000, 19.

CHAPTER 5

1. Fox 2003, 279.
2. See Fox 2003 and 2006.
3. Gallup Poll, January 2010.
4. Ferrin 2012.
5. Pew Research Center Forum 2011b, 17.
6. Gallup Poll, August 2010.
7. Pew Research Center Forum 2011b, 14.
8. Ibid., 15.
9. Ibid., 14.
10. Ibid., 14–15.
11. Poll 1967, 135–36.
12. Simpson 2007, 797.
13. Ibid., 797.
14. Firmage 1998, 54.
15. Andrus 1967, 123.
16. Doctrine and Covenants, 98:6.
17. Ibid., 101:77–80.
18. Ibid., 109:54.
19. *Journal of Discourses* 1885–86, 2:182.
20. Benson 1986, 12.
21. Ibid., 12.
22. Ibid., 1–2.
23. Ibid., 11.
24. Ibid., 10.
25. Oaks 1992.
26. Ibid.
27. Clark 1973, 172.

28. Oaks 1992.

29. Mosiah 29:34.

30. Benson 1986, 2.

31. Ibid., 4.

32. Ibid., 4–5.

33. Ibid., 6.

34. Ibid., 9.

35. King 1970, 12.

36. Doctrine and Covenants, 56:16.

37. Ibid., 42:30.

38. See Doctrine and Covenants, 78:3 and 82:17–20.

39. King 1970, 12.

40. See "Consecrate, Law of Consecration" in the LDS Guide to the Scriptures at http://www.lds.org/scriptures/gs/consecrate-law-of-consecration?lang=eng.

41. Riley 2012, 1.

42. King 1970, 14.

43. Ibid., 17.

44. Matthew 25:35–36.

45. See "2011 Welfare Services Fact Sheet" at http://www.lds.org/bc/content/shared/content/english/pdf/welfare/2011-welfare-services-fact-sheet.pdf.

46. This can be found at http://www.providentliving.org/.

47. Doctrine and Covenants, 109:8.

48. This can be found at https://www.lds.org/family/family-well-being/home-storage/longer-term-food-supply?lang=eng#1.

49. Malachi 3:10.

50. See "2011 Welfare Services Fact Sheet" at http://www.lds.org/bc/content/shared/content/english/pdf/.

51. Ibid.

52. See "Mormon Welfare Schemes," *The Economist*, 2002.

53. Weaver 2012, 1.

54. Ibid., 2.

55. Taylor 2011, 1.

56. Ibid., 2.

57. See chapter 9 of Handbook 2 at http://www.lds.org/handbook/handbook-2-administering-the-church/relief-society?lang=eng.

58. Corinthians 13:8.

CHAPTER 6

1. Juergensmeyer 2008, 233.

2. Ibid., 237.

3. Ibid., 238.

4. Ibid., 242.

5. Ibid., 11.

6. As discussed more thoroughly in chapter 7.

7. Brooke 1994, 266.

8. Flake 2004, 9.

9. O'Dea 1957, 138.

10. Ibid., 139.

11. Brooke 1994, 213.

12. Abanes 2002, 287.

13. Ibid. 290.

14. Brooke 1994, 255.

15. Abanes 2002, 292.

16. Ibid., 580.

17. O'Dea 1957, 247.

18. Fox 2006, 30.

19. Bushman and Bushman 2001, 66.

20. Abanes 2002, 311.

21. Moore 2003, 159.

22. Bushman and Bushman 2001, 70.

23. Fox 2006, 31.

24. Ibid., 31.

25. O'Dea 1957, 107.

26. Bushman 2006, xi.

27. Ibid., xii.

28. Flake 2004, 164.

29. Ibid., 148.

30. Bushman 2006, 51.

31. Ibid., 52.

32. O'Dea 1957, 139.

33. Abanes 2002, 419.

34. O'Dea 1957, 140.

35. Bushman and Bushman 2001, 79.

36. Fox 2006, 44.

37. See Appendix.

38. Bushman 2006, 125.

39. Bushman 2008, 59.

40. Bushman 2006, 128.

41. Bawer 1997, 274.

42. Bushman 2006, 129.

43. Fox 2006, 44.

44. Ibid., 44.

45. Bushman 2006, 125.

46. Fowler 142.

47. McKinley 2008.

48. Wald and Calhoun Brown 2011, 302.

49. Bushman 2006, 127.

50. Campbell and Monson 2007, 124.

51. Ibid., 125.

52. Fowler 68.

53. Pew Research Center for the People and Press, http://www.pewforum.org/
Gay-Marriage-and-Homosexuality/Religious-Groups-Official-Positions-on-Same-Sex
-Marriage.

54. Young 2007, 62.

55. Bushman 2006, 125.
56. Krakauer 2003, 24.
57. Fox 2006, 44.
58. Campbell and Monson 2007, 111.
59. Mauss 1984, 440.
60. Fox 2006, 45.
61. Ibid., 139.
62. O'Dea 1957, 34.
63. Van Biema 2009.
64. Fowler 196.
65. Ibid., 123.

CHAPTER 7

1. Juergensmeyer 2008, 6.
2. Kniss 2003, 338.
3. Juergensmeyer 2008, 35.
4. Wald and Calhoun-Brown 2011, 52.
5. Demerath 2003, 354.
6. Casanova 1994, 159.
7. Micklethwait and Wooldridge 2004, 324.
8. Demerath 2003, 356.
9. Ibid., 356.
10. Harper 2006, 300.
11. O'Dea 1957, 165.
12. Brooke 1994, 62.
13. Ibid., 266.
14. Harper 2006, 301.
15. Brooke 1994, 268.
16. Brodie 1995, 208
17. Flake 2004, 19.
18. Brooke 1994, 287.
19. Bushman and Bushman 2001, 54.
20. *Journal of Discourses* 1855–86, 64.
21. Ibid., 64.
22. Abanes 2002, xx.
23. Ibid., xxi.
24. Benson 1986, 12.
25. Firmage 1998, 54.
26. Benson 1986, 12.
27. Mauss 1984, 447.
28. Bushman 2008, 94.
29. Brodie 1995, 267.
30. Ibid., 286.
31. Ibid., 287.
32. Flake 2004, 46.
33. Brodie 1995, 362.

34. Campbell and Monson 2007, 105.
35. Ibid., 107.
36. Ibid., 111.
37. Ibid., 116.
38. Ibid., 122.
39. Bushman 2008, 100.
40. Moore 2003, 188.
41. Bushman 2006, 59.
42. Bushman and Bushman 2001, 95.
43. Bushman 2008, 46. Usually this cost is about $500 a month. The Church provides no stipends.
44. Pew Research Center Forum, 2011b.
45. Brooke 1994, 296.
46. Bushman 2006, 62.
47. Ibid., 61.
48. Ibid., 67.
49. Moore 2003, 23.
50. Bushman 2006, 66.
51. "Military Relations." n.d.
52. Israelsen-Hartley 2010.
53. Boone 1975.
54. Fox 2006, 49.
55. The coursework can also consist of related fields such as pastoral counseling, social work, and religious administration.
56. Abanes 2002, 333.
57. Bushman and Bushman 2001, 75.
58. Ibid., 76.
59. Flake 2004, 154.
60. Bushman 2006, 145.
61. Fox 2006, 164.

CHAPTER 8

1. Beckford 2003, 174.
2. Juergensmeyer 2008, 242.
3. Ibid., 40.
4. Ibid., 41.
5. These sects are detailed in chapter 2.
6. Fox 2006, 5.
7. Fowler 2010, 12.
8. Beckford 2003, 118.
9. Hertzke 2009, 231.
10. Beckford 2003, 110.
11. Ibid., 110.
12. Fox 2006, 42.
13. Bushman and Bushman 2001, 100.
14. Fox 2006, 21.

15. Beckford 2003, 65.
16. Bushman 2006, 5.
17. Juergensmeyer 2008, 241.
18. Jenkins 2002, 66.
19. Embry 1994, 28.
20. Jenkins 2002, 66.
21. Fowler 148.
22. Fox 2006, 84.
23. Ibid., 50.
24. Ibid., 16.
25. Ibid.
26. Brooke 1994, 216
27. Ibid.
28. Beckford 2003, 101.
29. Bushman 2008, 111.
30. Abanes 2002, 62.
31. Embry 1994, 57.
32. Abanes 2002, 365.
33. Ibid., 366.
34. Embry 1994, 28.
35. Ibid.
36. Mauss 1984, 448.
37. Abanes 2002, 368.
38. Embry 1994, 27.
39. Bushman 2008, 111.
40. Abanes 2002, 370.
41. Fowler 196.
42. Fox 2006, 161.
43. Ibid., 111.
44. Embry 1994, 94.
45. Ibid., 59.
46. Ibid., 157.
47. Ibid., 78.
48. Bushman and Bushman 2001, 111.
49. Bushman 2006, 100.
50. Ibid., 103.
51. Mauss 1984, 449
52. Murphy 1999.
53. Ibid.
54. Juergensmeyer 2008, 263.
55. Referring to Max Weber's well-known sociological observations about the impact of Protestant Christian values on the development of modern capitalism.
56. Lipset 1959, 73.
57. Davis 1951, 240.
58. Harriss and Renzio 1997, 919.
59. Wald and Calhoun-Brown 2011, 301.
60. Ibid.

61. Beckford 2003, 175.
62. Fox 2006, 128.
63. Campbell and Monson 2007, 120.
64. Ibid., 116.
65. Juergensmeyer 2008, 225.
66. Ibid., 228.
67. Wald and Calhoun-Brown 2011, 301.
68. Juergensmeyer 2008, 255.

CHAPTER 9

1. Demerath 2003, 6.
2. Juergensmeyer 2008, 29.
3. Beckford 2003, 32.
4. Ibid., 35.
5. Ibid.
6. Juergensmeyer 2008, 5.
7. Demerath 2003, 6.
8. Beckford 2003, 71.
9. Demerath 2003, 125.
10. Fowler 323.
11. Demerath 2003, 229.
12. Juergensmeyer 2008, 240.
13. Ibid., 242.
14. Fox 2006, 44.
15. Juergensmeyer 2008, 5.
16. Mauss 1984, 446.
17. Abanes 2002, 295.
18. Fox 2006, 31.
19. Bushman 2008, 92.
20. Bushman 2006, 111.
21. Ibid., 112.
22. Ibid., 117.
23. Ibid., 121.
24. Young 2007, 625.
25. Campbell and Monson 2007, 111.
26. "The Family: A Proclamation to the World." n.d.
27. Mauss 1984, 449.
28. Ibid.
29. "The Family: A Proclamation to the World."
30. Brooke 1994, 295.
31. Fowler 311.
32. Fox 2006, xi.
33. Mauss 1984, 440.
34. Ibid.
35. Embry 1994, 119.
36. Fox 2006, 35.

37. Embry 1994, 120.
38. Ibid., 121.
39. Fox 2006, 49.
40. Ibid.
41. Gardner 1922, 142.
42. Ibid.
43. Ibid.
44. Brooke 1994, 281.
45. Ibid.
46. Embry 1994, 16.
47. Ibid.
48. Young 2007, 627.
49. Brooke 1994, 295.
50. Ibid.
51. Bushman 2006, 4.
52. Mauss 1984, 447.
53. Bawer 1997, 164.
54. Jenkins 2002, 86.
55. Ibid.
56. Abanes 2002, 384.
57. Ibid., 385.
58. Ibid., 386.
59. Bushman 2006, 5.
60. Krakauer 2003, 322.
61. Bawer 1997, 265.
62. Van Biema, 2009.
63. Stephanie Meyer is the author of the widely read *Twilight* series.
64. Juergensmeyer 2008, 257.
65. Ibid., 258.
66. Fowler 330.
67. Bushman 2006, 133.
68. Harper 2006, 304.
69. Ibid.
70. Fox 2006, 84.
71. Fowler 66.
72. Ibid., 68.
73. Marty 2000, 164.
74. Ibid., 138.
75. Ibid., 21.
76. Wald and Calhoun-Brown 2011, 303.
77. O'Dea 1957, 171.
78. Harper 2006, 303.
79. O'Dea 1957, 223.
80. Fowler 12.
81. Casanova 1994, 160.
82. Abanes 2002, 384.
83. Ibid., 375.

Bibliography

Abanes, Richard. *One Nation under Gods: A History of the Mormon Church*. New York: Four Walls Eight Windows, 2002.

Andrus, Hyrum. "Mormonism and the American Dream." *Dialogue: A Journal of Mormon Thought*, 2.3 (Autumn 1967): 123–126.

Ballard, M. Russell. "A Chance to Start Over: Church Disciplinary Councils and the Restoration of Blessings." *Ensign*, September 1990. http://www.lds.org/ensign/ 1990/09/a-chance-to-start-over-church-disciplinary-councils-and-the -restoration-of-blessings?lang=eng.

Bawer, Bruce. *Stealing Jesus: How Fundamentalism Betrays Christianity*. New York: Crown, 1997.

Beckford, James A. *Social Theory and Religion*. Cambridge: Cambridge University Press, 2003.

Benson, Ezra Taft. *The Constitution: A Heavenly Banner*. Salt Lake City, UT: Deseret Book Company, 1986.

Black, Susan, Randy Bott, Dee Darling, and Fred Woods. "Preface." In *Out of Obscurity*, edited by Susan Black, Randy Bott, Dee Darling, and Fred Woods, vii–ix. Salt Lake City, UT: Deseret Book Company, 2000.

Boone, Joseph F. "The Roles of the Church of Jesus Christ of Latter-Day Saints in Relation to the United States Military, 1900–1975." PhD diss., Brigham Young University, 1975.

Brodie, Fawn M. *No Man Knows My History: The Life of Joseph Smith*. New York: Vintage Books, 1995.

Brooke, John L. *The Refiner's Fire: The Making of Mormon Cosmology, 1644–1844*. New York: Cambridge University Press, 1994.

Bushman, Claudia, and Richard Bushman. *Mormons in America*. New York: Oxford University Press, 1999. New York.

Bushman, Claudia L. *Contemporary Mormonism: Latter-Day Saints in Modern America*. London: Praeger, 2006.

Bushman, Claudia, and Richard Bushman. *Building the Kingdom: A History of Mormons in America*. New York: Oxford University Press, 2001.

Bushman, Richard. *Joseph Smith: Rough Stone Rolling*. New York: Vintage Books, 2005.

Bushman, Richard. "Mormons and Politics: Are They Compatible?" [Event Transcript]. May 14, 2007. http://www.pewforum.org/Politics-and-Elections/Mormonism-and-Politics-Are-They-Compatible.aspx.

Bushman, Richard Lyman. *Mormonism: A Very Short Introduction*. New York: Oxford University Press, 2008.

Butler, Jon. PBS interview. May 16, 2006. http:www.pbs.org/Mormons/interviews/butler.html.

Campbell, David E., and J. Quin Monson. "Dry Kindling: A Political Profile of American Mormons." In *From Pews to Polling Places: Faith and Politics in the American Religious Mosaic*, ed. J. Matthew Wilson, 105–30. Washington, DC: Georgetown University Press, 2007.

Cann, Damon. "Religious Identification and Legislative Voting: The Mormon Case." *Political Research Quarterly* 62, no. 1 (March 2009): 110–19.

Casanova, Jose. *Public Religions in the Modern World*. Chicago: University of Chicago Press, 1994.

The Church of Jesus Christ of Latter-day Saints. Political Neutrality Statement. March 26, 2012. http://www.mormonnewsroom.org/official-statement/political-neutrality.

Clark, J. Reuben, Jr. *Stand Fast by Our Constitution*. Salt Lake City, UT: Deseret Book Company, 1973.

Coe, Michael. PBS interview. May 16, 2006. http://www.pbs.org/mormons/interviews/coe.html.

Cohen, Jon, and Jennifer Agiesta. "Race, Gender Less Relevant in '08." *Washington Post*, February 27, 2007. http://www.washingtonpost.com/wp-dyn/content/article/2007/02/27/AR2007022700283.html.

Cowan, Richard. "The Latter-Day Century." In *Out of Obscurity*, eds. Susan Black, Randy Bott, Dee Darling, and Fred Woods, 26–25. Salt Lake City, UT: Deseret Book Company, 2000.

Davis, Kingsley. "Political Ambivalence in Latin America." In *The Evolution of Latin American Government*, ed. A. N. Christensen, 224–47. New York: Holt, 1951.

Demerath, N. J., III. "Civil Society and Civil Religion as Mutually Dependent." In *Handbook of the Sociology of Religion*, ed. Michele Dillon, 348–58. Cambridge: Cambridge University Press, 2003.

Doherty, Carroll. "Are Republicans Ready Now for a Mormon President?" July 5, 2011. http://www.people-press.org/2011/07/05/are-republicans-ready-now-for-a-mormon-president/.

Elisha, Omri. "Sustaining Charisma Mormon Sectarian Culture and the Struggle for Plural Marriage, 1852–1890." *Nova Religio: The Journal of Alternative and Emergent Religions* 6, no. 1 (October 2002): 45–63.

Embry, Jessie L. *Black Saints in a White Church: Contemporary African American Mormons*. Salt Lake City, UT: Signature Books, 1994.

"The Family: A Proclamation to the World." n.d. http://www.lds.org.

Ferrin, Josh. Infographic of 2011 Pew Forum Poll. January 12, 2012. http://www.deseretnews.com/media/pdf/722608.pdf.

Firmage, Edwin. "Reflections on Mormon History: Zion and the Anti-Legal Tradition." *Dialogue: A Journal of Mormon Thought* 31, no. 4 (1998): 53–62.

Flake, Kathleen. PBS interview. April 27, 2006. http://www.pbs.org/mormons/interviews/flake.html.

Flake, Kathleen. *The Politics of American Religious Identity: The Seating of Senator Reed Smoot, Mormon Apostle.* Chapel Hill: University of North Carolina Press, 2004.

Flanders, Robert Bruce. "The Kingdom of God in Illinois: Politics in Utopia." *Dialogue: A Journal of Mormon Thought* 5, no. 1 (Spring 1970): 26–36.

Fowler, Robert Booth, Allen D. Hertzke, Laura R. Olson, and Kevin R. den Dulk. *Religion and Politics in America: Faith, Culture, and Strategic Choices.* Boulder, Colorado: Westview Press, 2010.

Fox, Jeffrey C. "A Typology of LDS Sociopolitical Worldviews." *Journal for the Scientific Study of Religion,* 42.2 (June 2003): 279–289.

Fox, Jeffrey C. *Latter-Day Political Views.* New York: Lexington Books, 2006.

Gallup Polling Organization. "Mormons Most Conservative Major Religious Group in America." January 11, 2010. http://www.gallup.com/poll/125021/Mormons-Conservative-Major-Religious-Group.aspx.

Gallup Polling Organization. "Muslims Give Obama Highest Job Approval; Mormons Lowest." August 27, 2010. http://www.gallup.com/poll/142700/Muslims-Give-Obama-Highest-Job-Approval-Mormons-Lowest.aspx.

Gardner, Hamilton. "Communism among the Mormons." *The Quarterly Journal of Economics* 37, no. 1 (1922): 134–74.

Garr, Arnold. "Joseph Smith: Campaign for President of the United States." *Ensign,* February 2009, 48–52.

Givens, Terryl. "New Religious Movements and Orthodoxy: The Challenge to the Religious Mainstream." *The FARMS Review* 19, no. 1 (2007): 201–20.

Givens, Terryl. PBS interview. June 22, 2006. http://www.pbs.org/Mormons/interviews/givens.html.

Gordon, Sarah. PBS interview. April 28, 2006. http://www.pbs.org/mormons/interviews/gordon.html.

Harper, Steven Craig. "Dictated by Christ: Joseph Smith and the Politics of Revelation." *Journal of the Early Republic* 26, no. 2 (Summer 2006): 275–304.

Harriss, J., and P. Renzio. "Policy Arena: 'Missing Link' or Analytically Missing?: The Concept of Social Capital. An Introductory Bibliographic Essay." *Journal of International Development* 9, no. 7 (1997): 919–37.

Hartley, William. "Missouri's 1838 Extermination Order and the Mormons' Forced Removal to Illinois." *Mormon Historical Studies* 2, no. 2 (Fall 2001): 5–27.

Hertzke, Allen D. "Emerging Trends in Religion, Society, and Politics." In *The Future of Religion in American Politics,* ed. Charles W. Dunn, 229–55. Lexington: University Press of Kentucky, 2009.

Hickman, Martin. "The Political Legacy of Joseph Smith." *Dialogue: A Journal of Mormon Thought* 3, no. 3 (Autumn 1968): 22–27.

Hinckley, Gordon. PBS interview. January 2007. http://pbs.org/Mormons/interviews/hinckley.html.

Hinkle, Lynda. "Tithing to the Vortex: The Secrecy of Financial Records in the Church of Jesus Christ of Latter Day Saints and the Case of D.I. v. Corp. of the Bishops of the Church of Jesus Christ of Latter Day Saints." *Rutgers Journal of Law and Religion* 10, no. 8 (2008): 1–21.

Holland, Jeffrey. PBS interview. March 4, 2006. http://www.pbs.org/mormons/interviews/holland.html.

Israelsen-Hartley, Sara. "Military Missionaries: Mormon Soldiers Spread the Gospel in Post-war Japan." *Deseret News*, December 6, 2010.

Jenkins, Philip. *The Next Christendom: The Coming of Global Christianity*. New York: Oxford University Press, 2002.

Jensen, Marlin. "May the Kingdom of God Go Forth." In *Out of Obscurity*, edited by Susan Black, Randy Bott, Dee Darling, and Fred Woods, 1–15. Salt Lake City, UT: Deseret Book Company, 2000.

Jensen, Marlin. PBS interview. March 7, 2006. http://www.pbs.org/mormons/interviews/jensen.html.

Johnson, Kirk. "In Olympic Success, Romney Found New Edge." *New York Times*, September 19, 2007. http://www.nytimes.com/2007/09/19/us/politics/.

Jones, Jeffrey. Some Americans Reluctant to Vote for Mormon, 72-Year Old Presidential Candidates. February 20, 2007. http://www.gallup.com/poll/26611/some-americans-reluctant-vote-mormon-72yearold-presidential-candidates.aspx.

Journal of Discourses. Liverpool: Miscellaneous, 1855–86.

Juergensmeyer, Mark. *Global Rebellion: Religious Challenges to the Secular State, from Christian Militias to al Qaeda*. Los Angeles: University of California Press, 2008.

Kaylor, Brian. "No Jack Kennedy: Mitt Romney's 'Faith in America' Speech and Changing Religious Political Environment." *Communication Studies* 62, no. 5 (2011): 491–507.

King, Robert, and Kay Atchinson King. "Mormons in Congress, 1851–2000." *Journal of Mormon History* 26, no. 2 (2000): 1–51.

King, David. "The Principle of Good Samaritan considered in a Mormon Political Context." *Dialogue: A Journal of Mormon Thought*, 5.4 (Winter 1970): 11–22.

Kniss, Fred. "Mapping the Moral Order: Depicting the Terrain of Religious Conflict and Change." In *Handbook of the Sociology of Religion*, edited by Michele Dillon, 331–47. Cambridge: Cambridge University Press, 2003.

Krakauer, Jon. *Under the Banner of Heaven: A Story of Violent Faith*. New York: Doubleday, 2003.

Kranish, Michael, and Scott Helman. *The Real Romney*. New York: HarperCollins, 2012.

Kranish, Michael, and Michael Paulson. "Centered in Faith, a Family Emerges." *Boston Globe*, June 25, 2007. http://www.boston.com/news/politics/2008/specials/romney/articles/part2_main/.

"LDS Church Real-Estate Holdings Include Farms, Ranches, Buildings." *Deseret News*, July 2, 1991.

LeBlanc, Steve. "Fortunate Son: Mitt Romney's Life in His Father's Legacy." Associated Press, December 16, 2007. http://www.deseretnews.com/article/695236445/Fortunate-Son-Mitt-Romneys-life-is-his-fathers-legacy.html?pg=4.

Lipset, Martin. "Some Social Requisites of Democracy: Economic Development and Political Legitimacy." *APSR* 53, no. 10 (1959): 69–105.

Marty, Martin E. *Politics, Religion, and the Common Good: Advancing a Distinctly American Conversation about Religion's Role in Our Shared Life*. San Francisco: Jossey-Bass, 2000.

Mauss, Armand L. "Sociological Perspectives on the Mormon Subculture." *Annual Review of Sociology* 10 (1984): 437–60.

McKinley, Jesse. "Mormons Tipped Scale in Ban on Gay Marriage." *New York Times*, November 15, 2008, p. 1.

Medhurst, Martin. "Mitt Romney, 'Faith in America,' and the Dance of Religion and Politics in American Culture." *Rhetoric and Public Affairs* 12, no. 2 (2009): 195–222.

Micklethwait, John, and Adrian Wooldridge. *The Right Nation: Conservative Power in America*. New York: Penguin Press, 2004.

Mikkelsen, Craig. "The Politics of B. H. Roberts." *Dialogue: A Journal of Mormon Thought* 9, no. 2 (Summer 1974): 25–43.

"Military Relations." n.d. http://www.lds.org/pa/library/0,17905,4880-1,00.html.

Mooney, Brian. "Taking Office, Remaining an Outsider." *Boston Globe*, June 29, 2007. http://www.boston.com/news/politics/2008/specials/romney/articles/part6_main/?page=full.

Moore, R. Laurence. *Touchdown Jesus: The Mixing of Sacred and Secular in American History*. London: Westminster John Knox Press, 2003.

"Mormon Welfare Schemes." *The Economist*. February 14, 2002. http://www.economist.com/node/988818.

Murphy, Thomas. "From Racist Stereotype to Ethnic Identity: Instrumental Uses of Mormon Racial Doctrine." *Ethnohistory* 46, no. 3 (Summer 1999): 451–80.

Newport, Frank. "Americans' View of Mormon Religion." Gallup News Service, March 2, 2007. http://www.gallup.com/poll/26758/Americans-Views-Mormon-Religion.aspx?version=print.

Oaks, Dallin. "The Divinely Inspired Constitution." *Ensign*, February 1992. http://www.lds.org/ensign/1992/02/the-divinely-inspiredconstitution?lang=eng&query=constitution.

O'Dea, Thomas F. *The Mormons*. Chicago: University of Chicago Press, 1957.

Olson, Steven. "The Theology of Memory: Mormon Historical Consciousness." *The FARMS Review* 19, no. 2 (2007): 25–35.

Ostling, Richard, and Joan Ostling. *Mormon America: The Power and the Promise*. New York: HarperCollins, 1999.

Peterson, Daniel. PBS interview. February 27, 2006. http://www.pbs.org/mormons/interviews/peterson.html.

Pew Research Center Forum on Religion and Public Life. "Faith on the Hill: The Religious Composition of the 112th Congress." January 5, 2011a. http://www.pewforum.org/Government/Faith-on-the-Hill—The-Religious-Composition-of-the-112th-Congress.aspx.

Pew Research Center Forum on Religion and Public Life. Mormons in America. January 2012. http://www.deseretnews.com/media/pdf/722608.pdf.

Pew Research Center Forum on Religion and Public Life. "Mormons in America: Certain of Their Beliefs, Uncertain of Their Place in Society." January 12, 2012. http://www.pewforum.org/Christian/Mormon/mormons-in-america.aspx.

Pew Research Center Forum on Religion and Public Life. National Survey of Mormons. 2011b. http://www.pewforum.org/uploadedFiles/Topics/Religious _Affiliation/Christian/Mormon/Mormons%20in%20America.pdf.

Phillips, Richard. "The 'Secularization' of Utah and Religious Competition." *Journal for the Scientific Study of Religion* 38, no. 1 (March 1999): 72–82.

Poll, Richard. "Joseph Smith's Presidential Platform." *Dialogue: A Journal of Mormon Thought* 3, no. 3 (Autumn 1968): 17–36.

Prince, Greg. PBS interview. June 15 and 22, 2006. http://www.pbs.org/mormons/ interviews/prince.html.

Quinnipiac University. "Romney Leads GOP Pack, Runs Best against Obama, Quinnipiac University National Poll Finds; Mormons Near Bottom of Voter Comfort Scale." Press release. June 8, 2011. http://www.quinnipiac.edu/ institutes-and-centers/polling-institute/search-releases/search-results/release -detail?ReleaseID=1608.

Riley, Niaomi Schaefer. "What Mormons know about Welfare." *The Wall Street Journal*. February 19, 2012. http://online.wsj.com/article/SB100014240 529 7020479240457722717 3888056682.html.

Romney, Mitt. "Faith in America." December 6, 2007. http://www.nytimes.com/ 2007/12/06/us/politics/06text-romney.html?pagewanted=all.

Saad, Lydia. "In U.S. 22% Hesitant to Support Mormon in 2012 Election." June 20, 2011. http://www.gallup.com/poll/148100/Hesitant-Support-Mormon -2012.aspx.

Saad, Lydia. "Percentage Unwilling to Vote for a Mormon Holds Steady." December 11, 2007. http://www.gallup.com/poll/103150/Percentage-Unwilling-Vote-Mormon -Holds-Steady.aspx.

Saslow, Eli. "A Mission Accepted." *Washington Post*, December 10, 2007. http:// www.washingtonpost.com/wp-dyn/content/article/2007/12/09/AR2007120901 473.html.

Simpson, Thomas. "Mormons Study 'Abroad': Brigham Young's Romance with Higher Education, 1867–1877." *Church History*, 76.4 (December 2007): 778–798.

Smith, Joseph. "General Smith's Views of the Powers and Policy of the Government of the United States." 1844. http://www.latterdayconservative.com/joseph -smith/general-smiths-views-of-the-power-and-policy-of-the-government/.

Stapley, Delpert. Letter to George Romney. January 23, 1964. http://www.boston .com/news/daily/24/delbert_stapley.pdf.

Swidley, Neil, and Stephanie Ebbert. "Romney Determined to Make Mark Early." *Boston Globe*, July 4, 2007. http://www.deseretnews.com/article/680196334/ Romney-determined-to-make-mark-early.html?pg=1.

Swidley, Neil, and Michael Paulson. "Privilege, Tragedy, and a Young Leader." *Boston Globe*, June 24, 2007. http://www.boston.com/news/nation/articles/ 2007/06/24/privilege_tragedy_and_a_young_leader/?page=2.

Taylor, Scott. "Mormon Welfare Services: Another Day, Another D.I." *Deseret News*, June 7, 2011. http://www.deseretnews.com/article/700142439/ Mormon-welfare-services-Another-day-another-DI.html.

Top, Brent. "A Lengthening Stride, 1951 through 1999." In *Out of Obscurity*, edited by Susan Black, Randy Bott, Dee Darling, and Fred Woods, 26–52. Salt Lake City, UT: Deseret Book Company, 2000.

U.S. Census Data. Table 231. 2010. http://www.census.gov/compendia/statab/2012/tables/12s0232.pdf.

van Biema, David. "The Storm over the Mormons." *Time*, June 22, 2009, 173, no. 24.

Wald, Kenneth, and Allison Calhoun-Brown. *Religion and Politics in the United States*. 6th ed. New York: Rowman & Littlefield, 2011.

Walker, Joseph. "LDS Advertising Campaign Elicits 'Significant Increase' in Website Visitors." *Deseret News*, June 28, 2011. http://www.deseretnews.com/article/700147893/LDS-advertising-campaign-elicits-significant-increase-in-website-visitors.html.

Walsh, Elsa. "Minority Retort: How a Pro-Gun, Anti-Abortion Nevadan Leads the Senate's Democrats." *The New Yorker*, August 8, 2005. http://www.newyorker.com/archive/2005/08/08/05080fa_fact.

Weaver, Sarah Jane. "LDS Church opens Bishops' Storehouse to Help 'Poor and Needy.'" *Deseret News*, January 26, 2012. http://www.deseretnews.com/article/700219362/LDS-Church-opens-bishops-storehouse-to-help-poor-and-needy.html.

Young, Neil J. "The ERA Is a Moral Issue: The Mormon Church, LDS Women, and the Defeat of the Equal Rights Amendment." *American Quarterly* 59, no. 3 (September 2007): 623–44.

Index

About the Authors

LUKE PERRY holds an MA and PhD in political science from the University of Massachusetts at Amherst and has published several works on various aspects of American politics, including religion and politics, the presidency, political thought, and political rhetoric. A Fulbright scholar, Dr. Perry worked at Southern Utah University from 2008 to 2011 prior to holding his current position of associate professor of government at Utica College in New York.

CHRISTOPHER CRONIN holds an MA and PhD in political science from the University of Massachusetts at Amherst. He has published works in the area of religion and politics, including his previous work examining the role of progressive Christianity in party politics. He is an assistant professor of government studies at Methodist University.